Envision

Persuasive Writing in a Visual World

Christine L. Alfano   **Alyssa J. O'Brien**
Stanford University   *Stanford University*

PEARSON
Longman

New York • San Francisco • Boston
London • Toronto • Sydney • Tokyo • Singapore • Madrid
Mexico City • Munich • Paris • Cape Town • Hong Kong • Montreal

Senior Vice President and Publisher: Joseph Opiela
Senior Acquisitions Editor: Lynn M. Huddon
Development Editor: Michael Greer
Marketing Manager: Deborah Murphy
Senior Supplements Editor: Donna Campion
Media Supplements Editor: Nancy Garcia
Production Manager: Charles Annis
Project Coordination, Text Design, and Electronic Page Makeup: Pre-Press Company, Inc.
Cover Designer/Manager: Wendy Ann Fredericks
Cover Photos: *top*, Jeff Greenberg/PhotoEdit; *middle*, James Montgomery Flagg/Corbis/
    Bettmann; *bottom*, Ron Krisel/Image Bank/Getty Images, Inc.
Photo Researcher: Photosearch, Inc.
Senior Manufacturing Buyer: Dennis J. Para
Printer and Binder: R. R. Donnelley and Sons Company
Cover Printer: Coral Graphic Services, Inc.

Library of Congress Cataloging-in-Publication Data
Alfano, Christine L.
    Envision : Persuasive writing in a visual world / by Christine L. Alfano and Alyssa J.
O'Brien.
        p. cm.
    Includes bibliographical references and index.
    ISBN 0-321-18327-4
        1. English language—Rhetoric. 2. Persuasion (Rhetoric) 3. Visual communication.
    4. Visual perception. 5. Report writing. I. O'Brien, Alyssa J. II. Title.
    PE1431.A55 2004
    808'.042—dc22

                                                                            2004044745

Please visit us at http://www.ablongman.com/envision.

ISBN 0-321-18327-4

3 4 5 6 7 8 9 10—DOC—07 06 05

Contents

Media Focus:
Photographs

Part II Inquiry: Research Arguments

Media Focus:
**Propaganda
Posters**

Part III Innovation: Presentations and Visual Arguments

This book emerged from our practical need as writing instructors for a resource we could use in the classroom to teach students how to understand, analyze, and write about visual rhetoric. As writing teachers, we found ourselves struggling to find materials that might provide solid rhetorical instruction in visual culture while leading students in concrete steps from analysis of visual culture, to crafting an argument about visual texts, to using the visual as an argumentative text in itself. We turned to the students themselves as collaborators in this writing: they provided suggestions for examples, creative approaches to the assignments, extensive feedback on each chapter in progress, as well as continuous support and enthusiasm.

> *Envision* teaches students the fundamentals of writing in powerful, effective ways. College writers using this book will learn how to analyze, craft arguments, research, and ultimately produce persuasive visual texts.

It is our hope that this book addresses the need presented by a national turn to the teaching of visual rhetoric in the writing classroom and helps students and teachers everywhere to become knowledgeable, experienced, and confident participants in shaping the contours of our increasingly visually saturated world.

To develop students' understanding of visual rhetoric—and, most importantly, move from **written analysis** to more complex work such as **argumentation**, **research writing**, and **visual production**—we'll present both lessons on diverse visual media and instruction in time-honored rhetorical strategies. Students will learn about rhetorical appeals, the Canons of Rhetoric, and many other tools of persuasion while also working through interactive lessons on crafting thesis statements, structuring argumentative essays, developing research topics, evaluating sources, integrating quotations, revising papers, and, finally, designing and delivering multimedia presentations and projects.

Theoretical Foundations

Envision is designed to teach students strategies for understanding the visual world around us, its powers of persuasion, and the ways in which they can harness the visual as a rhetorical act of writing. We seek to explore how "what it means to write" has changed in an era marked by what W. J. T. Mitchell termed "the pictorial turn," in which the visual is not merely decoration, or simply a reflection of reality,

> "[W]e still do not know exactly what pictures are, what their relation to language is, how they operate on observers and on the word, how their history is to be understood, and what is to be done with or about them."
>
> —W. J. T. Mitchell

but is rather a complex *visual discourse* which uses images—sometimes in combination with words—as a means of persuasion. Indeed, our discussion throughout **Envision** is premised on the idea that word and image are not antithetical, but rather reciprocal in nature. The perspective that recognizes the power and value of such hybrid rhetorical texts actually turns traditional learning on its head. This viewpoint counters one long held by traditional academic studies—that the image is inferior to the word and that attention to the visual necessarily dictates neglect of the verbal. But such a belief is far from true. From the earliest hieroglyphics to today's hypertext fiction and virtual-reality games, visual and verbal texts perform a complementary rhetorical act. Often, image and word work together to construct meaning, or one aspect will provide a wonderfully ironic counterpart to the other. In order to understand, appreciate, and use visual rhetoric, then, we need to develop skills to read both words and images; we need not only *verbal literacy* but also what is called **visual literacy,** or *learning how to read the visual world as a text.*

This approach to visual rhetoric draws on previous work from other disciplinary approaches to visual culture, and indeed we see this book as a collaborative venture with those teachers, writers, and theorists who have paved the way in the fields of English, art history, film studies, communications, visual culture, and new media. We seek to build on the foundation provided by others who have examined visual or hybrid texts, whether as decorative supplements to verbal texts or as aesthetic artifacts that teach us about our world.

FIGURE 1. The *Book of Kells* provides an early example of visual rhetoric as part of a written text.

Significantly, however, **visual rhetoric** as an emerging field offers a new angle on this work by assessing the visual text as a fundamentally persuasive mode of communication and asking how such a focus on the visual changes what we mean by "writing." We find that persuasive hybrid texts that combine words and images in powerful ways reach back historically to the first communicative acts of humankind, in cave paintings, the runic alphabet, and even the *Book of Kells*. This illuminated manuscript reproduces the four gospels from the Bible through such elaborate drawings that many details can only be appreciated with a magnifying glass. But as the reproduction of the *Book of Kells* in Figure 1 reveals, the visual is a signifying system—it has purpose and meaning as part of the text.

Academics have studied and theorized the relationship between the visual and verbal in such texts across the disciplines, but only recently are we shifting our focus to visual rhetoric in the *writing classroom,* where we find that students are increasingly selecting visual texts as subjects for their analysis and research argument assignments. The interest that students show in selecting such texts as material for study parallels the trend nationwide to analyze, theorize, and incorporate visual texts into writing curricula. Not finding a text that might lead students in the writing classroom from analysis to production, we have written *Envision* to fill that void.

> Visual rhetoric is different from earlier work in art history, film studies, photography, cultural studies, and even new media; *it has its own subject matter: the art of persuasion through visual images and multimedia forms.*

Structure and Sequence of Assignments

Students of *Envision* will develop the skills to become confident and persuasive writers through a three-part structure: *Exploration, Inquiry,* and *Innovation.*

Part I: Exploration: Analysis and Argument

This section aims to make students proficient, careful readers of visual rhetoric: we analyze visual texts and practice strategies of writing about them. This means looking both at purely visual texts, such as comics, political cartoons, and photos, as well as at texts that combine visual and written rhetoric, such as comic strips, advertisements, newspaper covers, and Websites. Chapters 1–3 explore the ways in which a particular image and caption collaborate to create a persuasive argument, and we consider how this rhetorical choice convinces a reader to understand the text in a certain way. Students learn how to analyze the forms of persuasion in visual texts and study how the interaction between visual and verbal rhetoric influences an audience. We focus on writing, from drafting thesis statements to formal strategies of argument, and we examine both conventional academic essays and contemporary popular articles.

Part II: Inquiry: Research Arguments

Chapters 4–6 focus on strategies of research argument as we shift from the exploration and analysis of visual rhetoric to the use of visual texts as the subject of sustained research projects. This section of the book takes students into the process of research inquiry as we work through the research proposal, understand how to use charts and graphs, and study strategies for positioning visual rhetoric as compelling material in substantial research-based arguments. We spend time learning how to gather and evaluate sources, integrate quotations, and work collaboratively on a draft. Students can consult sample papers as they develop their expertise researching and writing about the power of visual rhetoric in research-based arguments.

Part III: Innovation: Presentation and Visual Arguments

The final three chapters offer students an opportunity to produce presentations, visual arguments, and other multimedia projects with creativity and strategic design. As we turn from the first two sections of this book, where we focus on writing analytical essays and research arguments, to this last section, where we explore ways of presenting, producing, and creating oral and visual arguments, we again rely on solid rhetorical instruction, including the last two canons of rhetoric— memory and delivery. We examine presentations, poster sessions, photomontages, op-ads, and monuments as well as embodied rhetoric and the e-rhetoric of Websites. Students learn how to create memorable, effective visual rhetoric projects for a wide range of academic and professional purposes, including service-learning courses, public exhibitions, and public audiences.

Sequence of Assignments

Throughout this book, our discussion of visual rhetoric will evoke Aristotle and Plato, for in order to understand *the visual* as *a rhetorical act,* we need to return to rhetoric's classical foundations. In addition, we'll explore the rhetoric of the visual world across many academic disciplines and areas of contemporary culture by analyzing a range of images and texts, from cartoons to advertisements, from news photos to covers of scientific journals, from propaganda posters to Websites, film, and public monuments. As we cover both classical rhetoric and contemporary visual culture, we lead students through the concrete and class-tested writing assignments to achieve specific learning objectives, as shown in the accompanying table.

MAJOR ASSIGNMENTS AND LEARNING OBJECTIVES IN *ENVISION*

Chapter Title	Media Focus	Major Assignments	Chapter Learning Goals
1: Introducing Visual Rhetoric	Cartoons, comic strips, and editorial cartoons	■ Personal narrative essay ■ Rhetorical analysis essay ■ Peer review ■ Self-assessment	■ Understanding visual rhetoric ■ Understanding the rhetorical situation ■ Considering audience
2: Understanding the Strategies of Persuasion	Advertisements	■ Contextual analysis essay ■ Analysis of rhetorical appeals and fallacies ■ Comparison/contrast essay ■ Peer review	■ Understanding rhetorical appeals: logos, pathos, ethos ■ Abuses or exaggerated uses of rhetorical appeals ■ Strategies of argumentation ■ Importance of context and *kairos*
3: Analyzing Perspectives in Argument	Photographs	■ Position paper ■ Argumentative essay incorporating diverse viewpoints ■ Multiple sides of argument assignment ■ Peer review	■ Drafting thesis statements ■ Considering various perspectives on argument ■ Developing persona and rhetorical stance ■ Addressing opposing opinion in an argument ■ Formatting and genre considerations
4: Planning and Proposing Research Arguments	Propaganda posters	■ Research log ■ Informal research plan ■ Research abstract ■ Research proposal ■ Peer review	■ Generating and narrowing research topics ■ Prewriting strategies ■ Developing a research plan and abstract ■ Drafting a formal proposal
5: Finding and Evaluating Research Sources	Magazines, journals, and Websites	■ Critical evaluation of sources ■ Website assessment criteria ■ Field research contact assignment ■ Visual annotated bibliography ■ Research log	■ Research strategies ■ Locating sources ■ Evaluating sources ■ Distinguishing primary and secondary sources ■ Conducting field research ■ Best practices for note-taking

Chapter Title	Visual Rhetoric Focus	Major Assignments	Chapter Learning Goals
6: Organizing and Writing Research Arguments	Film and movie trailers	■ Visual map assignment ■ Formal outline ■ Peer review response ■ Visual evidence assignment ■ Draft and revision of research argument	■ Organizing and outlining arguments ■ Importance of multiple drafts and revision ■ Writing and peer response ■ Quoting from sources ■ Best practices in documenting sources ■ Avoiding plagiarism
7: Composing Presentations	Presentations, poster sessions, PowerPoint, and embodied rhetoric	■ Conversion assignment, written to oral discourse ■ Poster session assignment ■ Multimedia and PowerPoint ■ Collaborative presentation	■ Transforming written arguments into visual, spoken, hybrid texts ■ Strategies of design and delivery ■ Using technology to address a range of audiences ■ Learning effective oral communication skills
8: Designing Visual Arguments and Websites	Op-ads, photo essays, Web design and multiple media	■ Visual arguments, (opinion ad or photo essay) ■ Designing a Website ■ Tactile and audio projects (murals, montages, film)	■ Appropriate voice, tone, and decorum ■ Attention to audience, purpose, medium ■ Relationship between rhetorical situation and types of argument
9: Writing for Public and Professional Communities	Monuments, community structures, and professional projects	■ Community service projects ■ Plan for memorial ■ Proposal for Website ■ Collaborative "pitch"	■ Considering public audiences and public discourses ■ Collaborative writing

Pedagogical Applications

"Learn by doing."

—Jean-Jacques Rousseau

As writing teachers, we realize that the best pedagogy involves interactive learning where the students can apply the instruction through immediate practice. From John Dewey to Cynthia Selfe, researchers in rhetoric and composition have shown the advantages of student-centered classrooms and student-focused pedagogy. Moreover, the well-known Learning Pyramid depicting student retention rates demonstrates clearly the efficacy of active student engagement in the learning process (see Figure 2). This book has been designed around the pedagogical philosophy that students learn more when they interact with the course material and when they are challenged to teach each other than when they simply implement the lessons taught to them.

The material in *Envision*, emerging as it did for the classroom and in collaboration with students, puts into practice the benefits of *active learning*. We aim to maximize student engagement and retention through a variety of interactive, student-centered exercises and assignments. This methodology eschews the "banking model" disparaged by educational theorist Paolo Freire and positions students as experts in their own learning.

With this pedagogical model, our role as teachers becomes one of guide and facilitator. Yet effective learning necessitates the careful preparation of activities, assignments, and discussion prompts; preparation is crucial to establishing the structure and the environment in which such active learning can occur. It is our sincere hope that this book will help you with everyday practical instruction in the classroom; that it will facilitate learning about ways of writing and methods of analysis; that it will lead your students to becoming adept researchers and confident producers of arguments across a range of media. Finally, we hope that the pragmatic, student-centered, interactive approach we offer here will inspire your students to take learning into their own hands and become creative, enthusiastic participants in society by writing, researching, and producing compelling and careful projects to share with their communities.

FIGURE 2. The Learning Pyramid shows the benefits of interactive pedagogy.

Features of *Envision*

AT A GLANCE

These boxes, interspersed throughout each chapter, list key principles or instructions. They offer concise how-to's and summaries of skills to reinforce retention.

A Closer Look

These boxes refer students to related readings or resources in both print and multimedia formats. They also list links available through the *Envision* Website; they can be used by students individually or in class lessons.

Student Writing

Students can consult actual student papers through the *Envision* Website to generate ideas on how to complete assignments or to read student reflections on working with visual rhetoric.

Seeing Connections
These cross-references to other parts of *Envision* identify useful additional instruction to meet the learning needs of a given task.

CREATIVE PRACTICE

These short exercises, integrated strategically throughout every chapter, ask students to practice the instruction; the hands-on, interactive teaching technique allows for immediate engagement and boosts both comprehension and retention of the material.

COLLABORATIVE CHALLENGE

Interspersed within the chapter, these exercises serve the same pedagogical function as the Creative Practices; however they entail a greater degree of complexity, depend on collaborative effort for their completion, and ask students to work with materials outside the textbook.

PREWRITING CHECKLISTS

These brainstorming prompts facilitate critical thinking and initiate the writing process by asking students to analyze the specific media focus of each chapter.

WRITING PROJECTS

These major writing assignments ask students to implement learning. Several options are provided to meet a range of teaching and curricular needs.

FOR ADDED CHALLENGE

These assignments offer more complex, collaborative, or creative ways of writing about and with visual rhetoric. These projects frequently ask students to produce digital, audio, oral, or multimedia versions of assignments.

CHAPTER ON THE WEB

Resources and Readings	Exercises and Assignments	Student Writing
• Links to media resources to launch a project	• Provides interactive exercises	• Lists work by assignment
• Writing and rhetoric resources	• Lists key assignments	• Identifies topics completed by students
• Closer Look links	• Includes peer review forms	• Provides samples for students to study in depth
• Annotations of suggested readings and Web resources	• Includes student self-assessment sheets	

www.ablongman.com/envision

This feature provides a "preview" of Web resources for students; it describes the digital offerings on the *Envision* Website.

Strategies for Classroom Use

The following list of what is now called "Best Practices" offers advice on how to implement this book in your own curriculum, course, or classroom. We offer many more strategies on the *Envision* Website, along with interactive activities, readings and resources, expanded asignment guidelines, and student projects. You may also wish to consult the Instructor's Manual, available to qualified adopters, for more on visual rhetoric and visual literacy, strategies for using *Envision* in different types of writing courses, sample syllabi, and additional ideas for student projects.

- *Use examples from current events.* Draw on recent events to energize students and reinforce the connection between what they learn in *Envision* and what they experience in their everyday lives. Substitute another visual example, timely topic, or recent event.

  How we have done it: While drafting this book, current events such as the toppling of Saddam Hussein's statue, the California recall election, Michael Jackson's arrest, and even the infamous kiss between Britney Spears and Madonna at the 2003 MTV Video Awards launched provocative discussions about writing and visual rhetoric.

- *Take advantage of* Envision*'s versatility.* While we have structured *Envision* to move students progressively from analysis and argument to research and visual production, we also designed it to be flexible and easy to navigate. We encourage you to customize your use of *Envision* to suit your pedagogical needs: use the Seeing Connections boxes to bounce between chapters; change a chapter's visual rhetoric focus.

  How we have done it: We have begun a course with Chapter 4 to introduce students to research in the first week; we have asked students to read Chapter 3's section on thesis statements alongside Chapter 1; we have started service-learning courses with Chapter 9.

- *Modify the Creative Practices and Collaborative Challenges.* Refocus these exercises onto examples most productive to the thematic parameters of your class; make a Creative Practice more collaborative to increase student-directed instruction in the classroom; expand the exercises into full-fledged course assignments.

How we have done it: We've used Chapter 3's Collaborative Challenge on O. J. Simpson to develop an extensive research assignment on the rhetoric of photo journalism; alternatively we've adapted the Creative Practice in Chapter 4 on World War II posters into an exercise on contemporary posters put out by the U.S. military.

■ *Pursue Closer Look readings and resources.* Use the ***Envision*** Website (http://www.ablongman.com/envision) to locate supplementary resources and extensive lists or annotated links for your course; use the recommended print readings listed in the Closer Looks to help students begin an assignment.

How we have done it: We show the "Bush vs. Bush" mock debate from *The Daily Show with Jon Stewart,* from Chapter 5 and ask students to analyze its thesis and points of argument; we have students write their own reflection on Susan Sontag's "Looking at War," a Closer Look from Chapter 3.

■ *Consult student writing on the Web.* For most of our students, while visual rhetoric itself is not new, the opportunity to write about it may be, so we have found that they appreciate having concrete student models to refer to as they approach their own writing assignments. These documents, available through the ***Envision*** Website, provide a pedagogy of models and give students ideas for the possible ways to complete assignments in this book.

How we have done it: We show students rhetorical analyses to discuss how to craft a compelling thesis on visual rhetoric; we examine multiple sides projects in Chapter 3 to showcase diverse forms of argumentative writing and visual layouts; we use PowerPoint presentations from Chapter 7 to suggest the range of possibilities for presentations. In each case we ask, "What are the strengths? What could be done differently? What can you learn from this example?"

■ *Attend to students with disabilities and diverse learners.* To facilitate the learning experience of all students, we put resources on the ***Envision*** Website for alternative methods of instruction for different learning styles, links to electronic resources, and tips for improving the accessibility of materials for diverse audiences, including those with learning or physical disabilities.

■ *Collaborate with us.* Use the *Envision* Website to contribute ideas, suggestions, feedback, and even writing projects of your own. Have students email us with comments on the examples, instruction, and resources we offer in *Envision*. Working on this book has been a collaborative process from the beginning, and now we welcome you.

Acknowledgments

During one of our first conference calls with people at Longman publishers, Chris's daughter Miranda drafted her own contribution to *Envision*, a cover featuring the two authors joined together through collaboration on a manuscript. Now at the end of book, we are deeply grateful for all those who helped us transform *Envision* from an ambitious idea into a finished reality and who should, fittingly, be sketched into that early picture. Lynn Huddon, our editor at Longman, believed in our vision from the first and supported us every single step along the way. Michael Greer, our development editor by title, third co-author in practice, helped us find our voice and in truth wrote the book with us, across the Internet and phone lines. Joe Opiela's personal belief in our project rallied us through the journey and was matched only by his generosity as Editor-in-Chief. We'd also like to thank many of our colleagues in the production process: Esther Hollander, whose editorial assisstance provided us with essential support in the early stages; Shaie Dively and Warren Drabek, who rose to the challenge of securing image and text permissions for a visually-centered book under tight deadlines; Elsa van Bergen, whose copyediting moved the manuscript into the final stages; and Katy Faria, whose incredible speed and graciousness during production was matched only by her meticulous attention to detail.

FIGURE 3. *Envision* proposed cover design by Miranda Alfano-Smith, November 2002.

We also count as key collaborators our reviewers for their expert guidance and timely suggestions on various versions of the manuscript in progress: Margaret B. Graham, Iowa State University; Sally E. Green, University of Colorado, Boulder; Cynthia Haynes, University of Texas–Dallas; Billie Hara, Texas Christian University; Katherine

Heenan, Arizona State University; H. Brooke Hessler, Oklahoma City University; Mary Hocks, Georgia State University; Mary Colleen Jenkins, Shoreline Community College; Carrie Leverenz, Texas Christian University; Laura Mandell, Miami University; Barry Mauer, University of Central Florida; Randall McClure, Minnesota State University; Bruce McComiskey, University of Alabama–Birmingham; Margaret P. Morgan, University of North Carolina–Charlotte; Sharmila Mukherjee, Oakland University; Esther Quinlan, University of Colorado, Denver; Peggy L. Richards, University of Akron; Irving N. Rothman, University of Houston; Patricia Webb, Arizona State University; Will Zhang, Des Moines Area Community College.

We are deeply grateful for the support from Stanford University and the Program at Writing and Rhetoric: Professor Andrea Lunsford and Marvin Diogenes provided inspirational leadership, unfailing support, and the opportunity to grow both pedagogically and professionally; our teaching colleagues Stacey Stanfield Andersen, Jenn Fishman, Marjorie Ford, Lisa Haefele, Sohui Lee, Joyce Moser, Carolyn Ross, Malgorzata Schaefer, Ardel Thomas, Anne Watters, and Susan Wyle generously offered their guidance, encouragement, and practical help throughout this project. We're also greatly appreciative for the administrative expertise and constant good humor of Cristina Huerta, Emily Phillips, Rania Hegazi Sanford, and the technological magic that Corinne Arraez, Adelaide Davies, Dan Gilbert, and Bob Smith make possible every day in the PWR Wallenberg classrooms.

In the classroom, we had the good fortune to find creative collaborators in our students. With energy and enthusiasm, they shared their ideas and insights with us throughout the planning, writing, and revision of this book. We'd like to thank our Writing and Rhetoric classes from Fall 2002 through Spring of 2004; we're especially grateful to the 60 students from our Fall 2003 Visual Rhetoric classes, whose faithful chapter feedback and experimentation with our Creative Practices, Collaborative Challenges, and assignments helped us streamline *Envision*, making it into a book designed specifically to address our student audience. We also would like to thank those students who granted permission for us to showcase their writing as models, both in the book and on the *Envision* Companion Website. Our students have been our co-authors and collaborators, and we continue to learn about writing and visual rhetoric by allowing them to teach us.

We extend our greatest appreciation to those who visualized our success with this project and made it possible for us to devote the long days, late nights, and weekends necessary to complete the book. To our friends and our families: without your love and support, we could never have realized our hopes and ambitions for this project. But, most of all, we dedicate *Envision* to Chris, Miranda, Max, and Laird: thank you for your patience, your understanding, and your love.

CHRISTINE L. ALFANO and ALYSSA J. O'BRIEN
August 2004

Envision

Persuasive Writing
in a Visual World

PART I

Exploration: Analysis and Argument

Rhetoric's classic definition as the art of persuasion suggests a power. So much of what we receive from others—from family and friends to 30-second blurbs on TV—is intended to persuade. Recognizing how this is done gives greater power to choose.

—Victor Villanueva, Jr.

CHAPTER 1

Introducing Visual Rhetoric

We've heard the adage "a picture is worth a thousand words." But what does this mean, exactly? Does it mean that pictures tell the same story words do, only more efficiently? Does it mean that pictures are more truthful or more objective than words? What about political cartoons, such as the one shown in Figure 1.1, or advertisements, propaganda posters, or film, where the writer makes strategic choices about the arrangement of both visual and verbal elements? What kinds of influence or power do such images have over their viewers? How do they communicate ideas and convince readers to see the world in a certain way?

FIGURE 1.1. Mike Thompson's cartoon about Michael Jackson's arrest on charges of child molestation makes its point through visual argument.

Chapter Preview Questions

- What is visual rhetoric?
- How do we "read" texts visually and rhetorically?
- How do we write about and with visual rhetoric?
- What are our tools of analysis?
- How do we read cartoon images and sequences ?
- How can we draft titles for our essays?
- How can we get started on a rhetorical analysis?

Understanding Visual Rhetoric

We'll address the fundamental question, "What is visual rhetoric?" throughout this book by looking at how a political cartoon, an advertisement, a news photo, and many other visual texts can be considered a **rhetorical act**—that is, a form of persuasion we'll call visual rhetoric. Visual rhetoric is a complex concept, and we'll need to spend some time looking at each part of the term. For now, let's define **visual rhetoric** as a form of communication that uses images to create meaning or construct an argument.

Thinking about the Visual

You encounter many kinds of visual texts every day, even in just walking across campus. Let's follow one hypothetical student—we'll call her Alex—as she walks to class and note the visual rhetoric she sees along the way. First stop: the dorm room, your average institutional room, which Alex and her roommate have decorated with Altoids ads they've ripped from magazines. There's also a large poster for the women's basketball team on one wall and a small Garfield comic taped above the computer screen. As Alex turns off her PC, we notice what's on the screen: the Website for Amazon.com, complete with banner ads for new software and an annoying pop-up telling Alex she'll win $50 if she clicks now. But Alex doesn't click; she shuts the machine down, piles her glossy-covered textbooks in her backpack, and slams the door shut on her way out.

As she walks down the hall, past the photos of other students in the dorm pasted outside their doors, she passes the lounge where several of her friends are watching a news broadcast on CNN. Alex pauses for a moment in the doorway until the broadcast breaks for a commercial, then, the news segment over, she continues, down the stairwell decorated with student event flyers—a ski trip, a rally, a dorm meeting—and pushes her way out into the cool autumn air. She only has two minutes to get to class, so she walks briskly past the student union with its event bulletin boards and its large hand-painted sign, "Café Open 6 am–midnight." Two students at a small card table have painted their faces blue and they hand her a small blue card with the cartoon of a surfer on it. "Come to our Hawaiian luau at the fraternity Saturday night!" they call to her as she crosses the quad and heads toward the statue of the university founder on his horse. Alex then walks over the school crest embedded in the center of the walkway and past a group of upperclass students who are congregated outside the administration building, waving signs that protest the conditions of university janitorial workers. She turns left, weaving along the back of a cluster of gleaming steel and brick buildings that constitute the engineering quad. To her right, she passes a thin metal sculpture called *Knowledge and Life* that guards the entrance to the library. Finally, she reaches her destination: the English department. As Alex jogs up the stone steps, she stops momentarily to pick up the campus newspaper and scan the photos and headlines on the front page before folding the newspaper under her arm. Down the hall and into the classroom; she is late. The professor has started the PowerPoint lecture already. Alex picks up the day's handout from the T.A. and sits down in the back row.

So now that we've seen Alex safely to her seat, how many visual arguments did you notice along the way? Ads, posters, cartoons, Web sites, textbooks, television shows, flyers, statues, signs, news-papers, PowerPoint slides, even architectural design: each can be seen as an example of visual rhetoric. Once you begin to look for it, you'll see it just about everywhere. Visual rhetoric permeates our cultural landscape. We take in an immense quantity of visual infor-mation in the course of our daily lives. Recognizing the power of visuals to persuade is an important part of learning to engage in contemporary society. It is the first step in thinking critically about the visual, or developing **visual literacy:** learning how to read our visual world.

CREATIVE PRACTICE

The next time you walk to class, pay attention to the visual rhetoric that you find along the way; take notes to catalog the different types of visual persuasion you encounter and develop your visual literacy. Then, write up your observations into a personal narrative. Discuss which types of visual rhetoric were most evident, which were most subtle, and which you found the most persuasive.

Thinking about Rhetoric

Student Writing

Read Esmeralda Fuentes's short narrative about the visual rhetoric she observes during the course of one day.
www.ablongman.com/envision001

Does this lens on our multimedia world—on the images that surround us at all times—seem familiar? You may recognize this focus on the visual from courses in communication, art, film, computer science, or design. However, visual rhetoric as a discipline, in which we consider the image as a powerful persuasive text, is just beginning to emerge. If we think about the visual as *persuasive,* then we see it as making an argument. This emphasis on the visual's persuasive power means that it performs a *rhetorical function.*

In one of the earliest definitions of **rhetoric,** the ancient Greek philosopher Aristotle characterized it as *the ability to discern the available means of persuasion in any given situation.* Essentially, this means knowing what strategies will work to convince your audience to accept your message. Although rhetoric emerged in Greece around 500 BCE as a means of training speakers for public arguments, the principles of rhetoric continue to be taught in universities across a wide variety of media, including oral communication, writing, and, most recently, visual and digital communication. In each case, rhetoric is an inherently practical and widely applicable art. For, as we know from Aristotle, rhetoric entails figuring out and using the best strategy of persuasion that will convince a given audience. As shown in Figure 1.2, you always have to attend to the **rhetorical situation**—the relationship between writer, text, and audience.

"Rhetoric may be defined as the faculty of observing in any given case the available means of persuasion."
—Aristotle

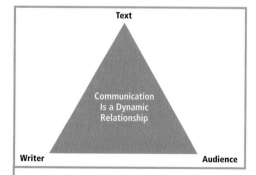

FIGURE 1.2. The rhetorical situation is a relationship between writer, text, and audience.

A Closer Look

For an interactive resource on classical rhetoric, visit Dr. Gideon Burton's Forest of Rhetoric.

www.ablongman.com/envision002

From the speeches of politicians to the advice of your parents, you hear persuasive arguments all the time. But you also use rhetorical strategies when you seek to persuade a coach to let practice out early, get an extension on a paper, or secure a summer job through your resumé and cover letter. Your verbal plea to your coach, your written email to a professor, your formal application for a job: these are all rhetorical acts in the form of oral and written arguments. Yet persuasion happens through visual means as well: how you stand and make eye contact, how you format your professional documents, even how you capitalize or spell words in an email. Moreover, when you insert an image in an essay, create a poster to advertise a club sport, or draw a cartoon spoofing university policy, you are moving into the realm of visual persuasion—"writing" with images. From photographs to Websites, political cartoons to advertisements, these visual texts use rhetorical means to persuade an audience. While some images may be more aesthetic than argumentative, many do in fact carry inherent or explicit persuasive messages. Think about brochures, movie trailers, flyers, commercial Websites, and even comics; these are all produced to create arguments. Since such strategies of persuasion occur through images—either alone or combined with words—rather than through words alone, we call this *visual rhetoric*.

The deliberately persuasive purpose of rhetoric makes such visuals distinctly more meaningful than simple decorative images. In other words, a text that uses visual rhetoric is one that is structured to produce an argument. A home video offers us a framed window into people's lives; a documentary is produced and edited specifically to suggest a particular point of view. The illustration in a children's book might provide a way to read a story; the sequential cartoons of a comic strip can offer powerful commentary on American society. In each example, the writer chooses the best visual representation for his or her message. The study of visual rhetoric provides you with the means to understand how and why such choices are made, and what the significance of these decisions is in the larger culture in which we live.

Writing about and with Visual Rhetoric

By writing about visual rhetoric texts, you'll be able to develop the skills that will equip you for larger, more complex writing projects. The goal of this book is to help you develop *as a writer* while we teach you the tools of analysis, argument, research, and production that you'll need for active participation in our multimedia world. At the same time, we will explore how we can think of the power of persuasion in these texts *as writing*. Today, the relationship between writing about images and understanding how visual texts work as powerful forms of writing is a fundamental concern. We need to be able to communicate not only in spoken and written form; we also need to understand what it means to "write" in a visual culture and through visual rhetoric as a medium.

What we think of as "writing" today is changing to include visual and multimedia texts.

In Figure 1.3, cultural critic Scott McCloud creates a diagram about the relationship between words and images to map out the complex nature of how we understand both pictures and written text. His argument gains more force from the fact that he uses visual rhetoric itself to convey his argument. In many ways, the work you do in the book will be similar: you'll analyze, study, and ultimately produce hybrid texts (involving both word and image) to present your arguments about how visual-verbal texts function as persuasive writing today.

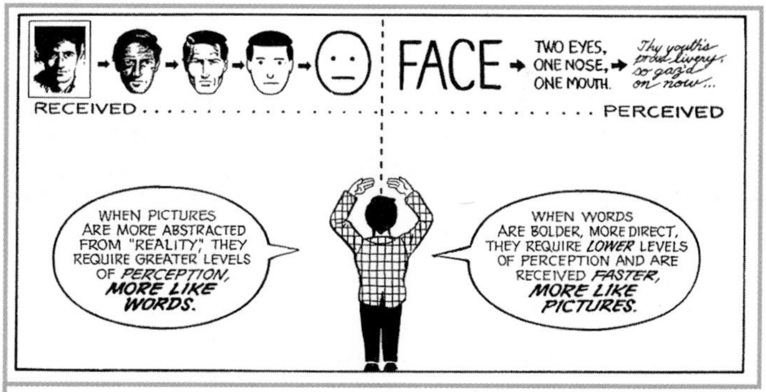

FIGURE 1.3. Scott McCloud uses cartoons to explain concepts.

We've chosen to explore various forms of comics and political cartoons in this chapter; by studying such texts, you'll develop skills as both a reader and a writer, learning how to read and analyze visual rhetoric, and, eventually, to create both written and visual texts that offer powerful arguments about the texts you encounter every day. In the process, you'll come to appreciate how writing as we know it is changing, causing us to approach it with a new set of eyes and rhetorical tools.

A Closer Look
Read Matthew Diamond's analysis of the importance of political cartoons in "No Laughing Matter: Post-September 11 Political Cartoons in Arab/Muslim Newspapers," *Political Communication* 19 (2002): 251–272.

Analyzing Images Rhetorically

Think of your favorite comics or political cartoons. Although they may seem purely aesthetic, merely informative about current events, or just plain funny, they do serve as an important mode of communicating ideas. As culture critic Matthew Diamond asserts, they "provide alternative perspectives at a glance because they are visual and vivid and often seem to communicate a clear or obvious message" (270). For example, the comic antics of Snoopy, Sponge Bob Square Pants, or Dilbert and Dogbert may not appear to carry any strong arguments about our society, human nature, or social relations. However, if you look closely at the composition of the image, or study its colors, layout, character placement, and line, then you can develop a deeper understanding of the cartoon's message. This can happen even if there are no words in the visual image.

Analyzing a Cartoon Frame

Consider the cartoon in Figure 1.4. While the cartoon is a complex set of frames, let's focus in first on the central, circular frame in the mid-

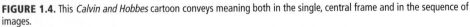

FIGURE 1.4. This *Calvin and Hobbes* cartoon conveys meaning both in the single, central frame and in the sequence of images.

dle of the strip. Even within the parameters of a single frame, we can see the power of visual rhetoric at work. When you look at the circular panel, what do you see?

You may see a split screen with two boys and two alien creatures; if you are more familiar with comic strips, you may identify the boy as Calvin from the cartoon *Calvin and Hobbes*. What is the *rhetorical function* of this image? The cartoon provides a dramatic enactment of a moment of crisis in this boy's life. The left-hand side portrays the "real" Calvin, cast in green liquid, an expression of alarm on his face. The white air bubbles surrounding him suggest his panic and amplify the impression of fear. In contrast, the right side of the cartoon features a different Calvin, his head opened up to reveal a mechanical brain, his eyes wide and staring like a boy possessed. It seems a standard body-snatcher science fiction scenario, complete with a pair of aliens, preparing to refasten Calvin's spiky blonde hair on top of this new brain. As an individual image, this panel taps into a message of fear and childhood imagining, with the aliens readying Robot Calvin to take over the functions of the real Calvin's life.

Now consider that panel as part of the larger strip. When read in conjunction with images of a stolen cookie jar, broken lamp, and discarded math book, Calvin's crisis takes on a slightly different meaning. As we arrive at the frame of Calvin gesticulating to his mother, her eyes narrowed with skepticism, we realize that the cartoon itself represents a moment of storytelling; the strip in effect juxtaposes Calvin's version of reality with his mother's. The final frame reveals the end of the tale, with Calvin banished to his room, staring out at the stars. These new elements add levels of meaning to the comic, as we are invited to ponder versions of reality, the power of childhood imagination, and the force of visual detail. Even Bill Watterson, reflecting on this comic strip years later, wrote, "I think much of the fun in this strip comes from the details in the drawing. The visual richness encourages you to look at the strip for a moment even after you get the joke." The cartoon, then, does have a persuasive function: the visual detail itself persuades readers to pause and think

AT A GLANCE

Selecting a Visual Rhetoric Image

When choosing a visual rhetoric text for analysis, ask yourself the following questions:

- Does the image attempt to persuade the audience?
- Are there sufficient elements in the image to analyze?
- What do you know about the author or the intended audience?
- What's your own interpretation of this image?

about the subjective nature of representation as well as the tensions between parent and child.

As you can tell, we gather a tremendous amount of information from seemingly simple cartoons. And indeed, different readers will make slightly modified interpretations of the cartoon. This is what we mean by **visual arguments:** each viewer makes a separate interpretation of the image. As we learn to develop our *visual literacy,* we can make more and better informed interpretations of such intriguing visual texts.

Analyzing Sequential Images

Let's think about how the meaning of a cartoon changes when it is integrated into a full strip. When we view still frames in succession, we find that meaning becomes more complex in a wonderful array of possible interpretations. Look at the sequential image in Figure 1.5.

FIGURE 1.5. In these sequential images, Watterson mocks naïve enthusiasm for a technology-driven future.

In this four-frame sequence, Bill Watterson uses his cartoon to participate in a larger cultural conversation about the dehumanizing effects of technology. Watterson could have written an article, or a series of essays, or even a full-length book on the subject. Instead, Watterson opted to use a different medium: comics. The message that Watterson's comic produces in this case is critical of naïve enthusiasm for computer technology: Watterson juxtaposes Calvin's idealistic but childlike view of a digitized future where machines will offer us a world with "No nuisance, no wasted time, no annoying human interaction" against Hobbes's more cynical but understated suggestion that such a techno-dominated world would offer us "No life."

Student Writing
Jack Chung's interpretation of a *Calvin and Hobbes* cartoon strip.
www.ablongman.com/envision003

This critique of the wired world speaks through a hybrid, visual discourse, not simply a printed verbal text. In Watterson's comic strip, not only do the words influence the reader, but also the visual associations link to each point of view. It is no coincidence that it is the prepubescent protagonist who voices what Watterson suggests is a naïve, egocentric point of view, and that it is an imaginary tiger who delivers the gentle yet toothed corrective that undercuts Calvin's idealism. Word collaborates with sequential images in this cartoon strip to make a persuasive point about our technologically mediated society.

Bill Watterson is not alone in the strategy of using visual texts to produce an argument; think of other cartoons that also use visual rhetoric to make persuasive statements. For instance, some cartoons, such as Aaron McGruder's *Boondocks* or animated cartoons such as Trey Parker and Matt Stone's *South Park,* offer sharper, more critical messages about society.

A Closer Look

Explore how cartoons make strong cultural statements in Alisa Coleman's article, "Calvin and Hobbes: A Critique of Society's Values." *Journal of Mass Media Ethics* 15.1 (2000) 17–28.

CREATIVE PRACTICE

Look at Figure 1.6. Jot down your analysis of the elements of the cartoon: color, composition, characters, and action. Then, ask yourself: what persuasive statement does the cartoon convey? What is its argument? What is the message for the reader?

FIGURE 1.6. *Boondocks* comments on American culture through both visual and verbal strategies.

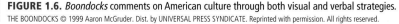

In your response to the Creative Practice, you might have noticed that the characters in this black-and-white sketch discuss the notion of Eurocentrism by referring to the popular television comedy, *Friends,* in large, bold font. But the layout and position of the image contribute in many ways to the cartoon's power as well. Note the expressions of scorn and naïveté on the faces of the characters; observe the long path to school that might signify the road of travails endured by African Americans. Look at the position of Huey in relation to Jazmine; how is he placed as the wiser one providing the polemical stance in this situation? Now look at another *Boondocks* cartoon in which Huey offers some of his own visual rhetoric for our analysis (see Figure 1.7).

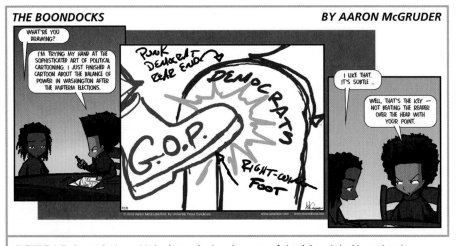

FIGURE 1.7. Cartoonist Aaron McGruder emphasizes the power of visual rhetoric in this comic strip.

In this instance, cartoonist Aaron McGruder refers to the power of political cartoons by demonstrating how Huey attempts to communicate his response visually to the electoral politics in Washington DC. The irony in his line "Well, that's the key—not beating the reader over the head with your point" reveals the very way in which *Boondocks* does in fact make its point explicit for readers of the strip. Note that McGruder subtitled his 2000 collection *The Boondocks: Because I Know You Don't Read the Newspapers*. That is, he casts his *cartoon* as a means of communicating arguments about current events, political controversies, and key issues concerning race in America. Thus, in the second frame of Figure 1.7, the main character turns to cartooning itself as a way to craft a persuasive political message. He makes a rhetorical statement with his visual image; the sequential image here is much more than an aesthetic, humorous, or informative text. It is a rhetorical act.

Specifically, in our analysis of the *Boondocks* strips, you probably assessed the cartoon's *rhetorical situation* in drawing your conclusions: the way the author (Aaron McGruder) took the audience (contemporary Americans) into consideration when creating the text (a comic strip, combining images and words). In fact, we can interpret McGruder's cartoon as offering a particularly striking example of a rhetorical situation: despite the fact that the Universal Press Syndicate had anticipated that this edgy strip would appear in somewhere between 30 and 50 newspapers, *Boondocks* was published in 160 newspapers for its first run in April of 1999 and was so popular with its audience that, by the beginning of 2000, it was carried by over 200 daily papers. McGruder's successful use of visual rhetoric to engage the topic of American race relations made his strip the most successful debut comic in the Universal Press Syndicate's history. His engagement with the audience shows how powerful the rhetorical situation can be not only for oral and written texts, but also for visual texts such as cartoon strips.

Visual Rhetoric as Types of Persuasion

As you can tell from our analysis of comics, visual rhetoric performs different kinds of rhetorical acts of persuasion. Part of your task in analyzing visual texts is learning how to read them carefully and make an argument about exactly how they function as visual arguments. Let's look at political and editorial cartoons to see more specifically the ways that visuals work.

Visual Rhetoric as Political Argument

Let's consider a type of cartoon with a more defined agenda: the political cartoon—or **editorial cartoon,** as it is also called—is one example of a rhetorical text that uses the visual in an explicit strategy of persuasion. The fact that cartoons offer a rich opportunity for social commentary has been recognized by cartoonists for over two centuries. From the densely symbolic eighteenth-century plates of

"The power and efficacy of political cartoons has long been recognized; because of their readability and visual immediacy, they appeal to and are understood by a wide audience"

—Lisa Melandri

William Hogarth, to the biting social satire of *Punch*'s illustrators, to the edgy work of political cartoonists such as Ann Telnaes and Mike Luckovich in this century, the editorial cartoon has emerged as a succinct, powerful apparatus for participating in dialogues on contemporary issues.

A Closer Look

Browse for political cartoons through Daryl Cagle's Professional Cartoonists Index.

www.ablongman.com/envision004

Indeed, the ability to engage a wide audience and convey a compelling message makes the political cartoon a particularly promising vehicle for communicating ideas. But often, even cartoonists themselves deny the persuasive power of their texts. In an interview with PBS anchor Jim Lehrer, for example, Pulitzer-prize-winning cartoonist Doug Marlette confessed: "I don't feel that it's my job to try and shape opinion. I wouldn't—you know, I have enough trouble trying to shape my own opinion, and . . . so I simply try to do a drawing that keeps me awake through the process of drawing it" (quoted in Lehrer, "Illustrated Men"). This notion that political cartoons serve primarily to express personal opinions often prevents us from taking them seriously. But if we approach political cartoons as important visual rhetoric texts, then we can develop a more sophisticated way of reading their persuasive power—and, in fact, of reading other visual media as well.

To develop our visual analysis skills, let's look at how Doug Marlette uses visual cues to comment on the political situation following the 9/11 attacks in the United States in Figure 1.8. When this political cartoon of an Arab man driving a Ryder truck drew death threats from the Muslim community, Doug Marlette responded by asserting that "the objective of political cartooning 'is not to soothe and tend sensitive psyches, but to jab and poke in an attempt to get at deeper truths, popular or otherwise'" (quoted in Moore). Look again at the cartoon and ask yourself *how* it attempts to jab or poke. What elements of composition, framing, shading, and layout suggest to you the target of Marlette's jab? What are the strategies of design, composition, and visual detail that construct the meaning of the cartoon? How might this cartoon

FIGURE 1.8. Marlette makes a controversial statement about stereotypes through a political cartoon.

be read differently by an American audience, an Arab audience, and an Arab-American audience? How might it be interpreted in the United States or in the Middle East as conveying a different persuasive message?

Political cartoons, according to Matthew Diamond, operate through "a kind of rhetorical 'tool kit' for constructing meaning."

Some might argue that the cartoon takes the announced threat of terrorists potentially using trucks to carry out nuclear attacks and reproduces it without irony. Another reader analyzing the cartoon could say that it mocks the government issuing the warning about post 9/11 terrorists. A third reader could point to the caricature of the driver and state that the cartoon makes fun of people of Arab descent. Recognizing these different ways of reading and responding to visual texts, think about the importance of the concept of *audience* as in the rhetorical situation shown in Figure 1.2.

Comparing Black and White to Color Images

For a very different kind of response to September 11, let's look at two political cartoons by another Pulitzer-prize-winning artist, Mike Luckovich, in which we see a compelling visual representation of the Statue of Liberty crying in the aftermath of the attacks on the World Trade Center twin towers. As you examine Figure 1.9, ask yourself: What is the persuasive message of this political cartoon? Write down your interpretation before reading further.

Perhaps, in your attempts to write a paragraph on the meaning of this cartoon, you commented on the statue's childlike features, suggestive of innocence or vulnerability. You might have remarked on the nose and hair as seeming particularly Caucasian and asked: what message does this send about "who is American"? You might also have integrated the history associated with this statue into your interpretation. Is Luckovich offering an argument about the way in which America's role as a haven for the oppressed and as a steward of peace and good-

FIGURE 1.9. Luckovich's "Statue of Liberty" circulated widely in newspapers and on the Internet after September II.

By permission of Mike Luckovich and Creators Syndicate, Inc.

will was attacked on September 11? Some students reading this cartoon have argued that it casts an ironic eye on the history of America; they read the Statue of Liberty as crying about the abuses of civil rights in the wake of the attacks. Others claim that the composition of the cartoon—the visual details of the crying eye and childish face—suggests that this country is more vulnerable than previously thought. As you consider the rhetorical situation for the cartoon (the way in which it was written in the wake of the attacks), reflect on how different audiences might respond to its power.

Now, compare the image in Figure 1.9 to the color one in Figure 1.10. What rhetorical function does color play in shaping audience response? Do we attribute different meaning, symbolism, power, and cultural resonance to the deep blue sky, the grayness of the statue, the brown smoke in her eyes? Write down your response to the color image.

Many students completing this exercise in our classes asserted that, to them, the black-and-white cartoon was more powerful than the color one, for they found black-and-white conveyed a somber, sad message, one in which the world was drained of color. These students felt that the color was inappropriate, for it suggested life and vibrancy that was no longer present. In contrast, other students thought that the color was effective, for the vivid blue brought home the shock felt by many on that day. What is your view?

As you look at the visual details of each cartoon and analyze them rhetorically for the messages they convey, your work with such texts shows that there is more going on with the visual image than mere fanciful illustration. Indeed, once we start paying careful critical attention to political cartoons as rhetorical texts and writing compelling analyses of them, then we can appreciate how such images convey powerful messages and meanings through the visual composition and arrangement of the text.

FIGURE 1.10. Luckovich's vibrant version shows the power of color in cartoons.

Images as Social Commentary

Let's look now at some examples of editorial cartoons that offer social commentary rather than a response to political issues. In the drawing by Daryl Cagle (see Figure 1.11), for instance, the face is recognizable to most twenty-first-century readers: the impish smile, the circular, black-frame glasses, and the prep-school tie identify this figure almost immediately as the young actor who plays Harry Potter in the first film of the series. However, through one strategic substitution, Cagle transforms this image from illustration into commentary; he replaces the famous lightning bolt scar on Potter's forehead with a dollar sign. Cagle's Potter has been branded not by

FIGURE 1.11. "Harry Potter," by Daryl Cagle, uses symbols as visual rhetoric.

his encounter with a nearly omnipotent wizard, but by his face-off with American capitalism. In this way, Cagle uses deliberate visual cues in his editorial cartoon to comment on the way in which this children's book hero has become a lucrative pop culture franchise.

COLLABORATIVE CHALLENGE

To begin writing about cartoons as powerful rhetorical acts, get into groups of three and turn to the Internet, a vast resource for finding visual rhetoric, to locate political cartoons that address the same issue from diverse national perspectives. Go to the *Envision* Website Chapter 1 resource page, and select two or three cartoons from Daryl Cagle's Professional Cartoonist Index. Compare how different countries craft persuasive visual arguments about the same issue with remarkably divergent messages. Working collaboratively, write out an analysis of each cartoon and prepare to share your interpretation with the rest of the class. Be sure to describe elements of the visual text in detail and discuss how each contributes to the rhetorical force of the image.

www.ablongman.com/envision005

The Visual-Verbal Connection

In your written analysis of cartoons so far, you may have focused on texts that rely primarily on images for rhetorical force. But often, visual rhetoric works as a combination of the verbal and visual. When we analyze visual rhetoric, we need to recognize the way that images and print texts can collaborate to produce an argument in what Robert Horn calls "the tight integration of words and visual elements." Indeed, in much of this book we join other scholars such as David Blakesley and Collin Brooke in "consider[ing] the visual and the textual as inextricably linked." We call such strategic combinations of words and images **hybrid texts**—rhetorical acts that involve both words and images.

Student Writing

See Jeff Enquist's analysis of a cartoonist's commentary on the media representation of Catholic priests as part of a larger social issue dealing with the place of religion in American culture.

www.ablongman.com/envision006

Consider the famous hybrid texts of *Saturday Night Live*'s Robert Smigel, who, in creating unique animation sequences called "TV Funhouse," overlays the words (his audio files of famous people speaking at a press conference or political speech) with images (his humorous animated cartoon) to create a subversive comment on today's current issues. This comic combination of word and image exposes and accentuates the rhetorical message he seeks to make. Similarly, political cartoons often appear as hybrid texts to increase the obviousness of their message.

In Figure 1.12, for instance, we find a commentary on the recent national debate over the Pledge of Allegiance. The drawing itself suggests a generic classroom in America: several elementary school students, diverse in terms of gender and race, face the flag in the standard, patriotic pose, their teacher looking on. The flag, as you might expect, is center stage—but it is significantly limp and uninspiring. This strategic rendering of the flag becomes complicated by the words that accompany the image: "one nation, under nothing in particular." Not only has "God" been removed from the pledge, but with the clever substitution of "under nothing in particular," cartoonist Gary Markstein

FIGURE 1.12. Gary Markstein conveys the controversy over the constitutionality of including the phrase "under God" in the Pledge of Allegiance.

speaks to the fear of raising a generation of Americans—and a future America—with no faith. He embodies his perspective in the disgusted teacher, whose mental thought, "God help us," voices an older generation's frustration and fear in the face of these young nihilists. This cartoonist has taken the controversy over the use of "God" in the Pledge of Allegiance to an extreme; he has used visual rhetoric to produce a statement on the "under God" debate as powerful as any written article found in a *New York Times* op-ed piece.

"The different ways in which words and pictures can combine in comics is virtually unlimited"

—Scott McCloud

CREATIVE PRACTICE

Using the political cartoon shown in Figure 1.13, create your own hybrid text. Think about the *rhetorical situation* of the cartoon: consider audience, author, and text. Now work on its argumentative content by filling in the blank tablet in the cartoon. When you are done, move into a small group, share your work, and discuss how each hybrid text produces a different rhetorical message.

FIGURE 1.13. John Deering's cartoon depends on both image and word.

By permission of John Deering and Creators Syndicate, Inc.

As you completed your work for the Creative Practice, you probably found that the addition of words altered the meaning of the cartoon in fundamental ways. You might have scripted a text that referred to OPEC, religion, September 11, or war with Iraq—a text that, through the combination of word and image, offers a very specific political message or social commentary. When we gave this exercise to our students, they offered the words "We support the USA" or "Women for equal rights!" Even more creatively, some suggested filling in the blank with a visual text—a drawing of a Muslim woman lifting her burka to expose her heels or a photo of Hillary Clinton. In the actual published version from the 2001 *Arkansas Democrat Gazette*, cartoonist John

Deering made the tablet present the ironic words "TO THE TALIBAN: GIVE US OSAMA BIN LADEN OR WE'LL SEND YOUR WOMEN TO COLLEGE." Deering used the ongoing search for Osama Bin Laden as a springboard for lampooning cultural differences in gender roles; his words suggest international and cultural differences between countries, and, as we have seen, political cartoons often use visual rhetoric to "jab and poke" at specific international issues and views. The visual-verbal connection thus often confirms the cultural resonance of a text suggested by the image alone. It is important to analyze *both* aspects when reading a visual rhetoric text.

FIGURE 1.14. The modified cartoon does not convey the persuasive point of the original.

Consider the way the persuasive power of the Pledge of Allegiance cartoon changes if we alter the balance between visual and verbal elements. In Figure 1.14, we have removed the figure of the appalled teacher and changed Markstein's clever rewriting of the Pledge of Allegiance (from "under nothing in particular") back to its original text, "one nation, indivisible, with liberty and justice for all." In this modified version, the cartoon is merely a visual-verbal representation, more of a descriptive cartoon about schools than a persuasive argument about that subject. As you approach your analysis of visual texts, make sure you pick a text that offers a persuasive point. Also, in your own writing, avoid simply describing the elements you see in comics, cartoons, and other visual rhetoric texts. Instead, zoom in on specific details and comment on their meaning. Make a persuasive argument by using visual evidence to support your analysis of how the cartoon succeeds at convincing an audience to see an issue in a particular way.

Writing an Analysis of Visual Rhetoric

As you turn to write your analysis of visual rhetoric, it is important also to keep in mind the social significance of this persuasive text. That is, you might include an opening line about the power of such visual-verbal rhetoric texts not only to persuade but also to shape public opinion in a certain way. This concern about the force of rhetoric on public opinion has a long history.

> **Rhetoric does not deal with absolute scientific truth**, but with probability and belief. This does not mean that rhetoric is automatically manipulative and false; it means that the world of human affairs simply does not involve the sort of absolute truths we find in mathematics or biology. **Rhetoric is, as Aristotle called it, the art of finding the available means of persuasion**, the art of solving problems that occur in the realm of human affairs and getting people to see that your solutions are good ones; in short, **rhetoric is an art of civic discourse**.
>
> —Mark Gellis, "Six Ways of Thinking about Rhetoric," (original emphasis)

Specifically, in one of the most influential texts on rhetoric—Plato's dialogue *Gorgias* from the fifth century BCE—Socrates criticizes the Sophist Gorgias for teaching rhetoric as a paid profession; Socrates describes rhetoric as the ability to "make people competent at speaking" and as an "agent of persuasion" that may not take into consideration moral or ethical considerations. Through Socrates, Plato voices his fear that "rhetoric is an agent of the kind of persuasion which is designed to produce conviction, but not to educate people about matters of right and wrong." It is from such moral anxieties about political motivations that we have developed the cliché *empty rhetoric.* Indeed, concerns about the truth or moral content of rhetoric continue to circulate today, as we are bombarded with the media's loose use of the term *political rhetoric*. In Plato's dialogue, however, Gorgias insists on proper moral character as a *precedent* to public speaking and *separate* from the communication strategies that he and the Sophists were teaching. Clearly, for the ancient Greeks as for politicans today, rhetoric's force on public opinion makes it an extremely valuable technique to learn. Its practical aspects have implications for society as a whole: through debate and persuasion, rhetoric facilitates the process of problem solving. This principle remains true from the debates in antiquity to our most current controversies.

AT A GLANCE

Visual Rhetoric Analysis Essays

- Do you have a sharp point to make about the visual text?
- Have you selected key visual details to discuss in support of your main point?
- Do you lead the reader through your analysis of the text by discussing important details in sequence? These include:

  Visual composition, layout, and imagery

  Verbal elements in the text

  Color, shading, and arrangement of items

  Caption or title of the image
- Do you have an effective title, main point, introduction, body, and conclusion?
- Have you included the image in the essay?

The Elements of Rhetorical Analysis

Seeing Connections
- For more on how to write a persuasive essay about your visual text, consult Chapter 2.
- Strategies for crafting an argumentative thesis are in Chapter 3.
- To learn how to incorporate research about the visual text in your writing, see Chapters 4–6.

When you write an analysis of a visual text, you perform a rhetorical act of persuasion yourself, and as such, you need to think about the crucial elements of analytical writing. These include having a point of interpretation to share with your reader, developing a coherent essay that proves your point by discussing concrete visual details as evidence, and leading your reader through the essay in an engaging and convincing way.

Also, spend some time brainstorming a title for your paper. Titles can set up your interpretation of the image and tell the reader not only what the analysis will cover, but also your angle on it. Try to play with language, linking your title to your main point, to the subject of the image, or to the larger issue raised by the visual rhetoric text. Test your working title by sharing with a partner in class.

COLLABORATIVE CHALLENGE

Peer Review your titles to check them against the following three criteria for Effective Titles.

- Informative (clear about the subject)
- Intriguing (cleverly catches audience's attention)
- Indicates your main point (conveys idea)

Practicing the Art of Rhetoric

Seeing Connections
For brainstorming strategies, explore the variety of approaches presented in Chapter 4.

In your own analysis of comics and cartoons throughout this chapter, you've probably come to realize the important role that writing can play in both the analysis and practice of visual rhetoric. As you move toward drafting your own written analysis of political cartoons or other image-based texts, consider the ways in which the lessons you've learned in this chapter can enrich your own writing. Specifically, think back to the cartoons or comics you found most striking in this chapter—perhaps the Michael Jackson cartoon, *Boondocks,* the Statue of Liberty, or the Pledge of Allegiance. Each of these texts conveys a powerful message through visual rhetoric. As part of your brainstorming process, keep in mind the need to think about the visual, analyze images both individually and sequentially, and then assess the elements of visual detail in order to offer a compelling reading of the text.

Student Writing

Eric Adamson examines the visual rhetoric strategies of economic forecasting charts and graphs.

www.ablongman.com/envision007

PREWRITING CHECKLIST
Comics and Cartoons

❏ **Topic:** What key issue is the comic or cartoon addressing?

❏ **Story:** On the most basic level, what is happening in the cartoon?

❏ **Audience:** In what country and in what historical moment was the cartoon produced? In what type of text did it first appear? A journal? A newspaper? Online? Was this text conservative? Liberal? Radical? Feminist? How does it speak to this audience?

❏ **Author:** What do you know about the artist? What kinds of cartoons does he or she regularly produce? Where does he or she live and publish? What kinds of other writing does this person do?

❏ **Argument:** What is the cartoon's message about the issue? Is there irony involved (does the cartoon advocate one point of view, but the cartoonist wants you to take the opposite view)?

❏ **Composition:** Is this political cartoon a single frame or a series of sequential frames? If the latter, how does the argument evolve over the series?

❏ **Word and image:** Does the cartoon rely exclusively on the visual? Or are word and image both used? What is the relationship between the two? Is one given priority over the other? How does this influence the cartoon's overall persuasiveness?

❏ **Imagery:** What choices of imagery and content does the artist make? Are his or her drawings very realistic? Are they caricatures? Does the artist include allusions or references to past or present events or ideas?

❏ **Tone:** Is the cartoon primarily comic or serious in tone? How does this choice of tone create a powerful rhetorical impact on the reader?

❏ **Character and setting:** What components are featured by the cartoon? A person? An object? A scene? Think about how character and setting are portrayed. What is the ethnicity, age, socioeconomic class, and gender of the characters? Do they represent actual people? Are they fictional creations? How are these choices rhetorical strategies designed to tailor the cartoon and its argument to its intended audience?

(continued)

❏ **Cultural resonance:** Does the cartoon implicitly or explicitly refer to any actual people, events, or pop culture icons? What sort of symbolism is used in the cartoon? Would the symbols speak to a broad or narrow audience? How does the cultural resonance function as a rhetorical strategy in making the argument?

WRITING PROJECTS

Visit the *Envision* Website for expanded assignment guidelines and student projects.

1. The Personal Narrative

Recall the Creative Practice from the beginning of the chapter (p. 7) when, after reading about Alex's observations of visual rhetoric on her way to class, you conducted a similar study of the visual rhetoric in your world. Write up your reflections into a *personal narrative essay.* Discuss which types of visual rhetoric were most evident, which were most subtle, and which you found the most persuasive.

2. The Rhetorical Analysis

Find a visual text that conveys a rhetorical argument and write an analysis. First, choose a political cartoon on a current issue. You might find an appropriate cartoon in a recent issue of *Newsweek*, in a collection such as Charles Brooks's *Best Editorial Cartoons of the Year*, or online through the *Envision* Website resource page for Chapter 1. Use the checklist on the preceding pages to help you write a rhetorical analysis of the cartoon.

FOR ADDED CHALLENGE

Visit the *Envision* Website for expanded assignment guidelines and student projects.

1. Comparative Rhetorical Analysis of Text and Image

Begin Assignment 2 above. Now, using either recent newspapers or newsmagazines as a source, or searching through a news database such as LexisNexis, find an article that addresses the same issue. Write a *comparative analysis of the text and the political cartoon.* What is each one's argument and what rhetorical strategies does each one use to effectively make that argument? You may want to use the prewriting checklist in looking at the political cartoon.

2. Comparative Rhetorical Analysis of Multiple Images

Follow the general guidelines for the Comparative Rhetorical Analysis project described above. Instead of comparing one article to a single cartoon, look at two or three articles and two or three cartoons that address the same issue. Introduce all your texts in the opening paragraph, and spend some time analyzing each one in detail. Make sure that your overarching argument raises a larger point about rhetorical attributes of all the texts you are comparing.

3. Historical Analysis of Visual Rhetoric

Choose several political cartoons from across the historical spectrum. Perhaps you want to consult the cartoons from *The Onion*'s "Our Dumb Century" or from online archives available through the *Envision* Website resource page for Chapter 1. For whatever texts you choose, write a *comparative historical analysis essay* in which you analyze how the cartoons use visual rhetoric to address a pressing issue of the time. Be sure to included specific visual details about each text.

CHAPTER 1 ON THE WEB

Resources and Readings	Exercises and Assignments	Student Writing
• Closer Look resources and annotated readings	• Interactive cartoon and comic exercises	• Personal narrative essays and blogs
• Links to Websites and online references on rhetoric	• The personal narrative essay assignment	• Visual rhetoric narrative reflections
• Links to comics, political cartoon archives, and image Websites	• The rhetorical analysis essay assignment	• Rhetorical analysis essays on cartoons, comics, international political cartoons, book covers, and economic graphs
• Further reading lists with annotations	• Peer review exercises	• Comparative rhetorical analysis essays
	• Self-assessment forms	• Historical rhetorical analysis essays
	• Focus on diverse learners and students with disabilities	

 www.ablongman.com/envision

Understanding the Strategies of Persuasion

What convinces you to buy a product, to make the decision to take a specific course, or to choose to attend a college? Some sort of text—a commercial, a course catalog, a brochure—undoubtedly influences your decision. Look at the college brochure in Figure 2.1, for instance. What strategies of persuasion does it use? Notice the way the brochure relies on a photo of a young female student working in the library. How does this picture catch your eye? Does it appeal to your enthusiasm for college study or make you identify with the student at the center of the ad?

Think now about other advertisements you have seen. How does the look of an ad make you pause and pay attention? Does a magazine ad show someone famous, a good-looking model, or characters that you can identify with emotionally? Does a television spot tell a compelling story? Does a brochure offer startling statistics or evidence? Perhaps it was not one factor but a combination of the above that you found so persuasive. Often, we are moved to buy a product, take a course, or select a specific school through persuasive effects that are so subtle we may not recognize them at first.

Brochures, ads, flyers, and other visual-verbal texts employ many of the same strategies as written arguments, often in condensed form. Applying our analysis of visual rhetoric to these texts

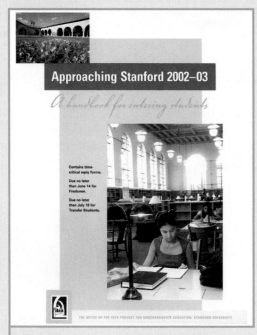

FIGURE 2.1. The cover of Approaching Stanford 2002–2003 functions as an ad for the university.

will help us understand how they work and how we can respond critically to them. In fact, you'll find that analyzing the strategies of persuasion in ads will help you assess conventional written texts with greater depth and understanding.

Chapter Preview Questions

- How do rhetorical strategies work?
- What are specific strategies of argumentation?
- What role do the rhetorical appeals of logos, pathos, and ethos play in persuasion?
- What is the effect of exaggeration in these appeals?
- How does parody work in advertisements?
- What is *kairos* and how does an awareness of context work to create a persuasive argument?
- How can you write a rhetorical or contextual analysis of advertisements?

Examining Rhetorical Strategies

Visual rhetoric, much like writing and speaking, operates through particular persuasive means we call **rhetorical strategies**—the techniques rhetoricians use to move and convince an audience. In this chapter, by focusing on advertisements, we will examine how such strategies work in powerful arguments across a range of texts. For, in our visually saturated world, advertisements represent one of the most ubiquitous forms of persuasion. In many ways, ads are arguments in incredibly compact and complex forms. There is little room to spare in an ad; persuasion must be locked into a single frame or into a brief 30-second spot. Yet, at the same time, ads offer us ample material with which to work as we try to understand exactly *how* visual rhetoric functions as persuasion.

Advertising is the most obvious place we might expect to find rhetorical figures (of which there are literally hundreds). In the first place, there is no doubt that someone is setting out deliberately to persuade; in the second place, there is little doubt that everything in the advertisement has been most carefully placed for maximum effect.

—Victor Burgin

CREATIVE PRACTICE

Examine the advertisements distributed by your university for prospective students: Websites, brochures, catalogs, and flyers in the mail. Look closely at both the images and the words. If the materials are advertising the "college experience," then what tools are they using to persuade you to attend the university? For example, what are the students doing? What types of activities do the photographs show and what kind of font, layout, and headings are used in the design of the ad? How do these choices construct a particular "character" for the school? Next, compare two different forms of ads, such as a brochure and a catalog. Is one more focused on sports photographs, pictures of teachers, or the landscape of the campus? What can you deduce from this selection of images? Now examine the school's Website. Does the page show students laughing, playing a sport or a musical instrument, or smiling in class? What kinds of emotions are such images designed to produce in you as the key audience and prospective customer?

Student Writing

Traci Bair analyzes the advertising strategies of Oklahoma City University's viewbook for prospective students in her essay, "In Loco Parentis."
www.ablongman.com/envision008

"Every time a message seems to grab us, and we think, 'I just might try it,' we are at the nexus of choice and persuasion that is advertising."

—Andrew Hacker

You may have noticed how the college Websites you explored in the above Creative Practice work as advertisements for potential students. These sites' use of carefully crafted visual rhetoric shows an attempt to target, attract, and secure a particular audience. We may not think of college Websites as ads; they seem to exist as purely informational texts. Yet clearly they have a rhetorical function: they want *you* to enroll at their college.

The promotional materials distributed by colleges and universities represent only a small fraction of the advertising circulating within our culture. As part of the "stuff" of our everyday lives, the average adult encounters 3000 advertisements every day (Twitchell, *Adcult* 2). This statistic becomes a little less shocking if you consider all the places ads appear nowadays: not just in magazines or on the television or radio, but on billboards, on the sides of buses, trains, and buildings, on computer screens, in sports stadiums, even spray-painted on the sidewalk.

You probably can think of other places you've seen advertisements lately, places that may have surprised you: in a restroom, on the back of a soda can, on your roommate's T-shirt. As citizens of what cultural critic James Twitchell calls "Adcult USA," we are constantly exposed to visual rhetoric that appeals to us on many different levels. In this chapter, we'll gain a working vocabulary and concrete strategies of rhetorical persuasion that you can use when you turn to craft your own persuasive texts. The work we do here will make you a sharper, more strategic writer, as well as a savvy reader of advertisements.

Thinking Critically about Argumentation

By looking closely at advertisements, we can detect the rhetorical choices writers and artists select to make their points and convince their audiences. In this way, we realize that advertisers are rhetoricians, careful to attend to the *rhetorical situation.* For instance, advertisements adopt a specific strategy of argumentation to make their case.

- They might use **narration** to sell their product—using their ad to tell a story.
- They might employ **comparison-contrast** to encourage the consumer to buy their product rather than their competitor's.
- They might rely upon **example** or **illustration** to show how their product can be used or how it can impact a person's life.
- They might use **cause and effect** to demonstrate the benefits of using their product.
- They might utilize **definition** to clarify their product's purpose or function.
- They might create an **analogy** to help make a difficult selling point or product—like fragrance—more accessible to their audience.
- They might structure their ad around **process** to demonstrate the way a product can be used.
- They might focus solely on **description** to show you the specifications of a desktop system or a new SUV.
- They might use **classification** and **division** to help the reader conceptualize how the product fits into a larger scheme.

Seeing Connections
For a review of the rhetorical situation, see Chapter 1.

These strategies are equally effective in both written and visual texts. Moreover, they can be used effectively to structure both a smaller unit (a paragraph, a part of an ad) and a larger one (the text as a whole, the whole ad).

Even a single commercial can be structured around multiple strategies. The famous "This Is Your Brain on Drugs" commercial from the late 1980s used *analogy* (a comparison to something else—in this case, comparing using drugs and frying an egg) and *process* (reliance on a sequence of events—here, how taking drugs affects the user's brain) to warn its audience away from drug use. In this 30-second spot, the spokesperson holds up an egg, saying, "This is your brain." In the next shot, the camera focuses on an ordinary frying pan as he states, "This is drugs." We as the audience begin to slowly add up parts A and B, almost anticipating his next move. As the ad moves to the visual crescendo, we hear him say, "This is your brain on drugs": the image of the egg sizzling in the frying pan fills the screen. The final words seem almost anticlimactic after this powerful image: "Any questions?"

FIGURE 2.2. This three-page Clairol hair-color spread utilizes several different strategies of argumentation.

These strategies function just as persuasively in print ads as well. For example, look at the three-page advertisement for Clairol Nice'n Easy hair color in Figure 2.2, an ad designed to move the reader literally through its visual argument. Coming across the first image, the reader would probably pause to contemplate the interesting visual and textual question posed by the ad, "Got hide-under hair?" The colloquial tone of the print text is echoed by the image: an extreme close-up of a young woman, making direct eye contact with the reader while hiding her hair beneath a floppy throw-pillow. She serves as an *example* or *illustration* of the ad's problem; turning the page, the reader finds the solution. In the two-page spread that follows, the reader is reintroduced to the model, her hair now uncovered, shining, and flowing, setting up a powerful *comparison-contrast* to the original image. To the right of the image, the ad showcases the secret behind this transformation: Nice'n Easy hair color. We can in fact read this ad as a *cause and effect* argument, one that uses a powerful visual strategy of argumentation to convey the benefit of using the product.

A Closer Look

For a particularly striking example of a television ad featuring comparison-contrast, view Apple's "Big and Small" laptop ad. www.ablongman.com/envision009

COLLABORATIVE CHALLENGE

Select a recent edition of a popular magazine. With a partner, look through it, selecting a few ads that you find persuasive. Discuss what strategies of argumentation you see at work in these visual rhetoric texts. Try to find an example of each of the different approaches; share the ads you selected with the rest of the class.

"There must be a fourth rhetorical appeal: HUMOS, the use of humor as a persuasive strategy."
—David Baron, Stanford student

Understanding the Rhetorical Appeals of Logos, Pathos, and Ethos

The rhetorical strategies we've examined so far can be filtered through the lens of classical modes of persuasion dating back to around 500 BCE. Their formal terms are *logos, pathos,* and *ethos.* It might be helpful to consider some preliminary definitions provided in the box to the right and then explore concrete examples of each of these appeals in turn.

These rhetorical appeals each represent a mode of persuasion that can be used by itself or in combination. As you might imagine, a text often will employ more than one mode of persuasion, such as "passionate logic"—a rational argument written with highly charged prose, "good-willed pathos"—an emotional statement that relies on the character of the speaker to be believed, or "logical ethos"—a strong line of reasoning employed by a speaker to build authority. Moreover, texts often use rhetorical appeals in combinations that produce an *overarching effect* such as irony or humor. You might also think of humor as one of the most effective forms of persuasion. Jokes and other forms of

AT A GLANCE

Rhetorical Appeals

• *Logos* entails rational argument: appeals to reason and an attempt to persuade the audience through clear reasoning and philosophy. Statistics, facts, definitions, and formal proofs, as well as interpretations such as syllogisms or deductively reasoned arguments, are all examples of means of persuasion we call "the logical appeal."

• *Pathos,* or "the pathetic appeal," generally refers to an appeal to the emotions: the speaker attempts to put the audience into a particular emotional state so that the audience will be receptive to and ultimately convinced by the speaker's message. Inflammatory language, sad stories, appeals to nationalist sentiments, and jokes are all examples of pathos.

• *Ethos* is an appeal to authority or character; according to Aristotle, *ethos* meant the character or goodwill of the speaker. Today we also consider the speaker's reliance on authority, credibility, or benevolence when discussing strategies of ethos. But while we call this third mode of persuasion the "ethical appeal," it does not mean strictly the use of ethics or ethical reasoning. Keep in mind that ethos is the deliberate use of the *speaker's character* as a mode of persuasion.

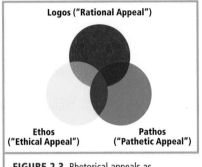

FIGURE 2.3. Rhetorical appeals as intersecting strategies of persuasion.

humor are basically appeals to pathos because they put the audience in the right emotional state to be receptive to an argument, but they can also involve reasoning or the use of the writer's authority to sway an audience.

Since they appear so frequently in combination, you might find that conceptualizing logos, pathos, and ethos through a visual representation helps you to understand how they relate to one another (see Figure 2.3).

As you read this chapter, consider how each visual text relies upon various rhetorical appeals to construct its message.

Appeals to Reason

As we defined earlier, *logos* entails strategies of logical argument. According to the second edition of the *Oxford English Dictionary,* the Greek word *logos* can be translated as "reason" or "word." We use the modern derivative of this word every day: whether you're an avid *Star Trek* fan or a philosophy student, you probably are quite familiar with the principle of logic. As a writer, you use logos when you construct an essay around facts and reason; in general, an argument based on logos will favor the use of logic, statistical evidence, quotations from authorities, and proven facts. But appeals to logic can also include interpretations of "hard evidence," such as found in syllogisms, reasoned arguments, closing statements in law, inferences in the form of statistical models, and appeals to "common sense" or cultural assumptions.

We see logos deployed in various ways—not just in formal logic or courts of law, but in advertisements. In fact, the majority of advertising utilizes an implicit *causal argument:* if you buy this product, then you or your life will be like the one featured in the ad. Sometimes the associations are explicit: if you use Pantene, then your hair will be shinier; if you buy Tide detergent, then your clothes will be cleaner; if you buy a Volvo, then your family will be safer driving on the road. Sometimes the *cause-effect argument* is more subtle: buying Sure deodorant will make you more confident; drinking Coke will make you happier; wearing Nike will make you perform better on the court. In each case, logos, or the use of logical reasoning, is the tool of persuasion responsible for the ad's argumentative force.

When we first look at the ad for Crest Whitening Strips in Figure 2.4 our eyes are drawn immediately to the model's white smile, posi-

The most amazing thing you can wear the first day of school? Your new smile.

The new jeans are great. Ditto for that new backpack. Now, let's focus on the twice a day for 14 days, anytime, anywhere. Then it's time for the premiere of your main event: that smile of yours. Two words: Crest Whitestrips. Just 30 minutes: whiter, brighter smile.

FIGURE 2.4. Crest Whitening Strips advertisement. Inset images offer visual evidence for the ad's argument.

tioned near the center of the two-page spread. Our gaze next moves up to her eyes and then down again to the two juxtaposed close-up shots of her teeth.

The two close-up photos of her teeth are captioned, but the visual images really carry the force of the argument. They are before-and-after stills, demonstrating in brilliant color the whitening power of Crest. The contrast between the two images makes a deliberate *logos* appeal by constructing a *cause-and-effect* argument. The captions—the words beneath the two boxes—confirm the message imparted by the visual image. The final small box insert shows the product and suggests the solution to the logical equation at work in this ad. That is, the graphic of the product box is our last visual stop. The fact that the ad's words, "Your new smile" appear beneath the smile—as the conclusion of the logical argument—reinforces the persuasive message that Crest indeed will give its viewers such white teeth. To put the logic

Student Writing

Fred Chang analyzes Apple Computer's reliance on logos in its advertising battle with Intel.

www.ablongman.com/envision010

FIGURE 2.5. Escort Passport Radar Detector ad persuades through the logical appeal of evidence and statistics.

plainly: if viewers use this product, then they too will achieve this end result. The images convey a visual promise of the product's performance. In this way, the ad relies on logos to attract and convince its audience.

As you can see, the mode of persuasion we call logos often operates through a combination of image and text. Consider the Escort Passport Radar Detector ad in Figure 2.5.

This ad relies at least in part on the strategic visual layout of its composition; in Western cultures, we normally read from top left to bottom right, and the ad uses this visual path to load up the space near the top with its evidence: a series of expert testimonies and recognizable headings from sources such as *Motor Trend, Car and Driver, Popular Mechanics* and *RadarTest.com*. This careful composition strategy reveals the importance of evidential material to develop the argument for the product's value.

Moreover, the ad places at the center a bold claim for being "the best" and cites statistics that compare the speed detector with its competitors and thereby "proves" its superiority. Such statistical evidence, comparative tables, and listing of "specs" or specifications are a proven marketing strategy for many technology-based products. While we can recognize them as appeals to logos, we might be wary of how data could have been modified to shape audience response.

Seeing Connections
See Chapter 5 for a discussion of the reliability of statistics.

COLLABORATIVE CHALLENGE

With a partner, find two additional ads that use logos as a persuasive appeal. Choose one that relies on images for its appeal and one that depends on the meaning of the words in the ad for its argumentative force. Together, draft a paragraph in which you compare the ads. Share your analysis with another group. How did your analyses differ? What did you learn from this exercise?

The different interpretations that you and your classmates produced for the Collaborative Challenge points to the way in which readers participate in shaping the meaning of texts. As cultural critic Paul Messaris asserts, because images don't follow the same principles of grammar and syntax as written language, additional responsibility is placed on the viewer to make connections and to construct the message of the advertisement. Indeed, even advertising experts attribute a great deal to the role of the audience in the rhetorical situation.

A Closer Look

See *Visual Persuasion: The Role of Images in Advertising,* by Paul Messaris (Sage Publications, 1997) for a theoretical discussion of how ads work.

It is my assertion that the carefully guided recall of a series of stored memories is the secret to powerful advertising. Do the words of your ad cause the listener to imagine a series of personal experiences? (The experiences can be real or imagined. The important thing is that they be recalled from the mind in such a manner as to actively engage the listener in your ad.) To put it plainly, the listener must be a participant in your advertising. You must cause him to imagine himself taking precisely the action you so artfully describe.

—Roy H. Williams

Logical Fallacies

Once you appreciate the way in which ads work through rational arguments, then you can recognize the care that must be taken in using appeals like logos. When crafting your own written analysis of advertisements, be careful not to rely upon mistaken or misleading uses of logos, commonly called **logical fallacies.** The causal strategy underlying most advertising can be seen as an example of faulty logic, for surely it is fraudulent to suggest that wearing a certain brand of clothing will make you popular or that drinking a certain beer will make

AT A GLANCE

Logical Fallacies

- **The post hoc fallacy:** confusing cause and effect

- **The hasty generalization:** drawing a conclusion too quickly without providing enough supporting evidence

- **The either-or argument:** reducing an argument to a choice between two diametrically opposed choices, ignoring other possible scenarios

- **Stacking the evidence:** offering evidence that shows only one side of the issue

- **Begging the question:** using an argument as evidence for itself

- **The red herring:** distracting the audience rather than focusing on the argument itself

you attractive to the opposite sex. For instance, consider the typical weight-loss advertisement. "I lost 31 pounds in 3 months!" one happy dieter exclaims on camera. The camera shows an old video clip of the subject at her previous weight, and then it moves to the newly trimmed-down version, usually with stylish hair style and tight-fitting clothes—a clear before-and-after strategy. However, more and more often, you now find these images captioned with one telling phrase: "These results not typical." This disclaimer points to advertisers' recognition that they, like other rhetoricians, need to be careful in their use of logos as an argumentative appeal.

Appeals to Emotion

Roughly defined as "suffering" or "feeling" in its original Greek, the term ***pathos*** actually means to put the audience in a particular mood or frame of mind. Modern derivations of the word *pathos* include "pathology" and "pathetic," and indeed we speak of pathos as *the pathetic appeal.* But *pathos* is more a technique than a state: writers use it as a tool of persuasion to establish an intimate connection with the audience by producing powerful emotions in the reader. We encounter ads that rely on pathos all the time, and indeed, the visual composition of an ad often taps our emotions in ways we barely recognize.

In our discussion of logos, we looked at how car companies rely on statistical data, authoritative testimony, and facts to sell their cars. But pathos is a compelling strategy that works well in many ads. Consider the Porsche commercial showing a sleek red car speeding along a windy mountain road, the Ford Explorer TV spot featuring the rugged SUV plowing through a muddy off-road trail, or the Volkswagen bug ad using nostalgia and uniqueness as a selling point for its small beetle-like car. Each of these ads uses pathos to produce a specific feeling in its viewer: I want to drive fast, wind in my hair; I want to get off the beaten path, forge into a new frontier; I want to stand out in a crowd, make a statement.

One famous ad campaign that relied on pathos to persuade its audience was the "Reach Out" campaign created by Bell Systems (now AT&T), one of the biggest telephone companies in the 1980s. In a recent revitalization of this concept, AT&T has launched a series of print and television ads that capitalize on an emotional connection with the reader. From the father, stranded in an airport, bonding with his 6-year-old daughter on the other end of a phone; to the commuting mother, stuck on a bus, listening to her son's piano recital on her cell phone; the newlywed couple making up through text messaging after a fight, each of these ads relies on the power of pathos as a driving force of modern persuasion.

Student Writing
Cyrus Chee's rhetorical analysis reads the appeals to pathos in two different poster ads for contemporary films about the Holocaust.
www.ablongman.com/envision011

In one ad from this series (Figure 2.6), AT&T employs pathos through a visual juxtaposition of images to suggest the way its wireless services connects people. When first looking at the ad, the viewer focuses on a snapshot of a grandmother, leaning forward, her lips slightly pursed as if preparing to blow out candles. Her posture then draws the reader's attention across the page to the festive birthday cake, with candles lit, and the small figure of a child whose gaze falls softly back on her grandmother's face. It is only after further reflection that the reader realizes that she is looking at not one image but two: a pair of overlaid photos linked by the theme of love and shared experience. The ad's argument is this: using AT&T wireless phones will connect us to our loved ones, no matter how distant, and allow us to be part of the special moments in their lives. In this way, the strong family ties suggested by the visual layout of the ad function as pathos, playing on our emotions by tapping our need for family connection, intimacy, and closeness with those we love.

FIGURE 2.6. This "Reach Out" advertisement relies on emotional appeal.

CREATIVE PRACTICE

Examine the ad sequence in Figures 2.7 and 2.8 and compare the rhetorical appeals used in each. Notice how the visual rhetoric of Figure 2.8 depends more on *pathos* (or an appeal to emotions) than does Figure 2.7, which relies mostly on *logos* (or an appeal to reason). Now write your own close analysis of each ad.

FIGURE 2.7. A somber anti-smoking ad.

FIGURE 2.8. A more emotional anti-smoking ad, also by the American Legacy Foundation.

As you worked through the Creative Practice, you probably noted the subtle distinctions between the ads, even without being able to decipher the handwriting to read the content of each letter. The woman in Figure 2.7 with resigned demeanor, professional dress, and downcast gaze, suggests a pensive, rational approach to the issue—an approach mirrored in the steady lines of her handwritten note. The woman in Figure 2.8 by contrast, engages the audience with her pained expression, contorted posture, and erratic handwriting, all reflecting her distraught emotional state. Each ad advocates the same message—that tobacco companies must take responsibility for the damaging effects of their products—but they do so through using pronouncedly different appeals.

In addition, *pathos* also works as an appeal to sexuality. You may have been waiting for this part of our analysis of advertisements, for clearly one of the most tried-and-true principles of advertising operates through the emotions produced by sexual imagery. Clearly, "Sex Sells." Look at Calvin Klein models posed in near nudity or a recent Abercrombie and Fitch catalog where models are more likely to show off their midriffs than a pair of khakis, and you can see how in many cases advertisers tend to appeal more to nonrational impulses than to our powers of logical reasoning. One Calvin Klein ad for cologne, for example, uses a strong red color, bold lines in the shape of an arrow pointing at a man's body, and the exposed chest of the model to attract a viewer's attention. The ad works cleverly to sell perfume, not on the merits of the scent or on its chemical composition, but through the visual rhetoric of sexuality and our emotional responses to it.

A Closer Look

For examples of ads that rely on sexuality as a persuasive strategy, link to the Unofficial Calvin Klein Website and others.

www.ablongman.com/envision012

COLLABORATIVE CHALLENGE

Find five advertisements from recent magazines—for instance, *Cosmo, Vogue, Seventeen, GQ, Details, Esquire*—that use sexuality to sell their products. In your group, compare the use of pathos in these different ads. When is this appeal an effective marketing strategy? When does it seem ineffectual or inappropriate?

Exaggerated Uses of Pathos

While these strategies of persuasion successfully move their audience, sometimes advertisers exaggerate the appeal to emotion for more dramatic effect.

Consider the case of exaggerated pathos found in the Listerine campaign from the early twentieth century. In the 1920s, Gerard Lambert introduced the term *halitosis* into the popular vocabulary as a marketing strategy; he used it to convince Americans that Listerine was their only alternative to public embarrassment from bad breath (Twitchell, *Adcult* 144). Regardless of the fact that Listerine's primary use at the time was as a hospital disinfectant, Lambert transformed American culture through his successful use of **false needs.**

In Figure 2.9, we see an example from the 1950s of this famous ad campaign. The words of the headline, spoken by the two women in the upper right corner ("He's Hanging Himself Right Now!") are a bit

AT A GLANCE

Exaggerated Uses of Pathos

- *Over-sentimentalization:* distracting the audience from evidence or relevant issues

- *The scare tactic:* capitalizing on the audience's fears to make a pitch

- *The false need:* amplifying a perceived need or creating a completely new one

- *The slippery slope fallacy:* suggesting that an event or action will send the audience spiraling down a "slippery slope" to a serious consequence

FIGURE 2.9. This Listerine ad uses numerous appeals to pathos to persuade viewers to use its product.

A Closer Look

James B. Twitchell provides a historical study of the ad campaign in "Listerine: Gerard Lambert and Selling the Need" in *Twenty Ads that Shook the World: The Century's Most Groundbreaking Advertising and How It Changed Us All.* (New York: Three Rivers Press, 2000): 60–69

cryptic so that the reader has to look to the image in the center of the ad to understand its message. The drawing of the man and woman makes a direct correlation between personal hygiene and romantic relationships, creating a sense of *false need* in the consumer for the product. In this case, the woman's averted head suggests her rejection of the suitor. Moreover, as you can see, the ad also uses the **scare tactic;** the disapproval on the women's faces produces a fear of rejection in the viewers. The way in which the woman's body turns away from the man augments this pathos appeal. Having deciphered the meaning of the ad from the image, the words now seem to confirm the idea in the headline that the man stands little chance of a romantic encounter. Image and word collaborate here to produce a powerful emotional reaction in the audience. Moreover, the threat of impending loss signifies a successful use of the **slippery slope:** first bad breath and then solitude.

The more contemporary advertisement campaign for Clearasil works in a similar way to the Listerine ad with regard to acne; the company defined a problem and then offered its product up as a solution. Take a moment now to think about times in your own life where you may have been motivated to purchase a product through *false needs:* have you ever bought a man's or woman's razor? pump-up basketball shoes? an angled toothbrush? curl-enhancing mascara? What other examples of exaggerated pathos can you recall?

Appeals to Character and Authority

The last of the three appeals that we'll look at in this chapter is *ethos*—literally "character." Perhaps you have used ethos in other disciplines to mean an argument based on ethical principles. But the *rhetorical* meaning of the term is slightly different: according to Aristotle, *ethos* works as a rhetorical strategy by establishing the good-will or credibility of the writer or speaker. In fact, as a writer you use ethos every time you pick up a pen or proofread your essay; you are constructing an argument in which your power to persuade depends on credibility. Let's look at how advertisements rely on *ethos* to construct compelling and memorable campaigns.

Seeing Connections
See Chapter 3 for a discussion of developing your ethos as an author through *persona*.

A Closer Look

To see one of American Express's most creative uses of celebrity endorsement, view their ads featuring "buddies" Jerry Seinfeld and Superman.
www.ablongman.com/envision013

One of the most prominent features of many contemporary advertisements is the celebrity endorsement. This form of ethos appears in ads everywhere. You can't turn on the television without spotting a familiar big-screen face promoting a small-screen product: NFL linebacker Terry Tate promoting Reebok; Michael Jordan selling Gatorade; Catherine Zeta-Jones arguing the merits of T-Mobile; even the Osbournes from MTV serving as spokespersons for Pepsi. While there is a rational appeal at work behind some endorsements—having basketball superstar LeBron James sell basketball shoes, for instance, makes sense—many campaigns rely not only on the celebrity's suitability for selling a product but also on the person's star appeal, character, and goodwill. Consider the power of the famous "Got Milk?" campaign. Here's the argument: if this celebrity likes milk, shouldn't we? Indeed, when we see Michael Meyers—or others, such as Venus Williams, Hillary Duff, Nelly, Jason Kidd, or Jackie Chan—sporting the famous milk moustache, we find the ad persuasive because these celebrities are vouching for the product. We look to their goodwill as public figures, to their character as famous people putting their reputation on the line.

If a celebrity's image takes a turn for the worse (think about the charges brought against Kobe Bryant or Michael Jackson in 2003), then we often find a quick severing of connections to avoid *guilt by association*. However, the power of advertising as a persuasive act is that, given the appropriate rhetorical situation, even a questionable reputation can be turned into a positive appeal. Consider, for instance, how child star Gary Coleman turned his own financial problems to his advantage as a spokesperson for CashCall, an online loan service; how tennis great John McEnroe used his hot-headed reputation to sell Heineken beer; how basketball coach Bobby Knight parodied his own bad temper to sell Minute Maid orange juice. In each case, these figures turned criticism and media scrutiny to their advantage, using their "bad boy" ethos to sell a product.

While the visual impact of a famous face can be a powerful use of ethos, celebrity endorsement is only one way to create this sort of appeal. Sometimes the *lack* of fame can be a strategic tool of the trade. Consider the Apple Switch ad campaign that featured everyday people stepping into the role of spokesperson for the Apple computer system. These ads featured the everyman or everywoman of various ages, nationalities, and professions speaking directly into the camera about their reasons for changing from PCs to Apple computers. The combination of an unknown spokesperson, a clear example, a simple white background, and a slightly choppy film style— designed to seem edited and somewhat amateur—brought an ethos to the campaign based not on star power but on no-nonsense use and everyday application. In assessing the rhetorical situation for creating their ads, Apple recognized an important fact: for a large part of their audience, ethos would derive not from the flash of a celebrity smile but from identification with real-life Apple users.

CREATIVE PRACTICE

Visit the Apple I-Pod, Apple I-Tunes, and Apple Switch links through the Chapter 2 resources on the *Envision* Website, and compare the use of this everyman-ethos appeal in the I-Pod, I-Tunes, and Internet-based Switch ads. As you look at these ads, jot down differences in the approach and strategies of argumentation. Having done so, write a paragraph-long analysis on one of the ads that discusses the rhetorical strategies Apple used to create its visual argument. In a second paragraph, verbally (or literally) sketch out an alternative campaign or ad that draws on different appeals and/or modes of argumentation to create a persuasive advertisement for this product.

www.ablongman.com/envision014

But advertisers do not always focus on an actual person in creating an argument based on character; sometimes an ad features a corporate ethos in order to establish the credibility of the company.

Microsoft's "We See" campaign, for instance, sells not software, but a company image. One representative ad (see Figure 2.10) from this campaign depicts a group of young children, lined up outside their school. They are in a variety of poses: looking expectantly at the teacher, stretching their arms in the air, or reading over notes. But what makes the ad visually interesting is not just the photograph, but the images sketched in white on

FIGURE 2.10. This Microsoft ad promotes its company image—and its corporate ethos—rather than a particular product.
Used with permission from Microsoft Corporation.

top of it. These drawings transform the children into an artist, an Olympic athlete, a scuba diver, a musician, and an astronaut. Complemented by the header "We see nothing small about them" and the closing tagline, "Your potential. Our passion," the photograph becomes a window into the future, Microsoft's rendering of the potential of the new generation. One element of the equation remains invisible: the Microsoft products that will help them reach that potential. But the message of the ad is nevertheless clear: Microsoft cares about America's youth and wants to help them realize their dreams. Does this ad sell software? Not directly—but it sells the idea of Microsoft as a forward-thinking company committed to helping its customers reach their potential.

The quest for a positive public image, actually, is nothing more than an issue of *ethos*. When Philip Morris runs antismoking television commercials, Toyota promotes its "Global Earth Charter to promote environmental responsibility" in *Time* magazine ads, or Budweiser launches a series of advertisements discouraging underage drinking, their underlying goal is to bolster the company's ethos. Visual rhetoric plays an important role in this process, encouraging readers to let go of old stereotypes and move to a fresh perspective.

COLLABORATIVE CHALLENGE

Many viewers were disturbed by the prominence of references to September 11th in the 2002 Superbowl commercials. In one spot, for instance, the Budweiser horses leave their idyllic country landscape to make a pilgrimage to New York City, where, pausing on the outskirts of the city, they bow reverently at the sight of the ravaged skyline. After the screen faded to black, the Budweiser logo appeared. This ad received mixed reaction; voted the best Superbowl ad by the viewers at Superbowl-ads.com, it also stirred other people to react against the company. Visit the "Budweiser Superbowl Ad" link through the Chapter 2 resources on the *Envision* Website, and watch the ad with your group. Divide your group in two; one subgroup should develop an argument suggesting that the ad was a respectful tribute to a national tragedy; the other subgroup should argue that the ad exploited the audience's emotions for commercial purposes. Debate the point, making sure that both sides rely on specific visual detail from the commercial to support each analysis. Afterward, as a class, discuss the relationship between patriotism, pathos, and ethos in American advertising.

www.ablongman.com/envision015

The Brand Logo as Ethos

In addition to calling attention to patriotism's relationship to ethos, the example discussed in the Collaborative Challenge points to another feature of advertising that relies upon the good character or reputation of the corporation: the brand *logo.* In essence, the brand logo is ethos distilled into a single symbol: it transmits in a single icon the entire reputation of a company, organization, or brand identity. From the Nike swoosh, to McDonald's golden arches, the NBC peacock, or the Apple computer apple, these symbols mark (or brand) products with ethos. In this way, a Polo horse on a shirt is an argument for the shirt's quality or stylishness; a Pepsi symbol on a can suggests a certain taste and quality of beverage; even a looped pink ribbon, pinned to someone's shirt, speaks to that person's good character as a supporter of breast cancer research. We read brand logos as signs of the character of these products: they provide powerful statements about ethos in very compact form.

Misuses of Ethos

One consequence of branding is that we come to trust symbols of ethos rather than looking to the character of the product itself. This tendency points us to the concept of **authority over evidence**—namely, the practice of overemphasizing authority or ethos rather than focusing on the merits of the evidence itself, a strategic exaggeration of ethos that helps entice audiences and sell products.

The most prominent examples of *authority over evidence* can be found in celebrity endorsements; in many commercials, the spokesperson sells the product not based on its merits but based upon the argument, "Believe what I say because you know me, and would I steer you wrong?" However, the American public has become increasingly skeptical of such arguments. Living in a world where rumors of Britney Spears's preference for Coke circulate on the Internet, Tiger Woods's $100 million deal with Nike makes front page news, and stars like former Sprite spokesperson Macaulay Culkin publicly announces, "I'm not crazy about the stuff [Sprite]. But money is money" (Twitchell, *Twenty* 214), the credibility of celebrity spokespeople is often questionable.

However, skilled rhetoricians can turn even such skepticism into a platform for a persuasive argument. During the late 1990s, Sprite produced a series of "anti-ads" that laid bare the financial motivations of many celebrity spokespeople. In this multilayered piece of visual rhetoric, Sprite showed NBA player Grant Hill in typical spokesperson pose, holding a bottle of Sprite and, in a mechanical and artificial tone of voice, offering up banal pronouncements on how much he liked it. However, every time Hill uttered one of his banalities, a little cutout of him holding two overstuffed bags with prominent dollar signs written on them would pop up and then disappear, accompanied by the loud "cha-ching" sound of a cash register, inviting the viewer to see how Hill's words translated into endorsement dollars. On the surface, this deliberate form of self-conscious advertising seems to undermine Sprite's ethos; yet, in this rhetorical situation, it actually enhanced credibility with its audience, who recognized in Sprite a company just as critical of the star-product cash nexus as they were. It was a strategy that served Sprite well.

A Closer Look

To see the Sprite ad in its entirety and hear a further discussion of such self-referential advertising and its relationship to teen marketing, view the *Frontline* documentary "The Merchants of Cool."
www.ablongman.com/envision016

Some companies are not necessarily as self-referential in their skepticism of ethos; one prominent advertising strategy involves criticizing a competition's product. You probably have seen ads of this sort: Burger King arguing that their flame-broiled hamburgers are better than McDonald's fried hamburgers; Coke claiming its soda tastes better than Pepsi's; Visa asserting its card's versatility by reminding consumers of how many companies "don't take American Express." The deliberate *comparison-contrast* builds up one company's ethos at another's expense. At times, however, this technique can be taken to an extreme, producing an **ad hominem argument**—that is, an argument that attempts to persuade through attacking an opponent's ethos or character. We see *ad hominem* at work most often in campaign advertisements, where candidates end up focusing less on the issues at hand than on an opponent's moral weaknesses, or in attacks on companies for the way they run their business rather than the quality of the products themselves. In other words, what this strategy does is try to persuade by reducing the credibility of opposing arguments.

AT A GLANCE

Misuses of Ethos

- *Authority over evidence:* placing more emphasis on ethos than on the actual validity of the evidence.

- *Ad hominem:* criticizing an opponent's character (or ethos) rather than the argument itself.

Exaggerated Ethos Through Parody

Another strategy of persuasion is attacking ethos through **parody,** or the deliberate mocking of a text or convention. Parody has long been recognized as an effective rhetorical strategy for making a powerful argument. You may have read "A Modest Proposal" by Jonathan Swift, in which he proposes quite seriously, and with ostensible goodwill toward his audience, that the Irish solve their overpopulation and poverty problems by cooking and eating their babies. Just as Swift turned a traditional political value system on its head in his mock proposal, extreme uses of ethos in visual discourse subvert traditional texts by imitating and mocking them. To see how this happens, let's turn to an ad designed by TheTruth.com, an innovative anti tobacco organization (see Figure 2.11). Through deliberate use of setting, character, font, and layout, this ad deliberately evokes and then parodies traditional cigarette advertising to make its claim for the dangers of smoking.

Seeing Connections Chapter 8 features a detailed discussion of parody in advertising.

Even if you are not familiar with the Masters Settlement Act, you probably have seen some of the Marlboro Country ads, often showing the lone cowboy or groups of cowboys riding across a beautiful, sunlit western American landscape. During the early part of their campaign,

FIGURE 2.11. This Truth anti-smoking advertisement attacks ethos through parody.

TheTruth.com recognized the impact of the long tradition of cigarette advertising on the public and decided to turn this tradition to its advantage. In the TheTruth.com parody version, however, the cowboy's companions do not ride proudly beside him. Instead, they are zipped up into body bags—an image that relies on exaggerated ethos and that employs pathos to provoke a strong reaction in the audience. By producing an ad that builds upon and yet revises the logic of Philip Morris's ad campaign, TheTruth.com could get past false images (the happy cowboy) to get at their idea of the "truth": that by smoking cigarettes "You Too Can Be an Independent, Rugged, Macho-Looking Dead Guy." The visual complexity of the image (and the combination of appeals) resonates powerfully by evoking the audience's familiarity with cigarette advertisements to pack some of its punch.

Student Writing

Amanda Johnson, in her analysis of a Barbie parody ad, and Georgia Duan, in her reading of cigarette advertising, explore the construction of body image in the media. www.ablongman.com/envision017

Kairos is "the right or opportune time to do something, or the right measure in doing something."

—James Kinneavy

Considering the Context of Time and Place

As you can tell from examining ads in this chapter, a successful argument must take into account not only the *rhetorical situation,* but also the context, or the right time and place. That is why a Hertz ad featuring O. J. Simpson hurdling over chairs in an airport could be so powerful in the early 1990s but would be a completely ineffective argument in late 1994 after his arrest for the alleged murder of his wife. In ancient Greek, rhetoricians called this aspect of the rhetorical situation **kairos**—namely, the contingencies of time and place for an argument.

In your own writing, you should consider *kairos* along with the other aspects of the rhetorical situation: audience, text, and writer. As a student of visual rhetoric, it is important to recognize the *kairos*—the opportune historical, ideological, or cultural moment—of a visual text when analyzing its rhetorical force. You undoubtedly already consider the context for persuasive communication in your everyday life: for instance, whether you are asking a friend to dinner or a professor for a recommendation, your assessment of the timeliness and the appropriate strategies for that time probably determines the shape that your argument takes. That is, you pick the right moment and place to make your case. In other words, the rhetorical situation involves interaction between audience, text, and writer *within* the context or *kairos.*

We can get a sense of how *kairos* works to create a powerful argument by turning once more to advertising for examples. Consider, for instance, Coca-Cola's ad campaigns. Coca-Cola has exerted a powerful presence in the advertising industry for many years in part due to its strategic advertising. During World War II, Coke ran a series of ads that built their beverage campaign around the contemporary nationalistic

FIGURE 2.12. This Coca-Cola ad used *kairos* to create a powerful argument for its World War II audience.

sentiment. What you find featured in these ads are servicemen, international landscapes, and inspiring slices of Americana—all designed to respond to that specific cultural moment. Look at Figure 2.12, an advertisement for Coke from the 1940s. This picture uses pathos to appeal to the audience's sense of patriotism by featuring a row of seemingly carefree servicemen, leaning from the windows of a military bus, the refreshing cokes in their hands producing smiles even far away from home. The picture draws in the audience by reassuring them on two fronts. On the one hand, it builds on the nationalistic pride in the young, handsome servicemen who so happily serve their country. On the other, it is designed to appease fears about the hostile climate abroad: as both the picture and the accompanying text assure us, Coca Cola (and the servicemen) "goes along" and "gets a hearty welcome." The power of this message relates directly to its context. An ad such as this one, premised on patriotism and pride in military service, would be most persuasive during wartime when many more people tend to support the spirit of nationalism and therefore would be moved by the image of the young serviceman shipping off to war. It is through understanding the *kairos* of this advertisement that you can appreciate the strength of the ad's rhetorical appeal.

A Closer Look

To explore how another soft drink company uses *kairos* effectively in a more recent ad, watch Pepsi's I-Tunes commercial. www.ablongman.com/envision018

Putting Persuasion into Practice

As you can tell from our work in this chapter, ads convey complex cultural meanings. Recognizing their persuasive presence everywhere, we realize the need to develop our own *visual literacy* in order to make more informed interpretations of ads around us. You can pursue your study of ads by conducting your own careful rhetorical analyses of these texts. You'll find over and over again that ads are a microcosm of many of the techniques of persuasion. From billboards to pop-up ads on the Internet, ads employ logos, pathos, and ethos to convey strong messages to specific audiences. We've learned how compact and sophisticated these texts are. Now it's time to apply those insights in your own writing.

Seeing Connections Read more about visual literacy in Chapter 1.

As you begin to perform your individual analyses of advertisements, consider the way in which your own writing, like the ads we've discussed, can "sell" your argument to the reader. Consider the rhetorical situation and the specific *kairos* of your argument: What *strategies of argumentation* and *rhetorical appeals* would be most effective in reaching your target audience? Do you want to use narration, a humorous analogy, or a stirring example to forge a connection with your reader based on pathos? Or is your analysis better suited to logos, following a step-by-step process of reading an ad, drawing on empirical evidence, or looking at cause and effect? Perhaps you will decide to enrich your discussion through cultivating your ethos as a writer, establishing your own authority on a subject or citing reputable work done by other scholars. It is probable that in your essay that you will use many different strategies and a combination of appeals; as we saw in the advertisements we examined earlier, from the Crest Whitening Strips to the Coca-Cola campaign, successful arguments utilize a variety of rhetorical strategies to persuade their audiences.

While focusing on the individual strategies, don't forget to keep an eye on the composition of your argument as a whole. Just as an ad is designed with attention to layout and design, so you should look at the larger organization of your essay as key to the success of your argument. As you approach the organization of elements in your essay to maximize your persuasiveness, even a question such as "Where should I insert my images?" has profound implications for your argument. Consider the difference between an essay in which the image is embedded in the text, next to the paragraph that analyzes it, or one with the image attached as an appendix. In your writing, use the persuasive power of visual rhetoric more effectively by allowing the reader to analyze the images alongside the written explanations. Use similar careful attention to organization, placement, and purpose as you craft your own analysis and begin your work with visual rhetoric.

Seeing Connections
Explore strategies of arrangement in Chapter 3.

PREWRITING CHECKLIST
Analyzing Advertisements

❑ **Content:** What exactly is the ad selling? An object? an idea? both?

❑ **Message:** How is the ad selling the product? What is the persuasive message that the ad is sending to the audience?

- ❏ **Character and setting:** What is featured by the ad? An object? a scene? a person? How are these elements portrayed? What is the ethnicity, age, socioeconomic class, and gender of any people in the advertisement? How do these choices relate to the ad's intended audience and reflect deliberate rhetorical choices?

- ❏ **Story:** On the most basic level, what is happening in the advertisement?

- ❏ **Theme:** What is the underlying message of the ad (beyond "buy our product")?

- ❏ **Medium:** What medium was the advertisement produced in? Television? print? radio? How did this choice suit the rhetorical purpose of the ad and accommodate the needs of a particular audience?

- ❏ **Historical context:** In what country and at what historical moment was the advertisement produced? How do the demands of context shape the persuasive appeals at work in the ad? How does the ad reflect, comment on, challenge, or reinforce contemporary political, economic, or gender ideology? How does this commentary situate it in terms of a larger trend or argument?

- ❏ **Word and image:** What is the relationship between the word (written or spoken) and the imagery in the ad? Which is given priority? How does this relationship affect the persuasiveness of the advertisement?

- ❏ **Layout:** How are the elements of the ads arranged—on a page (for a print ad) or in sequence (for a television commercial)? What is the purpose behind this organization? How does this arrangement lead the reader through—and facilitate—the ad's argument?

- ❏ **Design:** What typeface is used? What size? What color? How do these decisions reflect attention to the ad's rhetorical situation? How do they function in relation to the ad's rhetorical appeals?

- ❏ **Voice:** What voice does the text use to reach its audience? Is the language technical, informal, personal, authoritative? Is the voice comic or serious?

- ❏ **Imagery:** What choices did the advertisers make in selecting imagery for this ad? If it is a static print ad, does the ad feature a line drawing? a photograph? Is the photograph black and white? a close-up? a panoramic shot? If the advertisement is drawn from television, what is the pace and sequence of the images? Where does the camera zoom in? What does it focus on? Does the ad feature a close-up or a long shot? Is the image centered? completely captured in the frame? Is it cut off? If so, how? Does it feature a head-on shot? a three-quarter shot? Whose point of view, if any, is the viewer supposed to assume?

(continued)

❏ **Rhetorical appeals:** How does the advertiser use the images to work in conjunction with rhetorical appeals? For instance, does the image reinforce an appeal to reason? Is it designed to produce an emotional effect on the audience? Does the use of a certain style, such as black-and-white authority, contribute to the ethos of the ad?

❏ **Strategy of development:** What strategy of development does the ad rely upon? Narration? definition? comparison-contrast? example/illustration? classification and division? How do these strategies contribute to the ad's persuasive appeal?

❏ **Cultural resonance:** Does the ad use ethos—in the form of celebrities, famous events or places, or recognizable symbols—to increase its persuasiveness? If so, how does that establish audience or a particular relationship to a cultural moment?

WRITING PROJECTS

Visit the *Envision* Website for expanded assignment guidelines and student projects.

1. Visit an ad archive such as those linked through the Chapter 2 resources on the *Envision* Website, or look at old magazines in your school library. Choose two or three ads for the same product and write a rhetorical analysis on the strategies of persuasion these ads use to reach out to a specific audience. Use the prewriting checklist to help you analyze the appeals at work in the ads and to help you develop your ideas.

2. Using current print or television advertisements as your sources, find examples of ads that showcase an exaggeration of rhetorical appeals, such as logical fallacies, exaggeration of pathos, or misuse of ethos. Write an analysis of how these strategies operate within three of these ads and what the effect of this exaggeration is on the viewer. You could also include parody or self-referential ads for this assignment.

FOR ADDED CHALLENGE

Visit the *Envision* Website for expanded assignment guidelines and student projects.

1. Write a contextual analysis on the *kairos* of the Coca-Cola campaign. Examine, for instance, another Coke ad from the 1940s through the Adflip link on the *Envision* Website. Do some preliminary research and read about this era: explore the time, place, and culture in which the ad appeared. Ask yourself: How do the rhetorical choices of the ad you select reflect an awareness of this context? How does the ad use the particular tools of logos, pathos, and ethos to comment upon or criticize this cultural moment?

2. Working in groups, look at several ads from different time periods produced by the same company. Some possible topics include ads for cigarettes, cars, hygiene products, and personal computers. Each member of your group should choose a single ad and prepare a rhetorical analysis of its persuasive appeals. Now, share your analyses and collaborate to explore how this company has modified its rhetorical approach over time. As you synthesize your argument, be sure to consider in each case how the different rhetorical situations inform the strategies used by the ads to reach their target audience. Collaborate to write a paper in which you chart the evolution of the company's persuasive strategies and how this was informed by *kairos*.

3. Write a paper in which you compare two different ad campaigns and examine the ideology behind specific constructions of our culture. Does one campaign portray particular gendered or racial ideas? How do the tools of persuasion work to produce these messages? What larger message is conveyed by the reliance on such cultural ideals or notions of identity? What representations of sexuality, gender roles, or class are presented by these ads? Write up your findings and then present them to the class, holding up examples of the ads to discuss in support of your analysis.

CHAPTER 2 ON THE WEB

Resources and Readings	Exercises and Assignments	Student Writing
• Closer Look resources and annotated readings	• Interactive exercises with advertisements	• Rhetorical analysis of print ads, Superbowl commercials, and parody ads
• Links to Websites for understanding rhetorical appeals and fallacies	• Rhetorical analysis of ads	• Historical analysis essays of Got Milk? and Calvin Klein ad campaigns
• Links to advertisement resources on print ads	• Contextual analysis	
	• Peer review forms	
• Links to advertisement resources on television commercials	• Student self-assessment sheets	• Comparative analysis of movie poster ads and CD covers
• Further readings list with annotations	• Focus on diverse learners and students with disabilities	• Rhetorical analysis of ads developed into research papers

www.ablongman.com/envision

CHAPTER 3

Analyzing Perspectives in Argument

Imagine that it is February 2, 2003, and you have just heard the news of the tragic explosion that destroyed the space shuttle *Columbia* during reentry the day before. As you visit the newsstand to purchase your Sunday paper, you pause to reflect on the various front pages before you. Each uses a different cover photo with its lead article on the tragedy. One features a publicity shot of the smiling *Columbia* crew (see Figure 3.1); another juxtaposes the image of the shuttle's midair explosion with a photo of a piece of debris found in Bronson, Texas; yet another presents a series of photographs of the world in mourning, from the devastated Israelis to the very somber president of the United States.

Based on these images, which newspaper would you buy? How are the visual texts themselves operating as arguments about the significance of the event? How does each photo tell a different "story" about exactly what happened? How does the choice of a particular photo present a specific point of view?

As this opening example makes clear, visual texts work through the tools of persuasion that we examined in earlier chapters; they provide arguments in themselves. Yet they also provide the opportunity for us to create arguments by using them as visual evidence. In this chapter, we'll look closely at photographs to continue our exploration of visual rhetoric as a disciplinary lens—that is, the way in which visual texts

FIGURE 3.1. The editors of the *Sunday Telegraph* decided to run a photo of the crew on the front page rather than print an image of the space shuttle exploding as did many other papers.

shape our reality in particular ways—and you'll learn to write powerful thesis-driven texts that use both verbal and visual strategies of persuasion.

Chapter Preview Questions

- How do photographs function as both visual evidence and visual arguments?
- How does point of view influence written and visual arguments?
- What are the necessary steps for writing a powerful thesis?
- What roles do persona and rhetorical stance play in arguments?
- How can the canons of "style" and "arrangement" produce effective writing?
- How can multiple sides of an argument enrich the understanding of an issue?
- What are the ethical implications of visual arguments?

Perspective and Point of View

When we look at a photograph, we might think that it provides a window on another person's reality. Scenes from war, for instance, give us a perspective on battle that is often only accessible to us through photojournalism. Figure 3.2 was one of the first wartime photographs ever taken. It shows a young soldier lying lifeless on the battlefield, a number of guns strewn around his mangled body. We could use this image as visual evidence to construct an argument that war is savage and inhumane. However, we also could use it to support a more historically focused argument, perhaps one that suggests the importance of the siege of Petersburg for the Confederacy's ultimate defeat. Either argument could draw on the visual power of photographs like this one, using such images as expert witnesses to the events of history.

FIGURE 3.2. One of the earliest photographs showed a dead Confederate soldier with a gun in Petersburg, VA.

But what we must keep in mind when using photographs in this way is that, like all witnesses, their testimony may seem objective, yet it is actually informed by individual perspective and point of view. That is, the "reality" that photographs display is actually a *version* of reality created by a photographer's artistic decisions: whether to use color or black-and-white film; what sort of lighting to use; how to position the subject of the photograph; whether to opt for a panorama or close-up shot; what backdrop to use; how to crop, or trim, the image once it is printed. In effect, when we see photographs in a newspaper or art gallery, we are looking at the product of deliberate decisions of perspective, selection, placement, and framing—key elements of composition to consider when constructing arguments. In this way, photographs are a particularly powerful example of how visual rhetoric works to persuade an audience to accept a given argument.

"Photography helps
people to see."
—Berenice Abbott

Consider two famous photographs by Dorothea Lange (see Figures 3.3 and 3.4), which offer very different representations of migrant workers during the Great Depression. In each case, we see a migrant family huddled inside a tent. The subjects seem to be poor, hungry, and struggling to make a living. Their material conditions are bleak. What suggests this? The visual details of each photograph, such as the tattered clothing, the postures of each body, the woman's hand on her face, and the subjects' straggly hair as well as their sad or worried

FIGURE 3.3. Dorothea Lange's wideshot gives a stark sense of the experience of migrant farmers.

FIGURE 3.4. The close-up focuses on the struggles of the migrant mother.

expressions. But now notice the effect of the different perspectives. In Figure 3.4, we get an intimate look inside this woman's eyes, where we can see her concern. The lines on her face, visible in this close-up, are evidence of her hard life and worries. The photograph in Figure 3.3 has a wider frame, including the tent and the barren ground. This perspective makes a different kind of argument, one that addresses the condition of the soil, the landscape, the living quarters. We can hardly make out the woman huddled in the darkness of the tent of Figure 3.3. When we look for visual evidence of the living conditions of migrant workers in the American West during the 1930s, each photograph offers different angles on our argument. Which one would we use to support a thesis about the labor conditions of migrant workers? Which one would we use to argue that the human body was scarred by hardship? Depending on our purpose, we would choose one photograph over the other. Each one makes an argument that we can in turn select as evidence for our claims about the Great Depression.

COLLABORATIVE CHALLENGE

In groups of two or three, visit the Collection Highlights of "Suffering Under a Great Injustice: Ansel Adams's Photographs of Japanese-American Internment at Manzanar" through the Chapter 3 resources on the *Envision* Website. Browse through the contents and analyze the framing, cropping, and composition strategies of a selection of the photographs. Note that in some cases, clicking on an image will pull up a page comparing the print with the original negative so that you can better understand how Adams cropped his photographs to sharpen the argument conveyed by the images. Working from a comparison of photographs, or of photos and their negatives, make an argument about the perspective offered by each visual text about the experience of Japanese Americans interned during World War II.

www.ablongman.com/envision019

The Argument of the Image

While Dorothea Lange and Ansel Adams used their skills as photographers to make striking arguments about the conditions of Americans, these pictures do not represent *reality* as much as their interpretations of or perspectives on that reality; Lange and Adams both deliberately composed the shots to convey their points of view.

A Closer Look

Examine Alexander Gardner's photos and the controversy surrounding them through the "Case of the Moved Body."
www.ablongman.com/envision020

As savvy members of a multimedia society, we know that photographs can be staged, modified, and rearranged to serve a variety of purposes. In this way, their function as "evidence" becomes suspect, for they do not so much tell "the truth" as they provide an angle on whatever reality is represented in their window. Consider, for instance, the early photographic hoax perpetuated by Alexander Gardner, one of the first photographers on the battlefield to stage his subjects. While covering the Civil War, Gardner positioned discarded guns beside the bodies of dead soldiers to create a more effective composition. He even used the same photograph twice, once captioning it "A Sharpshooter's Last Sleep" and suggesting that the man was a Union soldier, and another time labeling the photo "Home of a Rebel Sharpshooter" in order to indicate that the soldier was a Southerner.

FIGURE 3.5. Snowball the Monster Cat fools many viewers with his huge size.

Indeed, since photography as a medium was invented in 1826, news journalists and amateur photographers alike have been using it both as a tool of social critique by offering an inside glimpse on often horrific realities and as a means of persuading viewers to believe that the visual is merely a mirror on reality. In fact, the term **photo manipulation** now describes photos that have been modified to produce a certain rhetorical effect.

You may be familiar with photographic spoofs, such as the enormous cat, "Snowball" in Figure 3.5, a popular image which circulated on dorm chat lists that offers a rather humorous version of photo manipulation. In this image, the cat looks completely real, but in actuality it is nowhere near this large. This photographer created the image as a joke to share with his friends. Often, however, photo manipulation serves a more serious purpose.

As recently as April 2003, Brian Walski, a photographer for the *Los Angeles Times* was fired for sending an altered photograph from the 2003 war in Iraq that combined two distinct moments in time. The issue of photo manipulation was at the heart of a scandal, as the Editor of the *Los Angeles Times*, explained:

On Monday, March 31, the *Los Angeles Times* published a front-page photograph that had been altered in violation of *Times* policy. The primary subject of the photo was a British soldier directing Iraqi civilians to take cover from Iraqi fire on the outskirts of Basra. After publication, it was noticed that several civilians in the background appear twice. The photographer, Brian Walski, reached by telephone in southern Iraq, acknowledged that he had used his computer to combine elements of two photographs, taken moments apart, in order to improve the composition. *Times* policy forbids altering the content of news photographs. Because of the violation, Walski, a *Times* photographer since 1998, has been dismissed from the staff. (Editor's Note)

A Closer Look

Access "Brian Walski *LA Times* photos" for a detailed illustration of how Brian Walski altered his photos from Iraq.
www.ablongman.com/envision021

In modifying the photos, Walski created a new visual image, one that conveyed what he felt was an accurate representation of the current situation in Iraq. In effect, the modified, composite image was his *argument* about the American presence in Iraq. In one original, the soldier with gun drawn extends a warning hand at a relatively sedate group of Iraqi citizens. In its companion original photo, the soldier himself seems calm, while an Iraqi man, holding a small child, stands up as if moving toward him. Walski's modified image presented the striking result of combining these images: the composite portrays the soldier with an aggressive posture as if warning back the civilian who is advancing toward him. The altered photo offers a more tense, confrontational view on the war. Indeed, the Walski incident gets to the heart of the complex relation between reality and photographic representation: visual images do not necessarily convey actual reality, although they may reflect it in compressed or reshaped form.

"Photographs are as much an interpretation of the world as paintings and drawings are."
—Susan Sontag

The Parallel Between Photography and Writing

In class discussion of these photographs, students raised many questions concerning the motivation behind Walski's changes:

Was the purpose of altering reality to offer a more compelling composition? to merge two distinct moments in time? to be more effective visually?

Was it to offer a condensed "still shot" of an action scene?

Was it to provide a particular argument about the purpose of American soldiers in Iraq?

Does this revision to the image parallel the work we do in writing, when we compress moments in time, give a summary, construct a paraphrase, or offer excerpts?

One of the most crucial points raised by students is contained in the last question: the parallel between working with words and working with images, a connection that is productive for our understanding of argumentation. For no image is a neutral or objective window on reality, as photos demonstrate so well, and we can begin to grasp the persuasive power of all language by thinking about the power of images to shape and create realities for readers.

Your own writing, too, is a text informed by perspective and point of view. In your writing, you are like a photographer, making important compositional decisions: What will be the subject of your text: an individual, a group, an institution? How will you pose that subject to best convey your own perspective? Should you zoom in, focusing on one particular example as a way of addressing a larger concern? Or should you take a step back, situating your argument in relation to the broader context that surrounds the issue? What should the tone of your argument be? Should you cast it in the deep sepia of early photographs, rich in tradition and nostalgia? Or should you color it with the complexities of technicolor? Finally, how will you present your final product? With an ornate and highly structured frame that identifies it as part of a serious academic discussion? Or in a more flamboyant, informal frame that marks it as part of popular discourse? The choices you make will determine the ultimate impact of your argument: like photographs, effective writing creates an argument that persuades the viewer to look at a topic through the lens of the author's interpretation.

A Closer Look

Susan Sontag offers an extended discussion of the power of photographs to shape our understanding of real events in "Looking at War," *The New Yorker* (December 9, 2003).

Developing an Argumentative Thesis

Your task as a writer is to forge a powerful text that argues a point; your goal, in other words, is to convince others to see a particular perspective, usually your own. But when you hear the word *argument,* you may think of something antagonistic, such as a heated discussion or debate. Indeed, we often equate *argument* with *arguing*. An argument, however, does not need to be an aggressive, adversarial action. In fact, we use a range of rhetorical strategies when we debate—invoking pathos, using ethos or good character, or reasoning calmly with our listeners—so that an argument does not have to be a negative experience. In fact, the definition of *argument*, according to the *Oxford English Dictionary*, emphasizes *influence*, not *debate:* "a statement or fact advanced for the purpose of influencing the mind." You create arguments all the time without realizing it; you craft language with the purpose of persuading your audience. Similarly, as we have seen, visual and multimedia texts all around us function as arguments, that is, as texts crafted with the deliberate purpose of convincing an audience.

> "Anything is an argument which naturally and legitimately produces an effect upon our minds, and tends to make us think one way rather than another."
>
> —MOZLEY

The Importance of Thesis Statements

One way we recognize arguments is through their reliance on a **thesis:** a strong, concise statement of your main point. Often, the thesis will appear in the introductory paragraph of an argument to let the reader know the main point of the essay. In longer research projects, a thesis might comprise an entire paragraph: a complex nexus or connection of ideas to be developed in the rest of the essay. A thesis can't be a fact, an unsupported personal opinion, or a gross generalization. It has to be a sharp statement of your position or an interpretation that attempts to convince readers of its own validity. In other words, the thesis statement sets up your argumentative claim; the work of persuading the reader is done in the rest of the essay. Therefore, think of a thesis in terms of a promise of your complete argument.

Look at the four thesis statements below, all from drafts of papers on Dorothea Lange's visual representations of migrant workers. Which one sets up the most interesting argument?

> **Thesis #1:** During the Great Depression, Dorothea Lange took a series of photographs of a migrant mother and her family.
>
> **Assessment:** *This thesis statement merely states a fact rather than suggesting an interpretation of those photographs.*
>
> **Thesis #2:** Dorothea Lange's "Migrant Mother" photographs are masterpieces.

Assessment: This thesis relies too heavily on subjective opinion; the author offers no criteria for evaluating the photographs or a context for understanding the statement.

Thesis #3: Dorothea Lange's "Migrant Mother" photographs show the power of photography.

Assessment: This thesis statement rests too much on broad generalization rather than specific analysis.

Thesis #4: Dorothea Lange's "Migrant Mother" photographs put a human face on a debate over agricultural labor conditions that often focused more on economic consequences than its very real victims.

Assessment: Of the four examples, this thesis provides the most provocative articulation of the author's interpretation of the significance of Lange's photographs.

FIGURE 3.6. What argument appears in this photo of freed slaves at rest on a levee?

Thesis #4, with its concrete language, specific focus, and implied argument, offers the reader the most interesting insight into the Lange photographs. But how do you go about formulating an effective thesis statement such as this one? One way is by working through a series of questions. Imagine, for instance, that you want to write an argument about the photographs in Figures 3.6 and 3.7. Both images portray freed slaves in the nineteenth century. How might you develop a thesis statement to contribute to the debate about the condition of African Americans around the time of the Civil War?

You may want to start by jotting down what you see, making close observations about these photos. You then can use questions to bring your

FIGURE 3.7. What representation of history does this photo of a freedman's school provide?

argument into focus and to make a specific claim about these images. The end product will be a *working thesis statement*. The process of developing your argument might look something like this:

1. First, write down your observations.

> *Close observations:* These don't look like typical pictures of slavery. They don't show people toiling away or enduring abuse; the people look relaxed; they are on break; they are in groups, not photographed as individuals; there are no "masters" here, only a white schoolteacher; the setting of a schoolhouse is one that you wouldn't see in relation to slave photos.

2. Work with those observations to construct a preliminary thesis statement.

> *First statement:* Freedmen had a life different from that of slaves.

3. Refine your argument by asking questions that make your statement less general.

> *Ask yourself:* What kind of life? When? Where?

4. Revise your preliminary thesis statement to be more specific.

> *Revised statement:* Even before 1863, freed slaves in the southern United States were able to control their working conditions and attend school.

5. Again, refine your argument through a question, perhaps introducing the particular evidence that drives your claim.

> *Ask yourself:* How do you know this?

6. Revise your thesis again.

> *Revised statement #2:* Photographs from the 1860s prove that freed slaves in the southern United States were able to control their working conditions (taking breaks on the levee as shown in the image) and attend school (receiving instruction in a log cabin as shown in the image).

7. Further polish your thesis by asking questions about the implications of your working thesis statement.

> *Ask yourself:* What do you find interesting about this observation?

8. Write out your working thesis so that it includes a sense of the implications of your claim—here involving an

Seeing Connections
For more about the importance of the "So What?" in argument, see Chapter 4.

appreciation of the larger context of discussions about the 1860s. Sometimes we call this the "So What?" of your claim.

Working thesis: Photographs from the 1860s offer a glimpse into a history that often overlooked triumph against adversity; they suggest that freed slaves in the southern United States were able to control the parameters of their employment and attend school to receive an education.

The previous exercise shows how you can take a simple statement and turn it into an intriguing *thesis.* Keep in mind that the exact length of this process varies for each topic and writer; however, you should end the process with a question that pushes you to address the "So What?" of your topic: Why should your reader care about your claim? What are its larger implications? What is interesting about it? In many cases, addressing the "So What?" can make the difference between stating a fact and constructing a provocative thesis statement. In the example above, the attention to context in the working thesis should make readers curious about this often neglected chapter of history. It should encourage your readers to want to study your evidence and consider your essay's argument carefully. If after reading your thesis statement, your reader is prompted to ask "How so?"—then you know you have the foundation for a strong argumentative essay.

Sometimes your best writing tool is a Post-it Note that says "How so?" or "So what?"

AT A GLANCE

Testing Your Thesis

- Do you have a specific and interesting angle on your topic?
- Does it offer a statement of significance about your topic?
- Is the thesis too obvious (not sharp enough)?
- Could someone argue against it (or is it just an observation)?
- Is it too dense (trying to compact the entire paper) or too simplistic (not developing your point thoroughly)?

Peer Reviewing Your Thesis

Since every argument is essentially an attempt to persuade an audience to accept your view, you should test out your assertions on real people: share your views in conversation, in drafts, through Instant Messaging, on the phone, or in peer review groups. One great way to develop a sharper thesis statement is to exchange it with a partner and work through the checklist in the At A Glance box. Notice how a real audience is a fresh pair of eyes, allowing you to strengthen and improve your work.

As you can tell, a thesis statement takes a lot of work—questioning, drafting, discussing, rethinking, researching, and refining—to get it just right. But most of all, be sure that you have a point to make with your writing. What is the argumentative claim (or main idea) that you need to prove to readers as the essay progresses? Does the thesis function as a promise of that argument? If you answer yes to these questions, then you are on your way to crafting a compelling argument.

Your Angle on the Argument

Generating a strong thesis statement is only the first step in your task of persuasion. However, you may have established your main idea, but you need also to spend some time considering how you are going to convey that idea to your audience. The question becomes: How do you move from the thesis as a promise of your argument to fostering a strong relationship with your readers so that they will be most inclined to entertain your perspective? The answer lies in careful attention to developing *persona* and *rhetorical stance* in your writing.

Constructing Persona

When you select a certain image, a set of words, or a written phrase in order to shape your argument and try to persuade your audience, you are in effect constructing a **persona** for yourself as a writer and rhetorician. You may be familiar with this term from literary analysis. Indeed, often writers distinguish themselves from their literary personas. Chaucer's character named Chaucer in *The Canterbury Tales* is not the same person as Chaucer the author. The character is a persona—*a deliberately crafted version of the writer.* Similarly, in the film *Being John Malkovich,* the actor John Malkovich plays a persona named John Malkovich who is a version of the real person; his character is not the same as the actor. We call such deliberate, staged representations of identity examples of *persona.* A public figure will often use *persona* as a purposeful rhetorical tool. President George W. Bush might choose to give a speech about war dressed in army fatigues and flanked by a group of soldiers, but when addressing the state of the economy, he's more likely to hold his press conference from his ranch, wearing a casual shirt and blue jeans. In each case, he constructs a different *persona* designed to be the most appropriate and persuasive for his given rhetorical situation.

A Closer Look
For an in-depth look at the relationship between photography and George W. Bush's presidential persona, read Elisabeth Bumiller's article, "Keepers of Bush Image Lift Stagecraft to New Heights."
www.ablongman.com/envision022

COLLABORATIVE CHALLENGE

Bring to class a selection of photographs of yourself, including some informal shots and some more formal ones (such as your school yearbook photo). In a group, examine each other's photographs and discuss the differences in *persona* evident in each one. Be sure to take into account the details that construct the persona (expression, posture, pose, clothing, background scene, people of various professions in the photo, etc.) as well the composition of the image (color, layout, perspective, angle, lighting). Which picture would you want printed in the newspaper alongside an article describing a prestigious scholarship that you have won? Which photo would you include on the dust jacket of your first published novel? Which photo would you submit to your dorm newsletter? Which would you use on your personal Website? Discuss both your decisions and how your assessment of the different rhetorical situations influenced the *argument* you want to make through your persona.

The same principle of putting on an identity as a representation governs the writing process whenever you put pen to paper. When we compose texts (written, verbal, or visual), we decide how to use language to present a particular persona to the audience we wish to address. Through tone (formal or informal, humorous or serious), word choice (academic, colloquial), sentence structures (complex or simple and direct), use of rhetorical appeals (pathos, logos, ethos), and strategies of persuasion (narration, example, cause and effect, analogy, process, classification, or definition), we create portraits of ourselves as the authors of our argument. We must take care in creating persona: a well-designed one can facilitate a strong connection with our reader and therefore make our argument more persuasive. However, a poorly constructed persona—one that is, for instance, biased, inconsistent, or underdeveloped—can have the opposite effect, alienating the reader and undercutting our text's overall effectiveness.

Seeing Connections
Chapter 2 provides a detailed discussion of strategies of persuasion and rhetorical appeals.

Choosing a Rhetorical Stance

To be persuasive, you must assume a persona that responds appropriately to your specific rhetorical situation. Wayne Booth, one of the most important twentieth-century revivalists of classical rhetoric, defined the writer's position in relation to the rhetorical triangle as the

rhetorical stance and claimed that it is the most essential aspect of effective communication. He argued that communication failed between people (or a text failed to persuade a reader) if the writer assumed a position that ignored the necessary balance of the rhetorical triangle.

We see examples of inappropriate rhetorical stances constantly: the TV evangelist who moves his congregation with a polished sermon that completely distracts them from flaws in his own moral character; the used-car salesman who pads his sales pitch with offers of free gifts, rebate specials, and low percentage rates; the actor who uses his own celebrity status to drive the endorsement of a cause, rather than clearly articulating the merits of the cause itself. In each case, the *rhetorical triangle*—the relationship between author, audience, and text—is out of balance, and the argument itself, ultimately, is rendered less persuasive. In your own writing, therefore, you need to pay special attention not only to the persona you create, but to the stance you assume in relation to your specific rhetorical situation.

> ## AT A GLANCE
>
> ### Three Rhetorical Stances That Lead to Communication Failure
>
> - *The pedant or preacherly stance:* the text is paramount and both the audience's needs and the speaker's character are ignored.
>
> - *The advertiser's stance:* the effect on the audience is valued above all, ignoring the quality of the text and the credibility of the speaker.
>
> - *The entertainer's stance:* the character of the speaker is elevated above the text and the audience.

Working with Position and Persona

One way to experiment with persona and rhetorical stance is to draft a position paper on your topic. By definition, a **position paper** presents one side of an issue, allowing you the opportunity to construct a strong thesis statement and actively argue your main points. A position paper also can be an ideal medium for developing your persona and rhetorical stance. Angela Rastegar, for instance, experimented with persona during a project on photographic coverage of the war in Iraq. First, she provided a written argument about the issue from the perspective of an unnamed academic or journalistic commentator. Then, she revised the argument by writing a short paper representing an extreme position on the toppling of a Saddam Hussein statue by U.S. troops. Her first "position" offers the academic voice with an ostensibly objective perspective. Note that there is no obvious "I" speaking and yet an argument about the power of the media clearly emerges.

Angela Rastegar: Academic Position Paper

Imagine a chaotic world in which you cannot trust the media--newspapers, television reports, and magazines are full of lies about the world and politics. Picture trying to decipher current events or important situations without knowing whom to turn to or what to believe. Sounds far-fetched? Unfortunately, this is not far from the truth. Current newspapers are filled with subtle, clever methods used to deceive the public.

As you look at photographic images in widely respected newspaper articles, consider the techniques used to deceive the public. Concerning one incident--the April 9th destruction of Saddam Hussein's monument in Baghdad--the actual events of this day have been carefully concealed from the public. Although the media portrayed a "heroic" destruction of Saddam's symbol by American forces and mobs of Iraqi supporters, this event was essentially staged by the media.

We must use a cautious eye when viewing news stories and alert ourselves to subtle biases. The media has been called the "fourth branch of the government" because of the undeniable power it yields over the American public. No other source of information is so readily and unquestionably accepted. The government realizes this, and it often takes great measures to work with the media to create effective, captivating stories that not only portray Americans in a positive light, but will also sell papers. Examples of the media's influence are not by any means limited to this single event; however, wars provide the perfect opportunity for the media to influence the public. They open wounds in all Americans leaving viewers vulnerable, easily influenced, and starving for more information. As a result, studying the media's influence on any war opens a vast field of controversy. In this time of crisis, we must read the news with a wary eye.

Finding this voice to offer too much of the "advertiser's stance," Angela then experimented with first person to shape her argument into an analysis of a specific photograph (see Figure 1 in her letter to the editor). She developed this position paper as an examination of the image and named her persona "Elizabeth Grant," a concerned media activist.

Angela Rastegar: Writing a Letter to Editor as "Elizabeth Grant," Left-Wing Media Watchdog

I am writing in response to the astonishing display of deceit attempted by President G. W. Bush and the American government on Thursday, April 10th. President Bush's public address began with the words, "Iraqi citizens support overthrowing Saddam," which was illustrated by the enclosed photograph. It depicts an American marine tying the Iraqi flag around the neck of Saddam Hussein's 15-foot monument. Seconds later, U.S. troops connected the ropes and cables to the statue's neck and brought it crashing to the ground.

The photograph, which contains a brightly colored red and white Iraqi flag in the center, focuses the viewer's attention on this emblem. Did the Iraqi citizens request to use this flag? We don't know, but we can see how the government attempted to appeal to those watching by having a soldier tie Iraq's own flag to the chains.

The flag falsely suggests that the Iraqi people were behind the destruction of the monument and that America can work in harmony with the people of Iraq to overthrow Saddam. This message drastically distorts the truth; in fact, the soldier originally held an American flag, but his commanding officers ordered him

Figure 1. Laurent Rebours, Associated Press. *The New York Times: On the Web.* "Scenes from Baghdad." Online Posting. 9 April 2003. *The New York Times Company.* 14 April 2003.

to tie this particular flag to the chains. Thus the government's use of logos in this photo subtly attempts to convince the public that Iraq wanted to bring down Saddam's statue--when, in reality, the citizens there had nothing to do with it.

In this photograph, the picture also appeals to the viewers' emotions by placing a rope and chains around the neck of Saddam's image. In this sense, it evokes the American hatred for Saddam and creates a clear, understandable aim. The military is able to put a noose around the neck of a symbolic Saddam, displaying the government's ability to destroy him. The government draws on these emotions from the viewers to increase patriotism. Bush applies these same tactics to his public speeches, focusing on American strength to justify our intervention.

In addition, the photo strategically includes a U.S. marine to add to the photo's visual credibility. This symbol of America--a soldier in uniform-- forces the viewers to place more trust in the photographer and what we see here. My greatest fear is that the average American will hear Bush speak and see this photo without realizing that their goal is to convince the world of Iraqi support for American intervention. They claim that they are fighting to "free Iraq," but in reality, our government simply ties Iraq's fate to Saddam and destroys them both.

"The persona used in each article greatly influences the reader. The voice of a writer sways the readers' beliefs and the tone of voice develops ethos, thus changing how seriously he or she is taken."

—Angela Rastegar, Stanford student

In Angela Rastegar's first position paper, she writes about the power of photographs from a generalized, academic perspective, the voice of analytical assessment. But in her subsequent paper, she explores a specific point of view about media coverage of international politics. The persona of Elizabeth Grant, which she develops through careful attention to word choice, rhetorical appeals, and prose style, relies on the use of "I" and repeated use of strong language. As you can tell, the experimentation with *voice* itself was the most important product of her revisions: it allowed her to reach into her topic—and examine differences in *rhetorical stance*—in a particularly powerful way. As she moved into the final stages of her project, she brought the power of this writing to bear on her longer researched argument; although she wrote the final paper from her own perspective, working with the pro and con points of view enabled her to construct a sharper thesis statement and a more persuasive approach to the photographs she was discussing.

Exploring Multiple Sides of an Argument

Angela Rastegar's project opens up some interesting possibilities for developing your own persuasive arguments. Sometimes when we write from our own points of view, we get so locked into our individual perspectives that we fail to take into account the diverse or multiple sides of our topics. Such limited vision can weaken our persuasiveness; if we fail to consider or acknowledge alternative positions on our topics, we produce one-sided arguments that lack complexity or credibility with our readers. Recall our earlier discussion of photographs: each photograph suggests a different angle, a unique "version" of an event, and the perspective of a particular persona. When we bring these different sides to light, we find that suddenly an incident or issue that seems polarized—or "black and white"—is actually much more complex. The same holds true for the issues we confront every day as writers and rhetoricians: it is only through exploring the multiple sides of our argument that we can engage it persuasively and effectively.

Student Writing
See persuasive position papers by Katie Jones, about photography depicting the civil rights era, and by Ryan Kissick, on media depictions of baseball star Pete Rose.
www.ablongman.com/envision023

Let's take a look at one example of how exploring multiple sides of an issue provides a powerful strategy for developing an argument about some of our society's most serious problems. In the mid-1990s, contemporary playwright and performer Anna Deavere Smith was commis-

sioned to script a theatrical performance about the riots that rocked Los
Angeles in the wake of the 1992 verdict in the case of the police beating of Rodney King. To begin this project, she interviewed over two
hundred people, from police officers to gang members, store owners,
and jurors. However, instead of synthesizing that information into a single narrative thread or argument, she decided to celebrate their diverse
viewpoints, and wrote each interview up as an individual monologue,
preserving their characteristic diction, syntax, pacing, expression, and
arguments. The resultant performance piece, called *Twilight: Los Angeles,* is an exploration of multiple perspectives and multiple points of
view. On stage, Smith gave voice to each of these personas, using as
her script only their verbatim commentary on the events. As the film
stills from the photodocumentary of her play illustrate vividly (see Figures 3.8–3.10), she literally
assumed the identity of each of her interviewees;
from speech patterns, to dress, mannerisms, and
attitudes, she embodied these multiple perspectives
on the aftermath of the Rodney King beating that
led directly to the Los Angeles riots.

> **A Closer Look**
> To learn more about persona in
> performance, follow the link for Anna
> Deavere Smith's *Twilight: Los Angeles.*
> www.ablongman.com/envision024

The example of Anna Deavere Smith's multiple
arguments should encourage you to begin thinking about how experimenting with diverse perspectives can help you achieve a more thorough understanding of a complex situation. You may be tempted to
think of these different perspectives in oppositional terms—as the
"pro" or "con" of an issue. However, such a point of view closes off

FIGURE 3.8–3.10. Anna Deavere Smith embodies three distinct
personas in her performance for the play, *Twilight: Los Angeles.*

the richer complexity of the issue; think of arguments not in terms of right or wrong, but as a spectrum of different perspectives. As you turn to write your own arguments, consider how you can explore different viewpoints by trying out personas; by inventing diverse responses to your own point of view; and by exploring various writing strategies through experimentation with diction, syntax, style, image selection, arrangement of argument, and voice.

Writing Diverse Perspectives

When writing arguments, you might choose to explore more than one *persona* or *rhetorical stance* in order to see different sides of an issue. Student Aisha Ali, for instance, developed her project on the conflict in the Middle East by creating three different articles—or sides—around the same provocative photograph (see Figure 3.11). Using the image as the foundation for each discussion, she assumed the personas of an African photojournalist, an Israeli soldier, and, lastly, a Palestinian boy. Just as the diversity of Anna Deavere Smith's characters suggested the vast panorama of opinion on the Los Angeles riots, so Aisha's contrasting personas offered a series of riveting snapshots of the Palestinian conflict. To create this effect, the writer took extra care with word choice, sentence structure, and the development of her arguments. In her first side, she opened the piece by exploring the context of the Middle Eastern situation, and then moved with fluid and articulate language to the central narrative: the freeing of the doves in front of an oncoming tank. Her second side adopts a different approach; using

---

Occupation: Elementary School Student

Mohammed al-Durra Age: 8

My birds are gone. I had to let them go. I didn't want to, but we had to leave the house and I couldn't carry them. Mommy told me this morning that we would go to my Aunt Fatema's house in Jenin. I didn't want to go, but she made me. And today, in school, we were going to have Show and Tell, and I told her that, but she said that I could bring in Ali another time. Now I won't get to. Because I had to let him and Nayla and Hassan go free. They were my three doves and every day I gave them food and talked to them. I knew that sometimes they were scared because of the loud noises that came from town, but I would talk to them in their cage and let them know that it was okay. Mommy said that nothing bad would happen to us because we didn't do anything bad—but Daddy had to leave us and now, I lost my three best friends.

direct, informal speech, and biased language suitable to a soldier hardened by armed conflict, this persona launches immediately into the narrative itself. The last side also presents the story of the doves' release. However, as the excerpt from her work shows, the voice is clearly that of a child: from the simple sentence structures and word choice to the underlying pathos of the narrative, Aisha has brought to life the perspective of the young boy forced to free his doves in the shadow of military occupation.

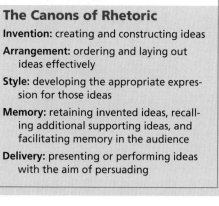
Together, this variety of perspectives enabled Aisha to avoid producing a simplistic argument about the violence in the Middle East, and instead to demonstrate its complexity. While the photograph Aisha used in her series of articles constitutes a powerful visual argument in itself through its striking juxtaposition of fluttering doves (a symbol of peace) and military tanks (a symbol of war), she was able to convey the meaning of the image for diverse viewers through powerful writing.

FIGURE 3.11. The powerful image of doves in front of a tank in the Middle East can be interpreted through a variety of lenses.

Understanding the Canons of Rhetoric

Looking at Aisha's exploration of persona gives you a unique opportunity to see the way in which all writing is informed by principles of **invention** (creating ideas), **arrangement** (organizing ideas in effective ways), and **style** (expressing those ideas in an appropriate manner). These three concepts constitute part of what classical rhetoricians called the **Canons of Rhetoric.**

Each one of these canons is necessary for a successful, or persuasive, communication,

AT A GLANCE

The Canons of Rhetoric

Invention: creating and constructing ideas

Arrangement: ordering and laying out ideas effectively

Style: developing the appropriate expression for those ideas

Memory: retaining invented ideas, recalling additional supporting ideas, and facilitating memory in the audience

Delivery: presenting or performing ideas with the aim of persuading whether that be through spoken word, written discourse, or, more recently, visual/multimedia/hybrid communication. However, for our discussion of developing arguments through persona and rhetorical stance, two canons assume particular importance: *arrangement* and *style*.

Working with Arrangement in Argument

In any written argument, ***arrangement*** should be a key consideration; the way in which you present material on the page will shape a reader's response to the ideas. In some cases, attention to arrangement takes the form of the way you order elements in your argument: for instance, whether you begin your paper with a strong thesis statement or instead embed an implied thesis in your introduction, saving the strongest statement of your argument for your conclusion. In more visual arguments, however, the idea of arrangement takes on a more literal meaning as well: it becomes a matter of layout and design—how you visually present material to your audience.

For instance, arrangement was a key consideration for one student who decided to take her exploration of multiple perspectives to a creative extreme. As part of a project on police brutality, Ashley Mullen created a newsletter that featured a cover story introducing the multiple sides of the argument. In designing this text, Ashley took into account not just the organization and development of her ideas; as the image in Figure 3.12 makes clear, she also considered questions of layout, placement of images, font size, color, and overall visual design. Her painstaking care with the arrangement of this text is evident in the power of her finished product. We can see here how visual rhetoric functions as a powerful tool in this exploration of argument. Inside the magazine, Ashley Mullen's choice of using three different photographs—each functioning as an individual visual argument—offered a graphic way of representing the complexity of the issue: each photo anchored each of three equally diverse personas. You might try working with three different photos to produce a range of arguments. Alternatively, experiment with the visual impact of multiple media in your layout; you could locate three different arguments as newspaper columns, magazine feature articles or cover stories, Web pages, or even personal letters.

FIGURE 3.12. Cover of Newsletter for Multiple Sides Project by Ashley Mullen.

Working with Style in Argument

In addition to structure, an argument's strength also resides in the way that it expresses its ideas—that is, its *style*. We often translate *style* into *voice* to indicate a writer's unique persona and rhetorical stance as it is manifested in word choice, syntax, pacing, and tone. In order to construct a successful argument, you need to be able to adopt the voice or style that best meets the needs of your rhetorical situation. If you are writing a feature article for *Time* magazine, for instance, you will most likely use accessible language, common expressions, and references to contemporary events. Your paragraphs may be only one or two sentences long, and you may use wit, humor, or pathos to try and move your audience. You might also include a color photograph or even a clip art drawing to convey your point to your readers. Such writing choices are all part of your persona as a popular writer. You would make very different composition choices if you were writing for an academic journal that would be read by the most distinguished scholars in the field. In this case, you might use disciplinary jargon or diction, longer paragraph structures, and references to other researchers. These rhetorical choices would distinguish your persona from that conveyed in the popular article. In both cases, your persona and your stylistic choices contribute to building your ethos and persuading your audience.

Perspectives and Possibilities

Experimenting with arrangement and style in these ways can help you understand the role of persona and rhetorical stance in all persuasive writing. Consider these examples of student work that attended to specific strategies of design, layout, and presentation in order to explore the multiple sides of an argument:

- Andrew Ardinger explored diverse angles of public reaction to the UNC Chapel Hill basketball coach as a *Daily Kansan* feature article, complete with ripped edges of a newspaper.
- Scott Chanatry investigated the controversy over the proposed monument for the Twin Towers in New York City by creating three feature articles from the *New Yorker*, as well as his own original cover for that fictitious *New Yorker* issue.
- Sean Bruich, in his examination of sports marketing, created a bound handbook, complete with ISBN number and promotional quotes on the back

Student Writing

Explore Multiple Sides Projects by Cyrus Chee, Sean Bruich, Janelle Cornwall, and many others.

www.ablongman.com/envision026

cover, and designed a variety of written arguments for inside, including an interoffice memo from the Oakland Athletics's marketing department, an AP wire story conveying a transcribed interview with the pitcher, and a biting review from a fan.

■ Derrick Jue worked through the implications of war photography by creating a Website modeled on the "Capture the Moment" site of Pulitzer-prize-winning photographs. The site featured the audio responses of three individuals (a soldier, the president of the United States, and the photographer) to an individual photograph.

■ Janelle Cornwall created a mock version of *Cosmo Girl* magazine that explored the issue of celebrity-endorsed Pepsi ads through a printed email, an IM conversation, a letter to the editor, and a closing interview with Britney Spears.

In each of these examples, the text's arrangement and style function as key components of the argument's persuasiveness; like Anna Deavere Smith's costumes, speech patterns, and theatrical gestures, they function as vital parts of the rhetoric of argumentation.

COLLABORATIVE CHALLENGE

Download two to three images from MSNBC.com's "Week in Pictures" accessible through the Chapter 3 resources on the *Envision* Website. As a group, select photos that convey different sides of a situation or event. Come up with three different personas—the voice of the person in the photo, the voice of the photographer, and the voice of an observer. Now, develop a thesis for each side and write a brief description of your imaged persona. Allow each person in the group to contribute a new perspective. Write up each of these sides; format them into a feature article or cover story for a newspaper or magazine, and when you are done, present your work as a group to the class.

www.ablongman.com/envision027

Representing Multiple Sides in Your Argument

While experimenting with multiple sides of argument allows you to develop a deeper understanding of the different viewpoints informing an issue, in many academic contexts, you will be asked to synthesize these perspectives into a single, thesis-driven text. The question then becomes: How do you write an essay that acknowledges diverse viewpoints without undermining the strength of its own argument?

We find an outstanding example of the successful balancing of an author's argument and other perspectives in Nora Ephron's article, "The Boston Photographs," published in *Scribble, Scribble: Notes on the Media* (1978). In this essay, Ephron offers us insight into the constant struggles that newspaper editors face in selecting photographs for publication—in this case, deciding whether or not to print the "sensationalist" images of a woman and child falling from a fire escape during a 1976 apartment fire. Ephron brings into her article at least three different perspectives, each embodying diverse rhetorical stances: her own perspective to that of photographer Stanley Forman and that of Charles Seib, the *Washington Post* ombudsman (the editor who monitors the content of the paper to ensure that it is not offensive to readers). She also represents in miniature other points of view through a series of brief quotations from letters to the editor published shortly after the incident. The writers of these letters each get a turn to argue their points from the basis of their own rhetorical stance. However, as you will see in reading the essay, the argument that ultimately is most persuasive is Ephron's own.

The Boston Photographs

"I made all kinds of pictures because I thought it would be a good rescue shot over the ladder . . . never dreamed it would be anything else. . . . I kept having to move around because of the light set. The sky was bright and they were in deep shadow. I was making pictures with a motor drive and he, the fire fighter, was reaching up and, I don't know, everything started falling. I followed the girl down taking pictures. . . . I made three or four frames. I realized what was going on and I completely turned around, because I didn't want to see her hit."

You probably saw the photographs. In most newspapers, there were three of them. The first showed some people on a fire escape—a fireman, a woman, and a child. The fireman had a nice strong jaw and looked very brave. The woman was holding the child. Smoke was pouring from the building behind them. A rescue ladder was approaching, just a few feet away, and the fireman had one arm around the woman and one arm reaching out toward the ladder.

The second picture showed the fire escape slipping off the building. The child had fallen on the escape and seemed about to slide off the edge. The woman was grasping desperately at the legs of the fireman, who had managed to grab the ladder. The third picture showed the woman and child in midair, falling to the ground. Their arms and legs were outstretched, horribly distended. A potted plant was falling too. The caption said that the woman, Diana Bryant, nineteen, died in the fall. The child landed on the woman's body and lived.

The pictures were taken by Stanley Forman, thirty, of the *Boston Herald American*. He used a motor-driven Nikon F set at 1/250, f5.6-S. Because of the motor, the camera can click off three frames a second. More than four hundred newspapers in the United States alone carried the photographs: The tear sheets from overseas are still coming in. The *New York Times* ran them on the first page of its second section; a paper in south Georgia gave them nineteen columns; the *Chicago Tribune,* the *Washington Post* and the *Washington Star* filled almost half their front pages, the *Star* under a somewhat redundant headline that read: SENSATIONAL PHOTOS OF RESCUE ATTEMPT THAT FAILED.

The photographs are indeed sensational. They are pictures of death in action, of that split second when luck runs out, and it is impossible to look at them without feeling their extraordinary impact and remembering, in an almost subconscious way, the morbid fantasy of falling, falling off a building, falling to one's death. Beyond that, the pictures are classics, old-fashioned but perfect examples of photojournalism at its most spectacular. They're throwbacks, really, fire pictures, 1930s tabloid shots; at the same time they're technically superb and thoroughly modern—the sequence could not have been taken at all until the development of the motor-driven camera some sixteen years ago.

Most newspapers editors anticipate some reader reaction to photographs like Forman's; even so, the response around the country was enormous, and almost all of it was negative. I have read hundreds of the letters that were printed in letters-to-the-editor sections, and they repeat the same points. "Invading the privacy of death." "Cheap sensationalism." "I thought I was reading the *National Enquirer*." "Assigning the agony of a human being in terror of imminent death to the status of a side-show act." "A tawdry way to sell newspapers." The *Seattle Times* received sixty letters and calls; its managing editor even got a couple of them at home. A reader wrote the *Philadelphia*

Inquirer: "*Jaws* and *Towering Inferno* are playing downtown; don't take business away from people who pay good money to advertise in your own paper." Another reader wrote the *Chicago Sun-Times:* "I shall try to hide my disappointment that Miss Bryant wasn't wearing a skirt when she fell to her death. You could have had some award-winning photographs of her underpants as her skirt billowed over her head, you voyeurs." Several newspaper editors wrote columns defending the pictures: Thomas Keevil of the *Costa Mesa* (California) *Daily Pilot* printed a ballot for readers to vote on whether they would have printed the pictures; Marshall L. Stone of Maine's *Bangor Daily News,* which refused to print the famous assassination picture of the Vietcong prisoner in Saigon, claimed that the Boston pictures showed the dangers of fire escapes and raised questions about slumlords. (The burning building was a five-story brick apartment house on Marlborough Street in the Back Bay section of Boston.)

For the last five years, the *Washington Post* has employed various journalists as ombudsmen, whose job is to monitor the paper on behalf of the public. The *Post's* current ombudsman is Charles Seib, former managing editor of the *Washington Star;* the day the Boston photographs appeared, the paper received over seventy calls in protest. As Seib later wrote in a column about the pictures, it was "the largest reaction to a published item that I have experienced in eight months as the *Post's* ombudsman. . . .

"In the *Post's* newsroom, on the other hand, I found no doubts, no second thoughts . . . the question was not whether they should be printed but how they should be displayed. When I talked to editors . . . they used words like 'interesting' and 'riveting' and 'gripping' to describe them. The pictures told of something about life in the ghetto, they said (although the neighborhood where the tragedy occurred is not a ghetto, I am told). They dramatized the need to check on the safety of fire escapes. They dramatically conveyed something that had happened, and that is the business we're in. They were news. . . .

"Was publication of that [third] picture a bow to the same taste for the morbidly sensational that makes gold mines of disaster movies? Most papers will not print the picture of a dead body except in the most unusual circumstances. Does the fact that the final picture was taken a millisecond before the young woman died make a difference? Most papers will not print a picture of a bare female breast. Is that a more inappropriate subject for display than the picture of a human being's last agonized instant of life?" Seib offered no answers to the questions he raised, but he went on to say that although as an editor he would probably have run the pictures, as a reader he was revolted by them.

In conclusion, Seib wrote: "Any editor who decided to print those pictures without giving at least a moment's thought to what purpose they served and what their effect was likely to be on the reader should ask another question: Have I become so preoccupied with manufacturing a product according to professional traditions and standards that I have forgotten about the consumer, the reader?"

It should be clear that the phone calls and letters and Seib's own reaction were occasioned by one factor alone: the death of the woman. Obviously, had she survived the fall, no one would have protested; the pictures would have had a completely different impact. Equally obviously, had the child died as well—or instead—Seib would undoubtedly have received ten times the phone calls he did. In each case, the pictures would have been exactly the same—only the captions, and thus the responses, would have been different.

FIGURE 3.13. The *Boston Herald American* chose to print the final, most sensational photograph in the series for its cover.

But the questions Seib raises are worth discussing—though not exactly for the reasons he mentions. For it may be that the real lesson of the Boston photographs is not the danger that editors will be forgetful of reader reaction, but that they will continue to censor pictures of death precisely because of that reaction. The protests Seib fielded were really a variation on an old theme—and we saw plenty of it during the Nixon-Agnew years—the "Why doesn't the press print the good news?" argument. In this case, of course, the objections were all dressed up and cleverly disguised as righteous indignation about the privacy of death. This is a form of puritanism that is often justifiable; just as often it is merely puritanical.

Seib takes it for granted that the widespread though fairly recent newspaper policy against printing pictures of dead bodies is a sound one; I don't know that it makes any sense at all. I recognize that printing pictures of corpses raises all sorts of problems about taste and titillation and sensationalism; the fact is, however, that people die. Death happens to be one of life's main events. And it is irresponsible—and more than that, inaccurate—for newspapers to fail to show it, or to show it only when an astonishing set of photos comes in over the Associated Press wire. Most papers covering fatal automobile accidents will print pictures of mangled cars. But the significance of fatal automobile accidents is not that a great deal of steel is twisted but that people die. Why not show it? That's what accidents are about. Throughout the Vietnam war, editors were reluctant to print atrocity pictures. Why *not* print them? That's what that was about. Murder victims are almost never photographed; they are granted their privacy. But their relatives are relentlessly pictured on their way in and out of hospitals and morgues and funerals.

I'm not advocating that newspapers print these things in order to teach their readers a lesson. The *Post* editors justified their printing of the Boston pictures with several arguments in that direction; every one of them is irrelevant. The pictures don't show anything about slum life; the incident could have happened anywhere, and it did. It is extremely unlikely that anyone who saw them rushed out and had his fire escape strengthened. And the pictures were not news—at least they were not national news. It is not news in Washington, or New York, or Los Angeles that a woman was killed in a Boston fire. The only newsworthy thing about the pictures is that they were taken. They deserve to be printed because they are great pictures, breathtaking pictures of something that happened. That they disturb readers is exactly as it should be: that's why photojournalism is often more powerful than written journalism.

How does Ephron present her own argument despite allowing so many voices in her piece? Let's look at the *arrangement* of her essay for insight into this question. Ephron begins with the voice of the photographer, Stanley Forman, using a direct quote as her opening paragraph to ground the reader in his perspective. From there, she moves to a pair of background paragraphs that provides context for Forman's recollections. It is only in the fourth paragraph that she gives her own assessment of the images—that they "are indeed sensational"—and, yet she refrains from providing a definitive thesis statement, allowing the multiple

A Closer Look

For an alternative perspective on the ethics of publishing "sensational" photographs, read Joe Klein's article, "PG-Rated War" in the April 7, 2003 issue of *Time*.

Seeing Connections
See Chapter 6 for strategies of formal outlining and help with structuring your own argument, arranging evidence, and developing a strong argument using research.

perspectives to play themselves out further before imposing her own viewpoint on the reader. She does so by next devoting an entire paragraph to the audience reaction to the photos. In the subsequent paragraph, she finally moves to the perspective of Charles Seib, the *Washington Post* editor who decided to run the photographs in that newspaper. She devotes over three paragraphs to a direct quotation from Seib on the issue. It is only now, after showcasing these voices, that she allows her own argument to openly enter the piece. Through a gentle qualification of Seib's argument—where she asserts its legitimacy while suggesting her own interpretation—she then moves to her own argument, which comprises the final three paragraphs of the piece. The piece ends very strongly with her own clear justification of the decision to publish the controversial photos.

As this analysis of Ephron's arrangement strategies reveals, she allows the multiple viewpoints to play themselves out, providing the reader with a firm grounding in the debate, before concluding with her own very strong point of view. However, Ephron's strategy is just one of many patterns of arrangement that could produce a persuasive text. You have multiple options available to you when dealing with opposing viewpoints. You could follow the classical method of arrangement (see table) or select a modified version, depending on your purpose.

AT A GLANCE

The Arrangement of Ephron's Argument

1. Quotation from photographer (1 paragraph)
2. Background paragraphs (2 paragraphs)
3. Ephron's general assessment of images (1 paragraph)
4. Reader reaction to photos (1 paragraph)
5. Editor's point of view (4 paragraphs)
6. Qualification of Seib's point of view (1 paragraph)
7. Her own argument (final 3 paragraphs)

The models of arrangement in the table are not designed to be rigid parameters. Instead, they should suggest possibilities and potentially productive strategies of arrangement; in your own writing, you will have to select the most productive way to lay out your topic and the diverse opinions that surround it.

You'll need to consider first the strength of the other perspectives on the issue. Do they corroborate your argument? Then you could include them as supporting evidence. Do they offer points of view that you can disprove? Then you might present the opinion and provide a **rebuttal,** or refutation of the points, demonstrating why they are not valid. Do they offer points of view that you can't disprove?

STRATEGIES OF ARRANGEMENT

A Classical Speech or Oration	Option A Use when you want to ground the reader in your argument before bringing up opposing perspectives.	Option B Establish opposing opinion up front so that the entire piece functions as an extended rebuttal or refutation of that line of argument.	Option C Treat diverse viewpoints as appropriate during the development of your argument and presentation of your evidence.
1. Introduction 2. Statement of facts 3. Division 4. Proof 5. Refutation 6. Conclusion	1. Introduction, identification of rhetorical stance 2. Thesis 3. Statement of background, definition, or context 4. Evidence and development of argument 5. Opposing opinion, concession, qualification, refutation 6. Conclusion	1. Introduction and opposing viewpoint 2. Thesis and identification of rhetorical stance 3. Evidence and development of argument 4. Conclusion	1. Introduction, identification of rhetorical stance 2. Thesis 3. Statement of background, definition, or context 4. Evidence, opposing opinion, concession, qualification, refutation 5. Conclusion

Then, you might *concede* the validity of their argument, but go on to *qualify* their points by showing why your own argument is nonetheless persuasive. The key is to treat these other voices with respect; always represent their points of view fairly and without bias, even if you disagree with them. In a sense, when you are dealing with multiple perspectives, some of which may run counter to your own argument, you face a question of ethics quite similar to that the editors faced with the Boston photographs: How do you present possibly volatile material in a way that is both fair and furthers your own persuasive purpose?

AT A GLANCE

Dealing with Multiple Perspectives in Your Arguments

When incorporating other viewpoints in your own writing, you could use them in one of three ways:

- **Evidence:** You could use the diverse viewpoints to support your own thesis statement.
- **Concession/Qualification:** You admit that the person has a strong point, but then explain why it doesn't diminish the persuasiveness or validity of your own argument.
- **Rebuttal:** You present an opposing opinion, fairly and respectfully, and then demonstrate why it is not a valid argument in this case.

CREATIVE PRACTICE

Rewrite the Nora Ephron piece from the perspective of one of the different personas that she mentions in her text: the editor, the photographer, or a disgruntled reader. As you do, incorporate the other perspectives into your argument, experimenting with arrangement and style to produce a piece that represents the diverse viewpoints while still making its own strong argument.

The Ethics of Visual Representation

In completing the Creative Practice concerning the Boston photographs, you may have realized that with photographs there is often a tricky ethical dilemma concerning the distribution, framing, and power of such images. As authors, we have debated over the ethics of including photographs such as the one of the Columbia space crew that heads this chapter (see Figure 3.1). We want to explore their power as visual rhetoric texts, but we don't want to rob them of meaning by reducing them to mere examples in this book. This presents quite an ethical quandary. Yet our study of visual rhetoric requires us to grapple with the political and ethical issues regarding the persuasive power of images.

The field of journalism has always had to wrestle with similar concerns surrounding publishing images and texts, and such issues have become even more pressing today in our world of ubiquitous multimedia coverage, live-feeds from war scenes, instantly distributed photographs over the Internet, and the increasing ease with which images can be altered to change their representations of reality.

The overwhelming reliance on visual communication in the media makes our study of visual rhetoric even more important and timely; consider the attempts by government officials to make sense of the political motivations of the kidnappers of Daniel Pearl by studying the video released by his Pakistani kidnappers. Or, consider the heated Internet debates over the possible "staging" of an Iraqi-led toppling of a statue

A Closer Look

Dan Kennedy provides a historical overview of photo ethics in his article, "Witness to an Execution," in *The Boston Phoenix* (13-20 June 2002).

www.ablongman.com/envision028

of Saddam Hussein. This is a perfect example of how even photographers are feeling the pressures of attempting to shape a story about reality by casting it through a particular lens. The media is beginning to respond to such concerns about visual representation and ethical responsibility. Consider the U.S. media's decision not to show photographs of people jumping out of the Twin Towers of the World Trade Center moments before their collapse, or the many articles in response to deliberately framed coverage of the 2002–2003 war in Iraq.

> No matter how the tools of journalism change, fundamental ethical concerns still apply. Displaying violent, sensational images for economic reasons, violating a person's privacy without a clear news sense for doing so, manipulating news-editorial pictures to alter their content, stereotyping individuals into preconceived categories, and blurring the distinction between advertising, public relations, and editorial messages were journalism concerns in 1902, are important topics in 2002, and will be carefully considered issues, no doubt, in 2102.
>
> —Christopher Harris and Paul Martin Lester

Photo Ethics in the Digital Age

As suggested by the example of Brian Walski's photo manipulation discussed earlier, the question of whether to publish a photograph has become even more complex with the advent of digital photography. The ease with which photographs can be digitally altered and the blurring of distinctions between photojournalism and photo illustration is nowhere more evident than in a controversy from the mid-1990s over a *Time* magazine cover. On June 27, 1994, top news magazines across America featured cover stories detailing the pursuit and arrest of former NFL running back O. J. Simpson for the murder of his wife. That week, *Newsweek* ran a cover based on Simpson's mug shot.

Time ran a very similar cover; however, in a controversial move, the magazine decided to darken the photo for rhetorical effect, sparking a widespread debate over the practice of photo illustration and its power in shaping a reader's understanding of the "reality" of representation.

COLLABORATIVE CHALLENGE

In a group, compare the June 1994 *Newsweek* and *Time* covers featuring O. J. Simpson with the June 27, 1994 *Time* cover, both linked through the *Envision* Website. What effect does the photo alteration of the original mug shot have on the message sent by the *Time* magazine cover? Think about the use of words and images in both texts. How do the different cover titles inform the audience's reaction to the image? As a group, compose a paragraph in which you argue a position about racism and the O. J. Simpson cover. Share your statement with the rest of your class and consider the different rhetorical strategies, appeals, and evidence that each group used in arguing its decision. For added challenge, read the managing editor's letter to the readers from *Time*'s July 4, 1994 edition. Consider the rhetorical strategies—in terms of both word *and* image—that he uses in this article in order to respond to the accusations of racism.

www.ablongman.com/envision029

The *Time* magazine cover image is only one of the most famous examples of photo manipulation; it actually has become a routine practice, from the February 1982 *National Geographic* cover that moved the Egyptian pyramids closer together to accommodate the space limitations of its cover design; to the July 2003 *Redbook* cover that created a composite image of Julia Roberts from two different photo shoots; to a University of Wisconsin-Madison admissions bulletin that digitally inserted an African-American student into a crowd photo to illustrate its commitment to diversity; to an airbrushed Mariah Carey CD cover and a 1997 *Newsweek* cover that straightened septuplet mom Bobbi McCaughey's teeth. The point of all these examples is that, as Plato believed, rhetorical acts have ethical and moral consequences. But the better we understand the power of rhetoric—in its verbal, visual, and hybrid forms—the better we'll be able to make choices about using rhetoric in a way that meets our own code of ethics.

Student Writing

See photo manipulation projects by Tiffany Yun and Chris Mathakul.

www.ablongman.com/envision030

Constructing Your Own Argument

In this chapter, you've learned to craft effective and focused thesis statements. You've developed strategies for constructing a persona and explored the value of rhetorical stance in argument. You've experimented with developing the multiple sides of an argument, and then integrated them into a single, thesis-driven argument. You've worked with the Canons of Rhetoric by inventing position papers, arranging your claims and evidence, and crafting your prose with diverse styles. Now it's time to implement these skills. Try working with images both as evidence for your own thesis-driven arguments and as arguments on their own (or in conjunction with written arguments). Practice inventing a thesis, constructing an argument, developing a rhetorical stance, and working on persona through style and arrangement. You might want to brainstorm first with the help of the prewriting checklist and then try out the longer writing projects described below.

PREWRITING CHECKLIST
Analyzing Photographs

❏ **Content:** What, literally, does the photograph depict? Who or what is the subject of the photo? What is the setting?

❏ **Cultural context:** What is the historical context of the photograph? If it "documents" a particular event, person, or historical moment; how prominently does this photograph factor into our understanding of this event, person or place? (For instance, is it the only known photograph of an event, or is it one of a series of pictures taken of the same subject?)

❏ **Material context:** Where was this photograph reproduced or displayed (an art gallery, the cover of a magazine, the front page of a newspaper)? If it was published elsewhere originally, does this source credit the original?

❏ **Argument:** What, thematically, does the photograph depict? What is its message to the audience? For instance, while the photo might *show* a group of people standing together, its argument might be about love, family unity across generations, or a promise for the future.

❏ **Photographer:** Who took this photograph? What was the person's purpose?

❏ **Genre:** Is this a news photo? a self-portrait? a piece of art? How does it fulfill or confound the expectations of this genre (i.e., the expectation for a news photo is that it clearly captures a person, moment, event; the expectation for a self-portrait is that it evokes an artist's sense of his or her own persona)?

❏ **Audience:** Was the photograph intended to persuade a larger audience or to function as a more personalized expression of a point of view?

(continued)

❏ **Purpose:** What is the photograph's purpose? Is it intended to be overtly argumentative and to move its audience to action? Or is the argument more subtle, even to the point of "seeming" objective or representational?

❏ **Rhetorical stance:** How does the composition of the photo convey a sense of the rhetorical stance or point of view of the photographer? Pay attention to issues of focus (what is "in focus"? this may differ from the ostensible "focus" of the picture), cropping (what is "in" the picture, and what has been left "out"), color (is the picture in black and white? color? sepia?), setting (what backdrop has the photographer chosen?), perspective (are we looking down? up?).

❏ **Representation versus reality:** Does this photograph aspire to represent reality, or is it an overtly abstract piece? Is there any indication of photo manipulation, editing, or other alteration? If so, what rhetorical purpose does this serve—what argument does this alteration make?

❏ **Word and image:** Does the photo have a caption? Does it accompany an article, essay, or other lengthy text? How does the image function in dialogue with this verbal text? Does it offer visual evidence? Does it argue an independent point? Does it provide a counterargument to the print text?

WRITING PROJECTS

Visit the *Envision* Website for expanded assignment guidelines and student projects.

1. Write up an argument about an issue that moves you; base your argument on your analysis of a powerful image, and include your interpretation of the image as part of your writing. Develop a strong thesis, pick your persona, decide on your strategy of arrangement, and write with particular attention to style. You might select to write a popular article, such as a letter to an editor of the campus newspaper, a "blog" on a Website, or a newspaper column such as *Newsweek*'s "My Turn."

2. Construct a persona in response to Susan Sontag's essay, "Looking at War" or Anna Deavere Smith's script for *Twilight: Los Angeles*. Invent a strong thesis, determine your voice or style, and write an argument for another way of seeing the images and issues at the center of each text.

3. Write three position papers or articles in the form of a Multiple Sides Project. That is, rather than composing one argument, compose three. Have each one comment on the previous one in turn so that the project forms a coherent whole. Give each persona a name, an occupation, a geographic location, and a strong perspective to argue in words. Each position can offer a new point of view on one image or can develop complexity about an issue by bringing in a new image as visual evidence.

FOR ADDED CHALLENGE

 Visit the *Envision* Website for expanded assignment guidelines and student projects.

1. Format your Multiple Sides Project as a feature article for a specific magazine or reading audience. Conduct a rhetorical analysis on the features of a chosen publication (*The New Yorker, The Economist,* a national newspaper, or a campus journal) and then format your three arguments as part of that publication. Include a cover page with an introduction by the editor and a closing assessment page, perhaps by a staff writer. You could also format your project as a Website or multimedia text (a bound book, a flash montage, or an animated photo essay).

2. Collaborate on your Multiple Sides Project by assigning the writing of each argument to a different member of your group. You might, for instance, write about the conflict between your college campus and the surrounding town: have someone interview locals, the sheriff, the administrators, and the students. Provide a series of arguments from each perspective and images to function as argumentative texts for each side. Be sure to include concession and refutation. Collaborate in the writing of the introduction and the conclusion as well as in the design, arrangement, and style of the project as a whole.

3. As a class, present your arguments in a conference format; set up the day as a showcase of arguments. Each speaker can project his or her argument and images on a screen and deliver the words of the argument in a powerful voice. You might pursue this option either individually, by having each person present the project in turn, or collaboratively, by having each member of a team present an argument and the images that inform and direct that point of view. Decide if you want to provide written feedback for each person, and award a prize to the most effective use of visual rhetoric, the most persuasive argument, and the best style.

CHAPTER 3 ON THE WEB

Resources and Readings	Exercises and Assignments	Student Writing
• Closer Look resources and annotated readings • Links to resources on arrangement, style, and developing thesis statements • Links to photography collections and exhibits • Position paper	• Multiple Sides Project • Cover and Contents Project • Media analysis form • Peer review sheets • Focus on diverse learners and students with disabilities • Position papers	• Multiple Sides Project • Formatted feature articles • Reflection letters on photography

 www.ablongman.com/envision

"THE ONLY TRULY 'ESSENTIAL' MOVIE OF THE YEAR" THE FACE
"A BOLD, BLACKLY COMIC MASTERPIECE" BBCi FILMS
★★★★
A film by Michael Moore
BOWLIN
FOR
COLUMBIN
ARE THEY A NATION OF GUN NUTS OR ARE THEY
www.bowlingforcolumbine.com www.penguinbooks.co.uk/stupidwhitemen

PART II

Inquiry: Research Arguments

Research is never completed. . . . Around the corner
lurks another possibility of interview, another book to
read, a courthouse to explore, a document to verify.

—Catherine Drinker Bowen

CHAPTER 4

Planning and Proposing Research Arguments

What can you learn about visual rhetoric from the propaganda poster shown in Figure 4.1? Speculate about the arrangement of elements: Why the juxtaposition of a menacing Soviet officer with a contemporary college student listening to downloaded music? Comment on the layout and look: Why the deep red background color and the placement of characters with the officer looking over the student's shoulder? Assess how words work with images: Why is *Communism* so large and visually echoed by the hammer and sickle? Such observations will help you make an argument from your analysis, but in order to back up or substantiate your claims about the meaning of this image, you would need to do research. That is, it is necessary to place the rhetorical elements of the poster in their original historical context.

As you seek to understand the 1950s Cold War era in which such propaganda posters originated, you need to study the ideas, the historical developments, and the social trends of that period. Similarly, as you try to grasp the significance of conveying the RIAA's position in terms of a parody of anti-Soviet propaganda, you need to investigate the political and legal controversy surrounding file-sharing. Research is one way to gain access to a specific period of time or set of issues. You can also conduct research to find out how other writers have approached and analyzed texts such as these, or your research might entail interviews with experts about your topic area or a survey of your peers.

FIGURE 4.1. How does this parody propaganda poster use visual elements to undermine the RIAA's stance on file-sharing?

Chapter Preview Questions

- How do I generate a productive topic for a research paper?
- What prewriting techniques can I use to develop ideas and focus my topic?
- How do I keep a research log?
- What are the steps for writing a strong research plan and abstract?
- How do I transform my abstract into an effective research proposal?

Doing research lends depth and complexity to your own interpretation of a given text and positions your argument within a larger discussion on an issue. Such research entails more than going to the library and gathering sources. It's an inquiry that you pursue by exploring a variety of sources: online, in libraries, and through field research. In this chapter, we will guide you through the first steps of becoming an active participant in a research community in order to help you develop the skills for turning a research topic into an effective research plan and a solid research proposal.

> Research is "a social, collaborative act that draws on and contributes to the work of a community that cares about a given body of knowledge."
>
> —Patricia Bizzell and Bruce Herzberg

Asking Research Questions

We have chosen to focus our discussion in this chapter around a specific subset of persuasive images—propaganda posters—because such texts make very powerful public statements, and also because, for many of us, to understand the motivations behind them, we would have to perform a certain amount of research. Often, this research comes in the form of looking for answers to our questions about the propaganda poster in order to comprehend its meaning in the context in which it was created. In fact, most research papers begin with the act of asking questions.

One way that you can get started on your research is to pick a visual text that moves you and start brainstorming questions about it. Let's say that you came across the 1917 American enlistment poster shown in Figure 4.2 in an exhibit on campus or as part of a class discussion about World War I posters. Approaching it for the first time, you

FIGURE 4.2. This World War I propaganda poster offers a wealth of detail for historical analysis.

and your peers probably would start to analyze the visual rhetoric much as we did in the earlier chapters of *Envision*.

What are your eyes drawn to first? The words or the image? Maybe you would look first at the simian figure in the middle, roaring menacingly at you, then at the swooning, seminaked woman in his arms. In contrast, maybe the person next to you explains that her eyes first move upward, to the overarching and inflammatory bold yellow text, then to the bottom, where the words "U.S. Army" in black are superimposed on the imperative "ENLIST." In synthesizing various responses to the text, you most likely would find yourself with more questions than answers. This is actually good, for those questions can be the beginning of your research inquiry.

You might have asked: Is that gorilla King Kong? Following up on that question through research, you would find that the poster was made decades before the movie, ruling out the possibility of an allusion between the texts. Thus, *King Kong* could not be one of the meanings for the beast. Instead, you might find several books that discuss the wartime practice of casting enemies as subhuman creatures, and this might explain why the enemy nation is conveyed as a menacing gorilla in this poster. Adding to that your observation that "culture" is spelled "KULTUR" (on the club the gorilla is holding) would make you realize that the enemy here is suggestive of Germany.

Then, you might ask: What is the significance of that bloody club? Why is the woman unconscious and partly naked? More research might provide insight on how bestiality emerged as a wartime theme in such posters in order to inspire men to enlist. The idea was that if a nation's women were threatened with potential attack by such "monsters," then the men would surely step up to save and protect their wives, daughters, sisters, and mothers.

These very specific observations and questions about the posters should lead you to look up sources that will provide compelling answers and, eventually, to acquire new knowledge. In other words, by asking questions about your visual text, you can move beyond an initial response and into the realm of intellectual discovery.

In fact, your first questions about the text will lead you to ask more pointed questions about the context, political environment, key players, or social trends informing your visual texts. For the propaganda poster in Figure 4.2, such questions might include: What conflicts was America involved in during 1917? What was the meaning of the word on the gorilla's hat, "Militarism," at this time? How would an

> "Propaganda has a bad name, but its root meaning is simply to disseminate through a medium, and all writing therefore is propaganda for something."
>
> —Elizabeth Drew

appeal to *enlist* factor into that historical situation? Who is the audience for this poster and how is this poster part of a series of wartime propaganda images? If you were to work through these questions, you might begin to develop ideas for a feasible research topic—one that could yield an interesting research

A Closer Look
Explore online archives of propaganda posters to look for possible research topics.
www.ablongman.com/envision031

paper on war propaganda and the relationship between America and Germany in 1917.

But as you can tell, your questions will often expand your focus on the text to look at it from a comparative perspective or to widen your frame of reference to include a range of visual texts. Your questions then become more complex: Do other posters of the same time period use similar imagery and rhetorical strategies? How do the techniques used in early twentieth-century posters differ from those used during World War II? How are the rhetorical strategies used in this poster similar to or different from enlistment posters we might encounter today? In what ways have enlistment posters changed over time?

To answer these questions, you might perform a quick online search to yield some useful information. Perhaps you would need to visit the library, talk with a history professor, or study a museum poster exhibit. In all cases, what these questions are moving you toward is a focused *research topic* and, ultimately, a written project that draws upon and contributes to the arguments that others have made about such texts. As you can tell from Milessa Muchmore's work shown on the next page in Figure 4.3, generating a range of interesting and productive questions is the first step in any research project; the process of inquiry itself helps you to define a project and make it your own.

Constructing a Research Log

As you move from asking questions about a text to producing a feasible research topic for your paper, keep track of your ideas in a **research log.** This log will help you organize your ideas, chart your progress, and assemble the different pieces of your

AT A GLANCE

Constructing a Research Log

To start your research log, include a variety of entries related to the initial stages of the research process:

- Write freely on possible topic ideas
- Insert and annotate clippings from newspaper or magazine sources that offer interesting potential topics
- Paste in and respond to provocative images related to potential topics
- Write a reaction to ideas brought up during class discussion
- Insert and annotate printouts from emails or other collaborative work on research ideas
- Track preliminary searches on the Internet and in your library catalog
- Develop your research plan
- Vent anxieties over your topic

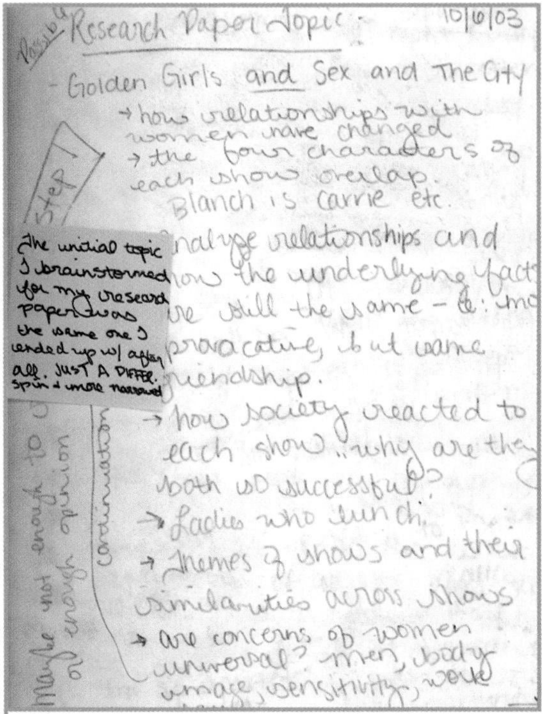

FIGURE 4.3. Milessa Muchmore used questions and preliminary searches to develop a topic in her research log.

research. It can contain primarily written text, as does the example in Figure 4.3, or it can include images as well. The log itself can take many forms, from a handwritten journal, to a series of Microsoft word documents, to an online Weblog. The key lies not in what form you choose, but in the way you use your chosen form to help you develop your topic into an interesting and provocative research project.

Generating Topics

One of the most crucial aspects of starting a research project is selecting a viable and engaging **topic.** The word *topic,* in fact, comes from the ancient Greek word *topos,* translated literally as "place." The earliest students of rhetoric used the physical space of the papyrus page—given to them by their teachers—to locate their topics for writing. Similarly, your teacher may suggest certain guidelines or parameters for you to follow when it comes to your topic. You may be given a specific topic (such as representations of race in Dr. Seuss cartoons) or you may be limited to a theme (the visual rhetoric of car advertisements).

In some cases, you may not have any restrictions at all. But despite the degree to which your topic has been mapped out for you, you still can—and should—make it your own. Partly, you do this by generating your own range of questions and your inquiry for where to look further; partly, you do this by responding to the rhetorical situation provided by your assignment. Even if your whole class is writing on the same topic, each person will present a different argument or approach to the issue. Some will use a different stance or persona, some will rely on different sources, some will use different rhetorical appeals, and all will argue different positions about the topic.

"Lists of topics were first written on papyrus rolls, and students who were looking for a specific topic unrolled the papyrus until they came to the place on the roll where that topic was listed."

—Sharon Crowley

COLLABORATIVE CHALLENGE

Get into groups of three or four and look at the series of posters in Figures 4.4–4.7, which fall under the broad topic of World War I enlistment posters. As a group, come up with a list of three different research questions that you might explore based on two to four of those posters. Now exchange your list with another small group and discuss the differences in questions. By the end of the session, come up with three or four concrete research topics you might pursue.

FIGURE 4.4. An American woman wears a Navy suit in Christy's propaganda poster.

FIGURE 4.5. A British mother and children watch male soldiers leave for battle in Kealey's 1915 poster.

FIGURE 4.6. This 1917 U.S. poster presents a direct message from a woman dressed for war.

FIGURE 4.7. Great Britain's John Bull points straight at the viewer in this 1915 poster.

As you completed the Collaborative Challenge, your responses to the posters undoubtedly varied. Perhaps you generated some of these topics:

- The different roles of women in the posters
- Crossing-dressing women and enlistment posters
- The use of sexuality in Navy propaganda
- The differences in portraits of men and women

A Closer Look

One of the earliest rhetoricians, Gorgias, became famous for offering a unique argument about a familiar topic: Helen of Troy. In his "defense of Helen," he argued that the power of language made her leave with Paris and led to the beginning of the Trojan War. Look at his approach in the "Encomium of Helen," and then ask yourself: If you had to write on this topic, what arguments could you make on this topic? www.ablongman.com/envision032

No matter what topics you and your collaboration partners wrote down, you all probably have one thing in common: you were drawn to themes that interest you with regard to the visual texts. The precise interest will vary from person to person, but the point here is that everyone focused on an aspect that intrigued him or her. This is key: successful research topics need to interest you, inspire you, or even anger you. Even with assigned topics, you should be able to find that aspect of the assignment that speaks to you. In general, there needs to be a *connection* between you and your topic to motivate you to follow through and transform it into a successful argument.

CREATIVE PRACTICE

Examine a copy of a school, local, or national newspaper for compelling stories or images that might offer interesting topics for research. Which would you be most likely to pursue? Which have you seen in the news for several days? Which touch on issues you've discussed before? Which ones seem to be workable research topics that you can explore through a sustained research inquiry? Write these ideas down in your research log.

Committing to a Topic

As you can tell, the most important part of a research project is deciding on a topic that is meaningful and interesting to you. It should be one that you want to write about, research aspects of, and contribute a new perspective on to a larger audience. To see how this works, let's look at one student's project on propaganda posters to see how

FIGURE 4.8. This Uncle Sam poster from 1917 was reissued for World War II.

FIGURE 4.9. Anti-Nazi propaganda relied on religiously-charged rhetoric.

FIGURE 4.10. American war efforts employed extreme visual messages to galvanize support.

he committed to a topic and developed a research plan. For his focus, student Tommy Tsai found himself interested in propaganda posters from World War II (see Figures 4.8–4.10).

Looking at these images, Tommy Tsai came up with a prospective topic: "The Rhetoric of World War II Propaganda." He wrote in his research log that he wanted to analyze these posters in their historical contexts: "In particular, I plan to focus on the propaganda posters that appeared in the three most active countries in that time period: the United States, Germany, and Japan. My research paper will report my findings from the comparison of the different rhetorical strategies employed by the three nations." In the process of asking questions about these posters, he became more committed to the topic. Now you examine the images. What topics and questions could you come up with? Such questions can lead to a research project based on these texts.

As you can tell, you might write about any number of images or issues. When considering potential topics, screen them by working through questions that test your interest in the area.

At this point, you might begin to think about the type of research you'll need to do for this topic; in fact, you might select your topic based mostly on the sorts of research it allows you to do. For

AT A GLANCE

Looking for the "Perfect" Topic

1. *Look inward.* Ask questions about yourself: What issues, events, or ideas interest you? Are there any hot-button topics that you find yourself drawn to again and again? What topic is compelling enough that you would watch a news program, a television special, or a film, or attend a talk on it?

2. *Look outward.* Ask questions about the people, structures, and issues you encounter every day. Walk through campus and look around: What are the central issues of student life on campus? Do you walk by a technology-enhanced classroom and see the students busy writing on laptops or using plasma screens? Topic: technology and education. Do you see a fraternity's poster about a "dry" party? Topic: alcohol on campus. Do you see workers outside the food service building on strike? Topic: labor relations at the university.

3. *Use creative visualization.* Imagine that you are at a party; you are chatting casually with a friend, when you overhear someone nearby talking about something. Suddenly, you feel so interested—or so angry—that you excuse yourself from your companion to go over and participate in the conversation. What would move you so strongly?

4. *Use the materials of the moment.* Perhaps the *topos* might be closer to the classical Greek model; although not a roll of papyrus, your class reading list or a single issue of a newspaper can house many topics. Scan the front page and opinion section of your school or town newspaper to see what events or issues people are talking about. Be sure to look at the pictures as well for hot issues or events. You might shift your perspective from local to global and pick up a national or international newspaper or a newsmagazine; what is gripping the community at large?

instance, a student writing on propaganda of the Prohibition era will work extensively with paper sources, which might involve archival work with original letters, posters, or government documents from that time period; a student writing on visual advertising for ethnic-theme dorms on campus will be more likely to complement paper sources with interviews with the university housing staff, student surveys, and first-person observations. Similarly, a student writing on sexualized visual rhetoric in student elections might take a poll, gather concrete examples, and research the newspaper's coverage of past and present elections. Think broadly and creatively about what kinds of research you might use. Tommy Tsai's research questions included specific concerns about finding and accessing information:

- What books/Websites would give me information and examples of propaganda posters from each of the three countries?
- What would be a good source for information about World War II in general?
- What previous analyses have been done on these propaganda posters?
- Where can I find information about the people who actually created the posters?

Reading Tommy's concerns, you might realize that it is important to determine if you actually can get your hands on the source material you need.

Seeing Connections
For a detailed discussion on the use and evaluation of print and electronic sources, consult Chapter 5.

CREATIVE PRACTICE

Brainstorm three possible research topics that use cartoons, advertisements, and photographs. You might start by looking up visual texts related to a topic that interests you. You can also choose your topic and then ask how it is filtered visually in the media and the popular press. Then, ask yourself the Screening Questions in the At A Glance box for each topic. Finally, look over your answers and consider: Which topic would you be most likely to pursue and develop into a full research paper? Why?

Bringing Your Topic into Focus

Once you have settled on a topic, the next step in the research project involves exploring your knowledge—and the limitations of your knowledge—about it. A productive way to do this is through **prewriting.** Defined literally, prewriting is writing that precedes the official drafting of the paper, but, practically speaking, it can take many forms. Lists, scribbled notes, informal outlines, and pictures—all of these different types of prewriting serve the same goal: to help you and your peers explore and focus a topic.

Graphic Brainstorming

As visual rhetoricians, we find that the practice of **graphic brainstorming** provides us with a great way to develop our topics through writing. This technique transforms traditional **brainstorming**—that is, jotting down a series of related words and phrases on a topic—into a more visible and visual process. Also called *webbing, clustering,* and *mapping,*

AT A GLANCE

Screening Questions for Topics

1. *Am I interested in the topic?* We write best about ideas, events, and issues that touch us somehow—through curiosity, passion, or intellectual interest.

2. *Can I argue a position on this topic?* At this stage, you may not have developed a stand on the issue, but you should see promise for advancing a new perspective on the topic.

3. *Will I be able to find enough research material on this topic?* Brainstorm some possible sources you might use to write this paper.

4. *Does this sort of research appeal to me?* Since you will be working with this topic for an extended period of time, it is best to have a genuine interest in it.

A Closer Look

To explore visual texts related to potentially interesting topics, consult the resources pages of the *Envision* Website. Search through propaganda posters, advertising banks, photography exhibits, and political cartoon archives.

www.ablongman.com/envision033

the goal of *graphic brainstorming* is to help you develop your topic through exploring relationships between ideas. You can brainstorm by hand or on a computer; in either mode, begin by writing a topic in a circle (or square or rectangle, if you prefer). In Figure 4.11, we've taken this first step for a paper generated out of the World War I posters discussed earlier.

FIGURE 4.11.

Next, brainstorm ideas and questions about that topic, and then arrange them in groups around your main circle to indicate the relationships between them. As you answer each question and pose more developed ones in response, you begin to bring your topic into focus. You'll notice that in Figure 4.12 we've started to do this through questions that differentiate between the various posters and group them by gender issues.

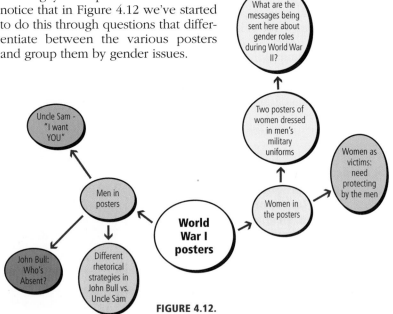

FIGURE 4.12.

You'll notice that in our visual brainstorming prewrite, we've used various types of notations—including words, phrases, and questions—and that we've inserted lines and arrows to delineate the relationship between concepts. We've even used color to further emphasize these associations. All these techniques help you to develop your argument about your topic and eventually lead you to your thesis.

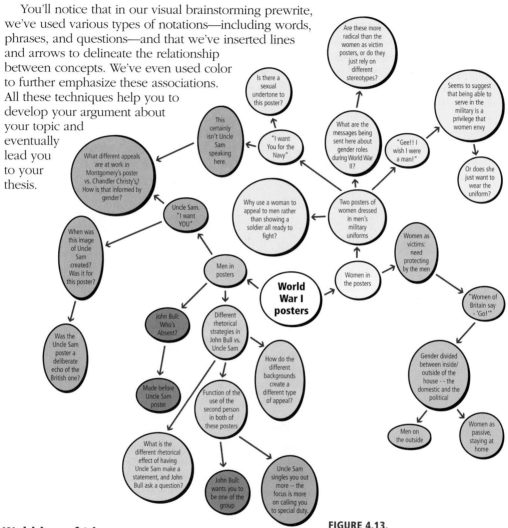

FIGURE 4.13.

Webbing of Ideas

As we continue to brainstorm—whether over the course of an hour or through several separate sessions—it becomes clear why some people call this technique **webbing:** in Figure 4.13, our graphic has turned into a web of ideas.

Apart from developing our ideas into a potential research plan, Figure 4.13 shows us that the topic of World War I posters seems too broad for a standard research paper assignment; there is simply too much material for a 10-15-page paper. Our web now offers enough ideas for an entire book on this subject. By looking over our diagram, however, we can see clues about what direction to take our project. We can pick a *subsection* of ideas to focus on in our writing.

Zooming in on a Topic

Recall the posters featuring men and women in the military (Figures 4.4–4.7). In our brainstorming questions, we moved toward an inquiry concerning the messages about gender roles in World War I posters. Let's now focus on these posters by zooming in on that one part of our diagram, color-coded yellow on our web of ideas, which asks key questions about representations of women in military posters.

Working with this part of the web, we could write a focused paper, one that performs a *comparative analysis* between representations of men and representations of women. We could begin to write about how women are pictured in men's clothing, or about how the military posters use the image of cross-dressing women as a deliberate appeal to the audience. To do so, we should again sharpen our questions about these images.

Webbing Questions to Focus the Topic:

1. First, write down your topic.

Topic Formulation: Gender roles in World War I

2. Work with that topic by asking a pointed question based on visual analysis.

1st Question: Is there a sexual undertone to the posters?

3. Refine your topic by answering the question.

Topic Narrowing: Yes, the women are standing in provocative poses and looking at the audience in a sexual manner.

4. Revise your narrowed topic to be more historically or contextually specific.

Revised Topic Formulation: The provocative sexual poses of women in World War I propaganda posters

5. Identify significant aspects of that topic to explore.

2nd Question: How so? In what way? What is the significance?

6. Use your answers to focus in on your topic.

Final Topic Focus: The provocative sexual poses of women in World War I propaganda posters range from the representations of "victim" to "fighter."

In working with the webbing process, we have just completed one of the most important steps in developing a viable research topic: **narrowing** a large subject to a more manageable one. By asking such questions—and we could come up with many others along different lines of inquiry (such as race, sexuality, international representations, and nationalism)—we begin to develop a *focused* topic that will offer us the opportunity for close analysis, rigorous historical research, and a sharp argumentative stance. That is, we can move from "World War I posters" to "Changing Gender Norms Reflected in World War I Posters from 1914–1919." With this focused and narrowed topic, we'll be able to contribute a new opinion about war posters and add to the ongoing scholarly dialogue that we find in our secondary sources.

A Closer Look

Read the scholarly article by Jose Luis Barrios, "Iconography Past and Present: Visual Constructions of Power in Post-PRI Mexico," *Discourse* 23.2 (Spring 2001): 26-43.

As our graphic brainstorming example suggests, the entire process of *narrowing a topic* is like photo editing: you enlarge the image, then crop or trim it in your own way to limit the field of vision and bring one part of the larger picture into sharper focus. If you don't narrow your topic, your paper risks becoming like a wide-angle, busy photo: there is too much going on to focus in on any one thing.

Seeing Connections
For additional discussion of photography's relationship to writing, see Chapter 3.

CREATIVE PRACTICE

Let's try out this practice of *narrowing a topic* with a pair of posters shaped around a familiar wartime phrase: "Loose lips sink ships." The saying originated during World War II when anxieties about information leaks were paramount. Examine the posters below (Figures 4.14–4.15), drawn from both U.S. and German sources, and then complete a *graphic brainstorm* in order to develop a feasible topic for your essay. Be sure that you narrow your topic from "Information Anxiety During World War II" to a more focused one that you might pursue in a 10-15 page research paper. You might decide during your graphic brainstorm to focus your topic by identifying which images you'd like to write about or by generating key questions to ask about particular texts: Why is the woman leaning on the man's shoulder? What is the dramatic impact of the sinking ship in the second poster? The more specific the questions you ask, the more focused your topic will be.

FIGURE 4.14. In this 1943 German poster, "The enemy overhears!"

FIGURE 4.15. This U.S. poster dramatizes the dangers of talk during wartime.

Developing a Research Plan

In completing the Creative Practice, you most likely constructed a set of web diagrams that, much as those found in Figures 4.12–4.13, alternated between asking and answering questions. This process will narrow your focus and provide you with a direction for your research inquiry. But did you find yourself concerned that you don't have the knowledge necessary to write this essay? Are you worried that the gaps in your own knowledge will prevent you from answering those rigorous questions in a satisfactory way? If so, then you are in good company. All researchers and scholars fear the limitations of their knowledge. The key is to use that lack of knowledge as a motivation and impetus for developing a more concrete **research plan.** This is the next step in the research process: putting your ideas on paper so that you can begin to formulate your approach to finding sources and building your argument. But there are many ways to get there, including answering questions to sketch your ideas, drafting those questions into a freewrite of a proposal, refining your ideas into a concrete and compact abstract, and completing a formal research proposal. We'll examine several of these methods as steps on the research journey.

> "If we knew what we were doing, it wouldn't be called research, would it?"
>
> —Albert Einstein

The Research Sketch

One way to start planning your research process is to jot down ideas in your research log. You might complete—in as much detail as possible—the questions in the At A Glance box in order to generate a rough **research sketch** explaining your ideas so far. Answering these questions will help move you from the work you did in narrowing on a topic to the work you need to do in gathering sources and developing a research outline.

AT A GLANCE

Generating a Research Sketch

- For my research project, I plan to write about . . .
- I already know this about my topic . . .
- I want to know more about . . .
- The specific aspects of this topic I hope to explore are . . .
- At this point, my key research questions about this topic are . . .
- I think that the interesting or important sources of information for my topic will be . . .

Student Writing
Consult students' research sketches on various historical topics.
www.ablongman.com/envision034

Student Writing

See Joseph Yoon's research free-write on the Vietnam War Memorials in the United States and in Vietnam.
www.ablongman.com/envision035

You might also want to try completing this sketch *orally* by talking the questions through with a friend, a peer in class, your instructor, or even a librarian.

The Research Freewrite

An alternative to the sketch is the **freewrite,** in which you draft detailed responses to the questions you need to take into account as you begin your research. This method provides an informal structure for your research plan, to help give it shape and sharper focus as you move deeper into the research process. Using the freewrite, you can develop your plan in even greater detail. To do so, follow a **three-paragraph model:** in the *first paragraph,* announce your topic and state a preliminary thesis so that you can begin the project with a critical and focused perspective; in the *second paragraph,* identify the sources you plan to use to investigate this topic; in the *third paragraph* speculate on obstacles or problems you might encounter in your research and how you might avoid or solve these problems.

Let's look at a freewrite from Bries Deerrose, who shaped his research inquiry around questions concerning a piece of contemporary propaganda, a leaflet dropped in Afghanistan by the U.S. military in the 2002–2003 campaign there.

AT A GLANCE

The Research Freewrite

- Allow yourself to write out complete sentences about your ideas
- Use a three-paragraph model to focus your answers

  Paragraph 1: Announce the topic and state your thesis

  Paragraph 2: Identify key sources

  Paragraph 3: Anticipate problems

This first paragraph introduces the research topic and describes what Bries thinks the main focus of his paper might be. At the end of the paragraph, he includes a tentative thesis to help him focus his interest and argument as he begins researching this topic.

Bries Deerrose: Research Plan

America's image has come increasingly under the scrutiny of our allies and enemies alike. In response, President George W. Bush established the Office of Global Communications, the stated purpose of which is "to advise . . . on utilization of the most effective means for the United States Government to ensure consistency in messages that will promote the interests of the United States abroad, prevent misunderstanding, build support for and among coalition partners of the United States, and inform international audiences." In this paper, I will examine how this Office has gone about this, especially through visual rhetoric. I will examine how the world has responded to such propaganda, especially the Middle East, and I will examine what image the Office portrays, whether this is an accurate image of America or an example of political rhetoric. Finally, I will discuss whether such marketing is beneficial or detrimental, from both a foreign and American perspective. **Tentative thesis:** America is actively projecting an image of itself using various forms of visual rhetoric; this image is both accurate and necessary for the dissemination of various liberal perspectives, in the hopes of providing more choice for the public and private lives of individuals worldwide, as well as ensuring meaningful, peaceful dialogue between America and the world.

To research this topic, I hope to examine firsthand government-generated materials: flyers, commercials, radio broadcasts, publications, etc. I will also attempt to find any commentaries on this effort as well as on domestic conceptions of what America is and what its image should be. I will compare this with foreign opinions regarding America's image and reactions to the American marketing techniques. To do this, I will need to find foreign commentaries, including visual rhetoric responding to our own visual rhetoric. I will need secondhand sources concerning foreign opinions.

In the second paragraph, Bries discusses the sources he intends to use. Notice the broad range of possibilities he considers: flyers, television commercials, radio broadcasts, and both American and international sources.

The most difficult part of this assignment will be determining foreign opinion, since I am not fluent in other languages. I will also need to form my own opinion about the effectiveness, morality, and accuracy of these rhetorical tactics (are we really projecting the objective truth, what is the objective truth, and should we really market ourselves at all?). Such philosophical issues are always sticky, and will require much thought and a wide array of perspectives.

In the third paragraph, Bries anticipates the difficulties he might face and how he can solve them.

Bries concludes with a concrete example of the visual rhetoric he will use in his research paper, a leaflet dropped in Afghanistan by the US in the 2002–2003 campaign.

Figure 1. Office of Global Communication Leaflet Air-dropped in Afghanistan. <http://www.psyop.com/afghan/afghanleaflet5.htm>

The Research Abstract

The research abstract is a condensed explanation of your research argument; it can predict or summarize a paper.

Another alternative step in moving from narrowing your topic to committing to a research plan is by writing what many academics call the **research abstract,** a professional genre designed not only to present the research topic, but also to lay out the tentative argument. There are many versions of abstracts depending on the disciplinary audience and the purpose of the writing. When applying to academic conferences in the humanities, for example, academics will need to write a "500-word abstract" that predicts the paper's argument, research contribution, and significance. Other times, especially for writers in the sciences or social sciences, abstracts are written *after* the paper has been completed to serve as a short summary of the article. You will undoubtedly encounter these abstracts when you begin searching for articles in the humanities and the social sciences; they often precede a published paper.

While you can use the abstract as a writing tool to help you conceptualize your research project, even while you may revise it after your paper is done in order to reflect more accurately the argument of your completed project. Abstracts can range from a few sentences to a page in length, but they are usually no longer than two paragraphs. The key is that writing the abstract helps you conceptualize and explain your research in one brief, coherent unit.

Student Writing
See many examples of research abstracts.
www.ablongman.com/envision036

AT A GLANCE

The Research Abstract

A concise summary of a planned or completed research project entails:

- A statement of the historical and scholarly context of the topic
- A statement about a central tension or problem related to the topic
- A statement about the paper's goals and a thesis *or,* if revised after the paper is finished, a summary of the paper's main argument and conclusions

Consider now the abstract Bries Deerrose produced as a follow-up to his research sketch. In this concise and compact research abstract, Deerrose has moved from the speculative nature of his research freewrite to a more tightly focused and clearly articulated statement of argument.

Within the abstract itself, Bries moves from establishing the context of his topic (in the first, blue section), to the presentation of the central tension or problem he is addressing (in the second, green section), to a final statement about his own intentions as a writer (in the third, red section). The benefit of this more focused version of his research freewrite is that he has refined what he finds intriguing about the topic and he has committed to the purpose of his project. Similarly, you could think of the abstract as a written form of your research plan that can help you begin your journey by capturing in prose your intentions for this research process.

Bries Deerrose: Research Abstract

Clearly, as the communications revolution sweeps the globe and geo-politics become increasingly interconnected, efficient, if not cooperative, dialogue between all parties is an absolute necessity for mutual existence. Unfortunately, as evidenced by the shocking and unexpected attacks of September 11, there seems to be a rather large deficit of communication, or at least of intelligible, productive communication between the United States and the Middle East. As taking lives is an ethically forbidden way to solve problems, something must be done to improve the dialogue between these two cultures in order to understand what went wrong, and how it could be prevented in the future. In "Selling Freedom: America's Communications with the Middle East," I examine (1) how the US is currently attempting to solve the communications problem (2) whether or not these attempts are effective and (3) what we should be doing, from a moral, ethical, and pragmatic point of view. I will argue that America's current efforts are moderately effective but insufficient. Instead, the US needs to advocate in both word and deed a true *dialogue*. That is, the US needs to promote free, informed discussion from the Middle East and from America.

Drafting a Research Proposal

Research proposals, like abstracts, are common in a wide variety of disciplines and professions. You'll find this writing form used to develop agendas for research communities, secure funding for a study, publicize plans for inquiry and field research, and test the interest of potential audiences for a given project. In the writing class-room, the research proposal provides a similar formal structure for developing a project, but it also serves another purpose: it is a more structured means of organizing your thoughts in order to help you solidify your topic and move into the next stages of the research process. For these reasons, the genre, organization, and content of the **research proposal** differ in important ways from other kinds of popular and academic writing that you might do.

Think of it this way: just as most travelers would not begin a trip without a clear sense of their itinerary and destination, so many

AT A GLANCE

Key Elements of the Research Proposal

- It introduces the narrowed *topic*.
- It presents the *rhetorical stance* or *thesis* that the writer will develop.
- It explains the *significance* of the research project.
- It lists possible *sources* for investigation.
- It outlines your research *methods* or planned approach to the research.
- It delineates a detailed *time line* for investigating the topic.
- It often anticipates any *difficulties* that might arise in pursuing this topic.
- It includes a brief *biography* of the researcher (usually a one-paragraph description of the writer's credentials, interests, and motivations).
- It includes a carefully chosen and representative *visual rhetoric text*.

successful writers begin their projects with a detailed road map for the journey through the research process. In mapping out this proposal, take into account many of the same issues that a hypothetical traveler would:

- *Background* (What do I know about where I'm going? What do I need to find out?)
- *Methods* (How am I going to get there?)
- *Timeline* (How long will it take to get to my destination, and how many stops will I make along the way?)
- *Ultimate goal* (What do I hope to accomplish with this trip?)

In the proposal itself, you need to explain your interest in your chosen subject and establish a set of questions to guide your inquiry. You also need to delineate the timeline for your research and writing process. Although this part may seem obvious, it is crucial for time management in order to help you shape the scope and range of your research. Some proposals may require you to have done some preliminary work with sources, while others may be designed to facilitate the very earliest stages of the research process.

As the last item on the At a Glance list indicates, you should incorporate an appropriate visual text—a sample propaganda poster to be analyzed or an editorial cartoon that introduces the issue—right into your proposal in order to show the readers a sample of the materials about which you'll be conducting your research. Use the image to introduce an issue, present the context, captivate your audience, provide a rhetorical stance, or offer insight into the complexity of your topic.

Student Writing

Examine Anastasia Nevin's research proposal on the historical mystery of the Romanov assassination, a study of archival photographs and artifacts.

www.ablongman.com/envision037

As you craft your research proposal, realize that it serves to clarify your research intentions but it should also *persuade* an audience of the feasibility and significance of your project. The abstract or proposal should be an example of persuasive writing, and consequently, it benefits from the inclusion of visual rhetoric as well as clear and compelling writing.

Shaping Your Research Hypothesis

By the time you begin writing your research plan—whether you choose the *sketch*, the *abstract*, or the full *proposal*—you will have decided upon a research topic, but defining your rhetorical stance in regards to that topic may be another matter altogether. So how do you make a claim about a topic that you have not researched completely yet? This is a key question, and it is often a frustrating one for many writers. Realize, however, that you've already taken the first step just by asking pointed questions about your topic. From these questions, you can develop a working thesis that makes an argumentative claim that you'll attempt to prove. Moreover, if you've chosen a topic that you've been thinking about for a while, then you might already have developed a thesis that you intend to prove. At this point, you might call it a **hypothesis,** rather than a *thesis,* in order to suggest its tentativeness. It is crucial for you to try and formulate a working hypothesis for your research plan in order to look at your project with an analytical eye. Of course, you may revise your hypothesis—and maybe your entire approach to the subject—several times over the course of your research. Indeed, most writers do modify their thesis statements, and this revision process is a natural part of what happens when you actually begin to read your sources and take notes about them in the research log. Nevertheless, stating your thesis or hypothesis is an important first step in focusing your argument and making the most out of the timeline available to you for research.

Seeing Connections
If you're having trouble thinking about how to make the transition from a topic into a thesis statement, review our discussion of thesis statements in Chapter 3.

A Closer Look
Explore propaganda leaflets in both English and Arabic that were dropped on Iraq during 2003.
www.ablongman.com/envision038

> Develop hypotheses early. . . . Objectivity seems to demand that you form no thesis before your research is complete. But if you have no thesis, you have no way of formulating questions for interviews or evaluating the importance of what you read. A better approach is to form a thesis—perhaps it would be better to call it a hypothesis—as early as possible, and then be prepared to change it as often as an honest interpretation of the data demands.
>
> —Douglas Hunt

Drafting the Hypothesis

One way to develop your detailed hypothesis is to rewrite one of your more narrowed questions from the research plan as a polished declarative statement that you intend to prove. For example, if you asked yourself, "How were representations of race used in World War II propaganda?" then turn that question into a potential thesis: "Representations of race deployed in World War II propaganda functioned as a way to justify the internment of innocent civilians." As you continue your research, you may come to disagree with that statement, but at least beginning with a tentative thesis gives you somewhere to start.

Let's take a look at how this process might play out for a research argument on propaganda posters. We're going to follow Tommy Tsai's research process as he developed his paper on propaganda posters entitled, "'This is the Enemy': Depravation and Deceitfulness of America's World War II Political Art."

First, Tommy completed the research sketch. His answers provide a useful example for arriving at a research hypothesis:

1. The opening sketch question sets forth the writer's familiarity with the topic.

Question: I already know this about my topic . . .

Tommy: The different styles of propaganda posters of the three countries during World War II. The United States exploited the nationalist feelings of Americans with their posters by using images like the American flag to represent the glory associated with "fighting for your own country." Germany also exploited nationalist feelings amongst its citizens; the German government did so by using the *ethos* appeal associated with its political leader Adolf Hitler. Japan used a more logical approach; many of their posters show images of Japanese soldiers as victors of a battle.

2. The next question moves the writer toward a specific argument.

Question: I want to know more about . . .

Tommy: The people who designed the posters and the work that went into the design process. Also, I would like to know more about the historical context (I've never taken history before, so basic information about the war would be really helpful).

Seeing Connections
To understand what Tommy Tsai means by ethos, logos, and pathos, see Chapter 2.

3. The last question begins to create a hypothesis for the project.

Question: The specific aspects of this topic I hope to explore are . . .

Tommy: The specific rhetorical strategies employed by each country, how these rhetorical strategies affected people in practice, and how effective each country's propaganda was.

Using this technique of asking questions, Tommy moved towards a hypothesis or tentative thesis in his research sketch and then used it in his full-length proposal.

Figure 1. Uncle Sam Poster.

Tommy Tsai's Working Hypothesis from His Research Proposal
I have conjectured that German propaganda made use of the *ethos* appeal of its fascist leader Adolf Hitler; that Japanese propaganda utilized the *logos* appeal by continually portraying images of a victorious Japanese army; and that American propaganda had for the most part employed the *pathos* appeal, by evoking nationalistic feelings and associating war with glory and patriotism (see Figure 1). These conjectures coalesce into my argument that the government of each nation is able to bring its political messages across effectively by employing the appropriate rhetorical appeal in its propaganda posters.

With this proposal, Tommy launched his research project, and he eventually wrote a compelling paper that examined U.S. propaganda posters against both Germans and Japanese nations. Some of this material was rather disturbing (see Figure 4.8–4.10), but Tommy felt compelled to work with these images. In his final reflection on the research paper, Tommy looked back at the development of his argument and even proposed ideas for future study. His reflection letter should show you that a research plan is

Student Writing
See Tommy Tsai's full Research Sketch and complete Research Proposal.
www.ablongman.com/envision039

only the beginning of your scholarly engagement with the issues that matter to you.

Tommy Tsai's Final Reflection Letter, Excerpt, March 2003

The final paper turned out to be very different from what I envisioned it to be at the beginning. First of all, my topic changed from World War II propaganda posters in general to a criticism of America's portrayals of their World War II enemies. Also, for my final draft, I had to cut out an entire section from my paper (the one about how America portrayed the political leaders of other nations) since it did not work well with my thesis. Instead, I concentrated on the two remaining sections in order to give my paper more focus. . . . I have also developed an interest in the topic. Perhaps the World Wars will make another appearance in one of the many other research papers I will have to write in my four years at Stanford.

Asserting the Significance of Your Project

"So What? This question vexes all researchers, beginners and experienced alike, because to answer it, you have to know how significant your research might be not just to yourself but to others."

—Wayne Booth

As you might have discerned from Tommy's closing reflection, perhaps the most important step in launching your own research inquiry is to address the issue of the significance of your project or, as some writing instructors call it, the "So What?" part of the project. It is the "So What?"—an awareness of the significance of the topic you're addressing and the questions you're asking—that moves the project from being a routine academic exercise to a powerful piece of persuasive writing. When addressing the "So What?" question, consider why anyone else would care enough to read a paper on your topic. Ask yourself:

- What is at stake in your topic?
- Why does it matter?
- What contribution will your discussion make to a larger academic community?

Student Writing

Go online to read "So What?" statements written by several students.

www.ablongman.com/envision040

These are difficult questions to answer, and they may be ones that you defer until later in your research when you have gathered evidence and developed your argument to support your thesis. However, the sooner you clarify the significance of your work, the faster you will move toward producing a rigorous and interesting piece of writing. Keep notes in your research log on how the answers to these questions change as you proceed with your research and your thinking about the topic.

Constructing Your Persona as a Researcher

In addition to stating the significance of the project, you should think carefully about how you will construct your own identity as the researcher and writer of this project. As we saw with the proposal, many academic or professional research plans have a space where you need to write a brief "biography" (or "bio") of the researchers on the project; this requirement reveals the way in which ethos functions as a tool of persuasion: the **research persona** you create establishes your credibility and authority for the project. Usually, this takes the form of a one-paragraph description of the writer's credentials, interests, and motivations for engaging in such work. You may feel that, at this point in your research, you have no authority. But, in the course of your research, you will in fact become an expert on your topic and produce an important contribution to an ongoing dialogue about your area of research.

Seeing Connections For a detailed discussion of persona, see Chapter 3.

It's helpful to convey that future sense of authority in the biography you construct for your research persona. The way in which you shape your "bio" will help persuade readers of the proposal that this is a project to be taken seriously.

Student Writing Read research proposal bios by Tommy Tsai and others. www.ablongman.com/envision041

Planning Your Research Project

Now that you've learned about the process of generating a topic; focusing the research questions for your topic; committing to an angle; and then writing up your plans for research in a sketch, an abstract, or a proposal, what can you argue about the first propaganda poster of this chapter (Figure 4.1)?

In answering this prompt, you might start to work through the projects related to the research process. You might develop a research focus that begins with questions and ends with a "So What?" statement of significance. You might try to incorporate visual images into a proposal that will conclude with a clear statement of your future authority on this topic as a researcher. Try the strategies for keeping track of your ideas and work in progress in a research log, a key tool that you'll be using in the next chapter as we turn to gathering and evaluating sources for your topic. It's time to get started on the research process for writing a persuasive argument about an issue that matters to you.

PREWRITING CHECKLIST
Analyzing Propaganda Posters

❏ What is the underlying message of this poster? What idea is it trying to convey to its audience?

❏ What are the specifics of the rhetorical situation informing this piece of propaganda? Who produced the poster? Who was its intended audience?

❏ What is the historical context for this poster? What country was it produced in, and what was the social and political situation of the time? How does an understanding of its context affect our understanding of its message?

❏ What type of rhetorical appeal does the poster feature? Does it rely primarily on logos, pathos, or ethos to make its point? How does attention to this appeal manifest itself visually in the poster?

❏ What is the relationship between word and image in the poster? How does this relationship contribute to its rhetorical appeal?

❏ How do design elements such as use of color, font, layout, and image selection (photograph vs. illustration) work as persuasive elements in this text?

❏ What strategies of argumentation does the poster use? Does it feature narration? comparison/contrast? example?

❏ Recalling the discussion of exaggerated use of appeals from Chapter 2, does the poster rely on any logical fallacies? Any exaggerated use of pathos? If so, how do these work to persuade the audience?

❏ Does the poster use stereotypes to convey its message? How do stereotypes figure as rhetorical devices in this situation? How does the stereotype place the poster in context of a larger cultural discussion?

❏ What research questions can you develop about this poster?

❏ What kinds of sources might you turn to in order to understand the context, meaning, and rhetorical force of this propaganda poster?

WRITING PROJECTS

 Visit the *Envision* Website for expanded assignment guidelines and student projects.

1. Create a *research sketch* by first writing out answers to the questions provided in the Prewriting Checklist, and then developing them into a three-paragraph research sketch. In the first paragraph, introduce your research paper topic and describe what you think the main focus of the paper might be. Include a tentative thesis in this paragraph. In the second paragraph, discuss the sources that you intend to use. In the third paragraph, speculate on what obstacles you foresee in this project and/or what you anticipate to be the most difficult part of the assignment. Use an appropriate image to complement your written text. Show your answers to your instructor or your peers for feedback.

2. Write a brief 3-5-sentence *research abstract,* describing the main focus of your research paper. In your abstract, move from the context of your topic, to the central problem or issue that you are addressing, to a final statement of your research question or anticipated thesis statement.

3. Write a *detailed research proposal* that uses visual rhetoric and discusses your plans, methodology, expectations, purpose, and research persona in depth. For more specific instruction, consult the Writing Guidelines on the *Envision* Website: www.ablongman.com/envision042

FOR ADDED CHALLENGE

 Visit the *Envision* Website for expanded assignment guidelines and student projects.

1. Collaboratively peer review your research proposals. Assume that you are on the review board granting approval and funding to the best *two* proposals of each group. Complete research proposal review letters for each member of your group. When you are done, discuss your letters and what changes you can recommend. Then, revise your proposals to make them stronger, better written, and more persuasive. Also, work on improving your use of visual rhetoric as a persuasive element of your research proposal.

For more specific instructions and for **Peer Review Forms** of the research proposal, consult the *Envision* Website: www.ablongman.com/envision043

2. Transform your research proposal into a Web-based showcase of your ideas that divides the prospective project into key sections, including overview, context, methodology, purpose, planned sources, timeline, writer's bio, and sample of images.

3. Present your proposal at a roundtable of research with other members of your class. At the roundtable, you should first present your proposal and then entertain questions from your classmates to help you fine-tune your topic and troubleshoot your future research.

CHAPTER 4 ON THE WEB

Resources and Reading	Exercises and Assignments	Student Writing
• Closer Look links	• Topic generating exercise	• Prewriting cluster webs
• Brainstorming and Pre-writing strategies	• Brainstorming exercises	• Research logs in various formats
• Links to propaganda archives and resources	• Keeping a research log	• Three-sentence and three-paragraph abstracts
• Annotated readings	• Detailed guidelines for the formal research proposal	• Formal research proposals
	• Peer Review forms	• Student bios
	• Focus on diverse learners and students with disabilities	• "So What?" statements

www.ablongman.com/envision

Finding and Evaluating Research Sources

As you move from planning to conducting research, you'll need to investigate resources of all kinds and evaluate them for use in your project. Look, for instance, at the covers of two magazines in Figures 5.1 and 5.2; while they focus on the same research topic—the Human Genome Project—the visual rhetoric of the covers suggests that the content of each journal will be quite different. In fact, while both *Time* and *Science* include articles about the same scientific issue of gene sequencing, the audience or readership of each

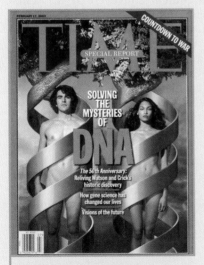

FIGURE 5.1. *Time* magazine's special report on DNA uses popular visual rhetoric to attract readers.

FIGURE 5.2. *Science* magazine chooses a different visual strategy for its cover.

Chapter Preview Questions

- What is the best way to locate research sources?
- What is the difference between primary and secondary sources?
- How do I critically evaluate both print and electronic sources?
- How do I pursue field research for my project?
- What do I need to record in my research log?
- How should I take notes while researching?
- What is a visual annotated bibliography and how can it help me?

differs significantly and, consequently, the writing style and arguments within the articles will be different as well. The distinctive cover of each magazine previews for the reader the distinct content inside; you can use your visual rhetoric analysis skills to begin to make important distinctions when locating, evaluating, and using sources for your own research project.

Specifically, the cover of *Time* magazine in Figure 5.1 conveys the way in which the editors chose to represent genetics to *Time*'s audience. Ask yourself: What is the argument conveyed by the visual rhetoric of the cover? Why are Adam and Eve shown intertwined in the helix strands of DNA? What kind of stance does this image suggest toward DNA research? What rhetorical effect does the use of bright color, vivid photography, a tree, and the biblical reference have on the audience? Are the cover designers attempting to make a very technical scientific endeavor accessible to a nonscientific audience, or are they suggesting a conflict between science and religion? Now compare *Time*'s cover to the one on *Science* in Figure 5.2. This cover also focuses on genetic research, but instead of a vivid image of Adam and Eve, the designers included a drawing, much like one found in the *New Yorker* magazine, a popular magazine with an intellectual readership. There are small images from scientific experiments—not religion—including a fly, a human anatomy model, a lizard, and several famous researchers. How do such different rhetorical strategies on this cover appeal to its very scientifically informed audience? As you can tell, in both cases, the editors of each magazine located, evaluated, and used materials for the cover that would indicate the type of contents found inside. As a researcher, you can use your skills in visual rhetoric analysis to help your selection process as you turn to find sources for your own research project.

CREATIVE PRACTICE

Visit *Nature* magazine online through the *Envision* Website and look at its cover from the February 10, 2001 issue, a special report on the Human Genome Project. How do the visual rhetoric strategies for this cover differ from those in Figures 5.1 and 5.2? Now, find a print copy of the *Nature* issue in your library and examine the cover closely. Considering that scientists were describing the genome sequence as a "mosaic," and that this cover was created by Professor Eric Lander, one of the leading participants in the project, how does this cover present a very specific visual argument about the Human Genome as a mosaic? Compare it to the examples in Figures 5.1 and 5.2, and think about how the rhetorical choices of covers shape both the audience's understanding of the topic and the setup of the contents of the magazine. Now consider that recently Lander said, "We've called the human genome the blueprint, the Holy Grail, all sorts of things. It's a parts list. If I gave you the parts list for a Boeing 777 and it has 100,000 parts, I don't think you could screw it together, and you certainly wouldn't understand why it flew." Building on one of these metaphors, sketch a design for a new cover for an upcoming issue of *Nature, Science,* or *Time* magazine. Use the cover to suggest an argument for a specific perspective on human gene sequencing and to provide a visual preview for the contents inside.

www.ablongman.com/envision044

Your task as a researcher will be quite similar to that of the editors of *Time, Science,* and *Nature.* As you begin gathering and evaluating sources for your own research-based argument, keep in mind that you will need to shape the argument into a paper addressed to a particular audience, whether that be your writing class, a group of scientists, a

A Closer Look

In a rich feature story, Sarah Gonser lays out in visual detail the process by which covers are selected for a national magazine: "Revising the Cover Story." *Folio: the Magazine for Magazine Management* 32.1 (March 1, 2003).

lobbying organization, an advertising firm, or browsers on the Web. To take part in any of these conversations, a researcher needs to learn what is being talked about (the *topic*), how it is being discussed (the *discourse*), and what the different positions are (*research context*). But your conversation about your research project also will extend beyond your audience; you will, in fact, be engaged in a discussion with the sources themselves.

FIGURE 5.3. The iceberg of research.

Visualizing Research

When you think of the act of research, what comes to mind? Surfing the Web? Looking through a library? Interviewing experts in the field? All these images represent different research scenarios. The material you gather in each situation will comprise the foundation for your research; this mass of knowledge will inform your essay, but not all of it will find its way into your final paper. Nevertheless, you need to research widely and thoroughly in order to be fully informed about your topic and write a compelling research-based argument. One helpful way of visualizing the relationship between the *process* and *product* of research is through the metaphor of the **iceberg of research** (see Figure 5.3). In essence, your topic represents only a starting point for your research project; beneath it lie the many different sources you'll need to explore in order to lend depth and body to your argument. Published books, journal articles, Websites, and field research all constitute the materials of your potential research. As you move beyond your surface knowledge of your topic, you will gather, assess, keep, throw out, and ultimately use a variety of sources. Moving into the depths of your project can therefore be quite exciting as you encounter a rich array of voices, knowledge, and opinions on your topic.

Sometimes, however, this process can be a bit overwhelming. We all share anxieties about writing a research argument. We all think of brilliant words penned by minds of genius, and we fear that we will have nothing new to add to the conversation. Or, we worry that we won't find anything interesting to say despite the richness of our sources. Both of these views are extremes. It is more helpful to think of research sources as texts written by people who were once, like yourself, struggling to add substance to their research ideas and seeking to fulfill the plan of their research proposals.

Student Writing

See icebergs of research for specific student projects.
www.ablongman.com/envision045

In this way, you might consider the process of gathering and assessing sources as a very social one, a process in which you respect and acknowledge the ideas of others and then you seek to add your own voice to an ongoing conversation. One way to begin that conversation is to discover what others before you have said, thought, written, and published, and to keep track of that process in your research log.

For the rest of this chapter, we address the fears and anxieties that are indeed very real obstacles on the research path. We'll rely on the metaphor of the *conversation* in order to accentuate the point that the research process is indeed an act of *composing a response to an ongoing dialogue about a topic;* that is, by gathering, synthesizing, and sorting the perspectives of others, you begin to shape your own stance on a research topic. By adding your own voice as a writer responding to others, you forge your contribution to the field. Research, then, is a *relationship* that you develop with the source material and the writers you encounter along the way.

AT A GLANCE

Using Your Research Log

As you begin gathering and evaluating sources, it is crucial to note where and when you find new ideas through a detailed and careful record, in what we called the research log. Keep track of your search terms, your discovery of source leads, and your developing ideas about this argument. Write down your findings, your notes and quotes from sources, your new thoughts, and your brainstorms for additional sources.

Seeing Connections
For concrete examples of research logs and how to begin one, consult Chapter 4.

Understanding Primary and Secondary Sources

Depending on your topic, you will use different kinds of sources to achieve your research goals. Scholars divide research into primary and secondary research, and sources, likewise, into **primary sources** and **secondary sources.**

To create an effective research argument, you will need to work with both *primary* and *secondary* sources. In Tommy Tsai's project in Chapter 4, for example, the propaganda posters were his *primary sources;* the articles, books, and transcribed interviews providing analysis of those posters were his *secondary sources.* His paper is now *another* secondary source, one that contributes to an ongoing intellectual discussion about the meaning and power of those posters.

But keep in mind as you search for your research materials, that no sources are *inherently* primary or secondary; those terms refer to

AT A GLANCE

Primary and Secondary Sources

- *Primary sources:* those materials that you will analyze for your paper, including advertisements, photographs, film, artwork, audiofiles, historical documents, and Websites. Primary sources can also include testimonies by those with first-hand knowledge or direct quotations you will analyze. Whatever is under the lens of your analysis constitutes a *primary source.*

- *Secondary sources:* the additional materials that help you analyze your primary sources by providing a perspective on those primary materials; these include scholarly articles, popular commentaries, background materials (in print, video, or interview format), and survey data reinforcing your analysis. Whatever sources you can use as a lens to look at or understand the subject of your analysis constitutes a *secondary source.*

how you use them in your paper. For instance, if you were writing about different visual representations of the Human Genome Project, you might use journal covers, including those in Figures 5.1 and 5.2, as primary sources, as well as press releases, posters, and Websites. For secondary sources, you might turn to articles that discuss different journal covers, a book about photo illustration in popular science magazines, and perhaps even an interview with a professor about ways in which scientific discoveries are communicated to the general public through words and images. However, imagine you shift your topic slightly, so that your new focus is that professor's approach to the visual rhetoric of popular science. Now, that same book you looked at before as a *secondary* source becomes a *primary* source for this new topic. As you can see, your inquiry will determine which sources will be primary and which will be secondary for your argument. In other words, you need to use a combination of primary and secondary sources in your research paper: the primary sources allow you to do your own analysis; the secondary sources offer you critical viewpoints that you need to take into account in your own analysis and integrate into your argument to build up your ethos. How you respond to and combine your primary and secondary sources is a matter of choice, careful design, and rhetorical strategy. It is less important that you categorize sources exclusively into primary and secondary sources than it is to find as much material as possible and determine which sources you need depending on your paper's rhetorical situation. To conceptualize this process, look at the diagram created by Tynan Burke to represent the research process (see Figure 5.4).

The significance of Figure 5.4 is the way in which the diagram incorporates opposing opinion as well as revision into the visual representation of the research process. This image portrays the complexity of the research process. It shows that the author's

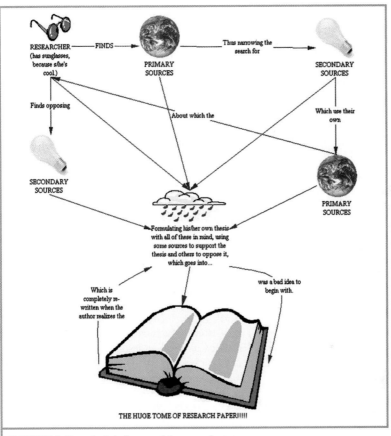

FIGURE 5.4. Tynan Burke's diagram of the research process.

argument operates in dialogue with other sources and evolves constantly. In essence, it maps out for the reader the complicated conversation of the research process.

Developing Search Terms

The first step in beginning this process lies in locating relevant and interesting sources to draw

Student Writing
Examine additional student diagrams depicting the research process as inspiration for your own model. www.ablongman.com/envision046

AT A GLANCE

Tips for Searching Sources

- *Web:* Use popular or colloquial terminology in your Internet searches because search engines pick up actual terms from pages as they crawl across the Web.

- *Library:* The Library of Congress has created a set of terms used by librarians to catalog information. These Library of Congress Subject Headings (LCSH), as they are called, may not be obvious to you. (For example, the Library of Congress calls the Vietnam War the "Vietnamese Conflict, 1961–1975," so you won't find anything if you put "Vietnam War" into a Subject Heading search in a library catalog.) You can find the LCSH terms in two ways: by looking at a library record online for the LCSH or by consulting the print index. By plugging the terms into your library catalog, you can access information for your project more efficiently.

- *Databases:* Since databases can house a range of materials, from academic publications to popular articles, you will have to customize your language based upon the database that you have selected; match your search terms in diction and formality to suit the type of resource you are exploring.

"Research is the process of going up alleys to see if they are blind."

—Marston Bates

into your conversation. This involves finding the best **search term** to use in searching for sources on your topic. This term will change depending on whether you are searching the Web, a library catalog, or an academic database. You will need to identify the most productive keywords for searching in each of these situations.

Let's take as our example a project about Internet advertising. Web engines using specific jargon, such as "pop-up ads," "banner ads," and "ethics & advertising online," would pull up different results than a search using the categorical terms "Internet advertising" or "Internet advertisements." Looking in a library catalog, you might discover that entering "pop-up ads" will yield fewer results than using academic terminology such as "Internet advertising," "electronic commerce," or "Internet marketing," because those terms appear in scholarly book titles. However, if you search a database such a LexisNexis (a resource for news articles as well as legal, medical, and political articles), your keywords should change again; here, "pop-up ads" will provide you with over 20 citations in popular magazines and journals. The point is this: the best way to explore a new terrain is to learn its language. Through such experimentation you come to find the search term that will yield you the most productive results.

Furthermore, experimenting with such a range of terms can provide you with a means of narrowing your sources by finding materials that you deem most relevant to your topic. That is, if your project on Internet advertising focuses on the legality of pop-up ads as an invasion of privacy, you will find that while using a term such as "Internet advertising" yields a range of materials (from how to advertise on the Web to the economics of the digital marketplace), using a Library of Congress Subject Heading such as "Internet advertising & law" in your library searches instead will lead you to helpful citations regarding the Unsolicited Commercial Electronic Mail Act of 2000 and the 2001 Anti-Spamming Act. By using your search strategies wisely, you can find the sites worth seeing.

CREATIVE PRACTICE

Perform a search on your topic, first on the Web, then in your library catalog, and then in a database. Experiment with your search terms and record your results in your research log. Now locate the Library of Congress Subject Headings for your topic, and use those terms in another catalog search. Do you achieve different results? Are your results more tailored to your needs or more general? Assess in your research log which search terms function best.

Evaluating Your Sources

Experimenting with effective search terminology provides you with access to many interesting sources, but how do you discriminate between them to find those that would be the most productive partners in your conversation? As in any collective exchange, the key rests in understanding the character and stance of the participants. At times, the source's stand may be self-evident: you may automatically gravitate toward experts in the field, well-known for their opinions and affiliations. It is just as likely, however, that you may not be familiar with the names or ideas of your sources. In either case, it is essential to develop a method for evaluating the integrity of the sources you encounter.

A Closer Look

In his article, Ted Gup provides a personal narrative about how directed searching through electronic resources has changed how we access and process information: "The End of Serendipity." *The Chronicle of Higher Education* November 21, 1997: A52.

Evaluating Websites

For many of us, when we hear the words "research paper," our first impulse is to log on to the Internet and plug our topic into a search engine such as Google (http://www.google.com). However, while you might encounter a vast number of "hits," you still need a method for assessing the credibility and usefulness of your findings. This need is especially pressing since initial searches may produce quantity rather than quality. For instance, if you decided to write a paper on the stem cell debate, you might perform a Web search on the term "stem cells," a search that could yield close to a million results. On the one hand, such a plentiful search gives you ample means to "eavesdrop" on the ongoing conversation about your topic; on the other hand, the sheer magnitude of hits can be slightly overwhelming. Faced with such a massive amount of material, how do you begin to sort through them to identify those most helpful to your research?

One of your most crucial resources in this situation is your skill as a visual rhetorician. While opening the different Web pages, consider how their visual and verbal elements suggest the sites' stances and points of view on your topic. The CNN.com "In Depth Special" on the stem cell debate (see Figure 5.5) provides us with a good example of how rhetorical analysis factors into the research process. As

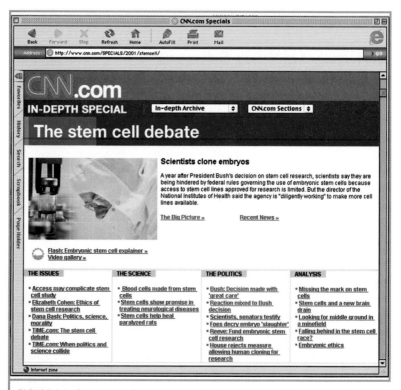

FIGURE 5.5. This CNN Web feature on stem cells deploys words and images in careful arrangement.

you study this page, three prominent aspects of the site probably stand out for you: the large CNN.com logo in the upper right hand corner, which establishes the ethos of the site; the topic header "The Stem Cell Debate," which identifies the focus and approach of the page; and the picture of the scientist at work. You probably then notice the finer details such as, for instance, that the topic is broken down into "The Issues," "The Science," "The Politics," and "Analysis," indicating the way the Website offers the reader exposure to diverse perspectives on the issue. By presenting a balanced and neatly compartmentalized approach, the site aims for what we might call an "objective" appearance: it is as if the entire issue of stem cell research has been dissected and laid out for our analysis. In a sense, then, the image of the scientist functions both as an organizing principle for the site and a point of identification. The reader enters the site with a purpose—to learn more about stem cell research—and accomplishes this task through a systematic exploration of the diverse parts of this research area.

A Closer Look

- Johns Hopkins, "Evaluating Sources Found on the Internet"
- Cornell University, "Five Criteria for Evaluating Web pages"
- Duke University, "Evaluating Web pages"
www.ablongman.com/envision047

In performing this type of analysis on the Website, you have in fact engaged in the most important part of Web research: evaluating your findings. You'll want to take special care in evaluating Web pages as sources for your own projects. The quality and reliability of Web pages varies widely across the Internet. Careful attention to the visual rhetoric of a site's "cover" is essential to understanding its argument and therefore its suitability as a source for your research project. After assessing the "cover" pages of each Web page, the next step is to move deeper into the site, to analyze its content and argument.

> Familiar print standards do not appear here. Websites can be aesthetically pleasing, yet contain no relevant information. On the other hand, a Web writer may have simply converted a groundbreaking thesis from a word processor to a text format and put it on the Web . . . A well-designed Web page means that the Web writer is good at writing HTML and designing an effective Web page, not that the information on that page is necessarily a reputable source for the students' needs.
>
> —Alan Rea and Doug White

COLLABORATIVE CHALLENGE

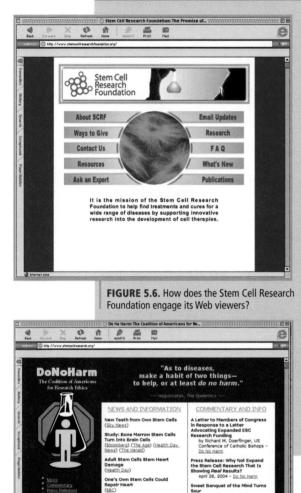

FIGURE 5.6. How does the Stem Cell Research Foundation engage its Web viewers?

FIGURE 5.7. Compare the visual rhetoric of the DoNoHarm site to the zone above.

In small groups, compare the CNN site in Figure 5.5 with two other Web pages generated from searching "stem cell" on Google: the "Stem Cell Research Foundation" site and the "DoNoHarm" site, (see Figures 5.6 and 5.7).

What rhetorical decisions are apparent from their cover designs? How do the images suggest different approaches to the stem cell issue? How does the organization of information, the menu, and the written text contribute to this impression? Follow the site links to explore how the rhetorical stance suggested by the cover is reflected in the site's contents. As a group, evaluate these two pages as sources for a paper on stem cell research. Develop a list of criteria for evaluating Web pages and share it with the class.

Seeing Connections
To move from evaluating Websites to creating one of your own, read Chapter 8 on visual arguments.

The list of criteria generated by the Collaborative Challenge may have varied from group to group, but most likely you all focused on issues of authority, accessibility, and suitability in assessing the Web pages. After your preliminary rhetorical analysis, you might have looked at the URL to establish the author or host of a Website; or, you might have examined the selection of images or the word choice for indications of bias or sensationalism; perhaps you looked for the "last updated" note to check the currency of the site or for the "contact" link to evaluate the author's sense of accountability for his or her work; you may have followed the links to see if the site was self-contained, linking only to its own materials, or whether it contained external links, connecting it to the broader conversation on the topic. You also probably tested it for ease of use and navigation by experimenting with the menu or search engine. In addition, you most likely evaluated the *type* of material the site contained: primary documents or secondary commentary. Each of these steps inevitably took you beyond the cover, deeper into the contents of the site, and closer to assessing its appropriateness as a source for your own research.

AT A GLANCE

Evaluating Websites

1. Who is the author of the Website? Is it a personal Website or is it institutionally affiliated? What sort of authority does it draw upon?

2. Does the author take responsibility for the page by offering a place for comments or an email link for feedback?

3. Who is the audience?

4. What is the purpose?

5. What is the rhetorical stance of this Website? Does it deal with both sides of the issue or only one side?

6. Is it self-contained, or does it participate in a dialogue? linking up to other sites? linking up to other sites on the Web?

7. How timely is the page? Does it have a date? Does someone maintain the Website? Are there broken links?

8. Is it an archive of primary material? If so, does it cite the original sources in a correct and complete manner?

9. Is it easy to navigate? Does it have a search engine?

10. How is it relevant to your specific topic?

CREATIVE PRACTICE

Perform a Web search related to your research topic. Using the evaluative strategies in the At A Glance box, select two Websites that are strong possibilities for use as primary or secondary sources and two that are more questionable for your project. Now list the reasons for these choices. What was it about each site that either drew you in or convinced you that you shouldn't use it? Write a short paragraph that considers the benefits and drawbacks of using the Web as a resource for a research paper and share it with your class.

Evaluating Scholarly Sources

While popular Websites might be important sources for your research project, the Internet also can serve another function: to provide access to more scholarly texts. Whether you are using an academic database or a library home page, you will find that many scholarly sites function as a gateway to productive research. For instance, while researching your topic online, you might have come across the Website for the Library of Congress, the largest and most famous library, which houses a copy of every single book ever published (see Figure 5.8). Notice the way in which the visual rhetoric of the site itself reinforces the authority and richness of this online collection. The page pairs the words "The Library of Congress" (placed for prominence in the upper left corner) with their visual equivalent—the impressive domed structure—in the upper right

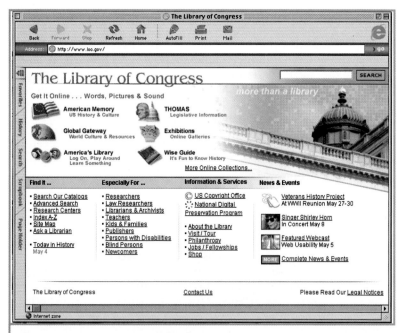

FIGURE 5.8. Explore the Library of Congress home page.

corner. The relationship between word and image is further underscored by the distinctive blue of both font and background. Other aspects of the design reinforce the ethos: the prominence of the flag reveals that this Website—and the library it represents—is a government institution; the abundance of links to exhibits and resources suggests the many ways in which the Library of Congress functions as "more than a library"; the helpful search tool and "contact" link at the bottom speak to the site's commitment to facilitating the visitor's research experience. Taken together, these elements construct the Library of Congress Website as an authoritative resource for finding texts related to your topic.

The movement from CNN.com to the Library of Congress site points us to an important observation about performing research: while Internet searches offer you immediate access to the current conversation on your research topic, in most cases you will need to seek out academically rigorous research materials to produce an effective argument of your own. This often means moving beyond the keyboard and mouse and into the physical structure of a library. Entering the phrase "stem cell research" into the Library of Congress search engine, for instance, generates an impressive list of sources. Yet rather than providing links to full texts, the Library of Congress offers bibliographic citations designed to guide you into the library stacks and toward related source materials of interest.

Once in the stacks, you might feel just as overwhelmed as you did after your initial Web search: facing the rows of books on your topic, most bound in plain-colored library bindings, how do you select those that would be most productive for your research? In order to select the best ones, you can once again use your rhetorical analysis skills to evaluate them based on concrete strategies of assessment.

> To avoid feeling overwhelmed, be rigorously selective in your research texts; use only the most promising sources.

First, you might assess the author. Perhaps someone recommended the author to you or you recognize the writer's name as someone well known in the field. If the author is unfamiliar, you might look this person up in a bibliography index or online to assess the *ethos* of the writer. You might also evaluate the ethos of the text by looking at the pages preceding the title page to see if there are any excerpts from published reviews. Check out the place of publication. Is it a university press (suggesting peer-reviewed scholarship) or a trade press (suggesting a commercial venture)? Is it published by a foundation or organization (suggesting a political

AT A GLANCE

Evaluating Academic Sources

- *Author:* Is the author an expert in his or her field? What professional or personal affiliations or experiences has this author had that might have influenced his or her argument or *ethos*?

- *Date:* When was the text published? If not recently, might it be out-dated? Is it a foundational text for your subject, one that sets a certain framework for discussion that other writers have since built on? Or does it offer a fresh, new perspective to an ongoing discussion?

- *Publisher:* Is the publisher an academic or popular press? Which would be most appropriate for your topic? Does the publisher have any connection to the topic under discussion?

- *Rhetorical stance:* What is the author's point of view on the topic? Is it moderate or extreme? How does that affect his or her treatment of the issue?

- *Audience:* For whom was this work intended—an academic or a popular audience? What level of specialized knowledge does the author assume that the audience has?

- *Relevance to your project:* How does this text relate to your argument? Does it provide background material? an opposing opinion? a supporting argument?

agenda) or self-published (suggesting the author's struggle to have his or her views accepted for publication)? Look also at the date. Is it a recent contribution or an out-dated study?

Next, go beneath the cover of the book. Open it and flip through the pages, looking for interesting arguments and judging the quality or complexity of the writing. If the book works with visual texts, turn your rhetorical analysis lens on those passages: does the writer analyze carefully, make insightful points, and offer material worth using in your paper? You may note the voice or tone of the book; is it written for specialists in the field or for a popular audience? You might study the table of contents and the index to see exactly what the book contains.

While all assessment questions are helpful, the most important one is how *useful* a source will be for your project. That is, you might want a disreputable author in order to demonstrate how there exists extremely exaggerated writing on your topic. Similarly, you might use a book published by a specific foundation to argue that there exists a political agenda concerning certain issues. Alternatively, an outdated book might be helpful to you even if it doesn't seem to be very recent. A description of the space program in the 1950s, for example, might not be the best secondary source for your paper, but it can become a primary source for a research argument on how representations of science have changed over the

Your key evaluation question is: How useful is this source? years. The bottom line is that above all you need to consider the usefulness of a source for your project and your potential argument. This principle applies to print and Web texts alike.

CREATIVE PRACTICE

Visit your school library's home page. How does it construct its own sense of *ethos*? Now take an online tour of its resources. Consult the list of resources, experiment with the search engine, browse through the photo galleries of rooms or collections, consult the floor plans, and locate key areas of the library: the reference desk, the stacks holding books, the room for current journals, the multimedia center (names of these areas will vary from school to school, so again, be flexible in your search terms). After exploring online, go to the building and do a walking tour of the library as well. Here are some questions to help you with both methods of exploration:

- What collections and areas of the library look particularly helpful to you and relevant to your research project?
- Where do you think you'll need to spend most of your time?
- What obstacles can you anticipate (need for photocopy cards, lack of scanners, even building hours)?

Write down your responses in your research log to keep track of your progress on your project.

Locating Sources for Your Research Argument

Once you understand the importance of search terms and evaluation criteria, you need to find specific resources to use in your paper, including both primary and secondary sources.

Finding Primary Sources

As previously explained, **primary sources** are usually original texts that you will analyze for your research paper. They come in many forms and can be some of the most exciting sources to work with in your research process. Consider, for instance, the sources that one student, James Caputo, used in his project on the media representations of the early years of the NASA space program. James had many fascinating primary resources he could work with: John F. Kennedy's inspirational speeches about the formation of the space program; front pages of both American and Russian newspapers detailing the successful completion of the first Apollo mission; publicity shots of the astronauts; the first images—both still and moving—from the moon's surface; and advertisements published after the first moon landing that capitalized on the space program's attempts to win public support. He chose to focus on multiple magazine covers and inset images for his primary source materials (see Figures 5.9 and 5.10).

For instance, the image in Figure 5.9 originally appeared in an article published in *Collier's* magazine on October 23, 1948, concerning the military applications of space travel. James analyzed it and found that it was intended to warn American readers graphically of the consequences of falling behind in the "space race" with the Russians. Similarly, Figure 5.10, a cover shot from *Time* magazine of July 25, 1969, relied on pathos to persuade the American readers to view the U.S. space program in a certain light. James found that the image, with its strong nationalistic overtones, cast the successful Apollo 11 mission once again in terms of the Cold War and the American-Soviet space race. He placed these primary sources at the center of his research argument, and then he turned to secondary sources to substantiate his own claims about them.

FIGURE 5.9. "Rocket Blitz from the Moon" provides a powerful primary source for analysis.

FIGURE 5.10. This magazine cover, a primary source, can be analyzed through research.

Such materials are more accessible than you might think. A range of primary sources can be found right in your library—in the general stacks, the special collections rooms, or in the video and multimedia collections—or at other sites on campus, such as in special exhibits in departments, galleries, and museums. Since these resources differ from school to school, it is best to ask your teacher and your librarian for guidance on where to locate collections relevant to your topic. Special collection departments and library archives are particularly rich resources for primary material, including the following:

- Original documents (perhaps a handwritten letter, penned by Mahatma Gandhi)
- Rare books (such as an illustrated first edition of William Blake's *Songs of Innocence and Experience*)
- Portfolios of photographs (for instance, photos of Japanese-American internment camps)
- Other one-of-a-kind texts (for example, AIDS prevention posters from South Africa, a noted artist's sketchbook, or a series of leaflets produced by the U.S. Psychological Warfare Department, distributed to the Vietnamese during the Vietnam War).

In many cases, you can work directly with these materials; they are brought to you straight from the vault, so you can perform your own first-hand analysis of that piece of cultural history.

Realize, however, that not all primary materials are kept under lock and key. Many circulate from the library collection—from bound collections of letters, to back issues of journals and full-length books. In addition, you may find more current examples of primary source material collected and displayed on the ground floor or near the entrance of the library; this is where many libraries house their most recent issues of national and international newspapers, popular magazines, and scholarly journals. Take advantage of their accessibility by looking through these materials to encounter the images and articles about a topic first-hand.

Keep in mind that while most recent issues of journals probably will be in your library's "current periodicals" section, issues more than a year old are bound into volumes and transferred to the library stacks.

While the best way to determine your own library's holdings may be to search your library catalog or to contact a reference librarian, an increasing number of academic institutions and organizations also digitize their collections to make them widely available to an international community of scholars. Your school's electronic access to primary sources might be as simple as a list on the library Website of holdings you can explore at the library itself. Alternatively, it might be as extensive as a complete set of digital reproductions or links to Internet archives of primary materials that you can analyze.

A Closer Look

Browse *Time*'s Person of the Year cover archive for a rich collection of primary sources.

www.ablongman.com/envision048

Time magazine, for instance, hosts an entire archive of primary sources on its Website. If you were beginning a project on media representations of women famous for challenging the status quo, you might consider browsing for primary sources in their collection and searching the "Person of the Year" covers from 1927 to the present.

The 2002 *Time* cover featured three women whose "courageous act of whistle-blowing" exposed the corporate corruption of Enron, WorldCom, and the FBI (see Figure 5.11). You might compare this representation of women on journal covers to the 1936 cover of Mrs. Wallis Warfield Simpson (see Figure 5.12). Her "courageous love" for Prince Edward of England changed the course of history, for Edward abdicated the throne to marry the recent divorcee, causing an entirely different kind of social scandal than the one brought about by American corporate greed. Taking these striking covers as a starting point, you might write about how the covers tell each story, how they shape social attitudes about both women and ethics, and even how the covers convey the women differently.

FIGURE 5.11. The serious pose of these women on the cover of *Time* begins to suggest the story inside.

FIGURE 5.12. *Time*'s 1936 issue again relies on body language to sell its story about a powerful woman.

COLLABORATIVE CHALLENGE

Browse the online cover collection generated either by *Time* magazine or *Life* magazine. Look at two to three covers on a particular topic, such as global warming, presidential elections, or computer technology. Generate a list of other primary source material—whether in electronic, print, or audio form—that you might use to pursue this research topic. Discuss with others in the class the benefits and drawbacks of using each of the sources you list.

www.ablongman.com/envision049

Searching for Secondary Sources

If you decided to develop your Collaborative Challenge topic into a persuasive argument, the next step would be to broaden your search to include **secondary sources**—that is, sources that offer some form of analysis or commentary on your primary material. Secondary sources help develop the substance of your argument. These are the voices that you will engage in scholarly conversation.

Your first stop in your search for secondary sources should be your library's reference area, the home of dictionaries, guides, encyclopedias, bibliographies, and other resource materials. These storehouses of important information can be invaluable in providing you with the foundational information for your project, including basic definitions, historical background, and brief bibliographies. Yet, while such "background" materials are necessary to help you construct a theoretical and cultural framework for your research argument, they represent only one part of your *iceberg of research*. For more rigorous analysis, you should turn to books and articles that provide detailed critical analysis and arguments about your specific research subject. To locate these more useful secondary sources, you might search your library catalog for relevant books and films and other published materials. However, you also have another valuable type of resource available to you: databases and indexes.

AT A GLANCE

Using One Source to Locate Additional Sources

After finding one relevant source through the catalog, locate it in the library stacks and then spend some time looking over books in the same area. By engaging in this physical equivalent of the computer "browse" search, you can more quickly move into a conversation with your sources, assessing their value to your project. Also, look at the bibliography in the back of your most useful book to locate sources helpful to its author; consult those sources to build your own iceberg of research.

AT A GLANCE

Finding Secondary Sources

You can use the following library resources to track down relevant secondary material:

- *Dictionaries, guides, encyclopedias:* Such foundational texts provide helpful background information for your topic.

- *Library catalog:* This engine allows you to search the library holdings for relevant books or documentaries.

- *CD-ROM indexes and bibliographies:* These CDs, which have been purchased by the library, can contain vast amounts of bibliographic information, but usually they can be used only in the reference section of the library.

- *Electronic databases and indexes:* These online databases are available on the Internet through subscription only; many provide access to full-text versions of articles.

- *Electronic journal databases:* Such databases offer access to e-journals on a range of topics and the full-text articles that are published within them.

You'll find databases and indexes indispensable to your research since they provide you with bibliographic citations for academic articles on your topic of interest. Keep in mind that databases can come in many different forms: they can be housed on CD-ROMs, online, or as collections of electronic journals. Additionally, while some databases provide only a bibliographic citation that you can then locate in your library catalog, many provide a detailed abstract summarizing a source's argument, and others will link you to full-text electronic copies of the articles you are searching for.

Let's say, for instance, that you decided to pursue the project on global warming that you began in the last Collaborative Challenge. After looking up foundational information in the *Encyclopedia of Environmental Information Sources* in the reference section, you search the library catalog for sources on your topic, returning from the stacks with a rather heavy collection of books. Despite the success of your search, you decide to track down some articles; journal articles, you reason, will provide balance to your research since they often represent the most current discussions on a topic. To find those articles, you begin searching the electronic databases that most closely suit the specific focus of your project: SciSearch; the Environmental Sciences and Pollution Management databases; LegalPeriodical; PAIS International; and the Consumer Index. You generate an impressive list of citations, and even a few full-text articles. Your next step is to search more news-related sources, including LexisNexis and ProQuest, to find a selection of references to popular newspaper and magazine articles focused on the issue of global warming that you can later search and find in your library. Lastly, you enter Project Muse and JSTOR—two electronic journal databases—and download several important essays on your topic.

Look for books in catalogs; look for articles in databases.

Your first search complete, you can now retreat to a quiet space and assess the significance and value of your findings. You can be relatively confident of the quality of the texts you've accumulated; since these databases are search and storage catalogs that your library must pay for in order to offer them to you, they provide a more rigorous screening of materials than an Internet search engine would. However, keep in mind that you'll still need to apply the same evaluation criteria to these texts as you would with less reliable sources. By assessing the visual rhetoric of the journal covers spread across your desk, you can begin the process of assessing topic, stance, and reliability. You might, for instance, have come across the two covers found in Figures 5.13 and 5.14. A rhetorical analysis reveals differences in purpose, audience, and focus: *Global Environmental Politics* prioritizes the ethos of its authors and con-

A Closer Look

Jocalyn Clark. "Babes and Boobs? Analysis of JAMA Cover Art." *British Medical Journal.* Dec 18, 1999, 1603. In this article, Clark examines the stereotypes often present in the covers of the *Journal of the American Medical Association*; not surprisingly, when Clark submitted the article to *JAMA*, they declined to publish it.

FIGURE 5.13. The strategically academic cover of *Global Environmental Politics* alludes to its audience.

FIGURE 5.14. A pair of hands and informal language cast *Alternatives* as a popular journal.

AT A GLANCE

Recording Searches in your Research Log

- Date each entry to keep track of your progress and show the evolution of your ideas.

- Write down complete identifying information for any source you consult, include images on the Web, articles online, journals or magazines in the library, articles from library databases, and chapters in books.

- Double-check transcribed quotations for accuracy while you still have the source before you, and include page numbers (or paragraph numbers for Website articles).

- Annotate the entry by including an evaluation of the source and an indication of how you might use it as part of your final paper; what is its relevance to your argument?

- If you are using Web sources, be aware that Websites tend to be updated or to simply disappear; to avoid losing important source material, print out significant Web pages and insert them into your log or download them to your hard drive and include them on a CD-ROM with your research log.

tent, whereas *Alternatives Journal,* with its powerful visual metaphor, suggests a more practical approach to environmental politics. Moving from the cover of the journal to the contents inside would confirm your observations. In this way, you can begin to distinguish between more and less important sources for the specific focus of your research topic.

As you continue to search for sources, remember that the best strategy for keeping careful track of your research process entails recording the dates, details, and relevance of your searches in your *research log,* as in the example below.

- **March 1:** conducted preliminary search on Internet. Found three articles related to my topic and printed them for folder "Primary Sources Online."

- **March 3:** conducted library search through university Web page. Came up with four books; checked them out. Might be good secondary sources. Recording their names below. Note that one is a collection of essays, suggesting multiple arguments I might consult. Note also that three books are published by university presses, promising rigorous arguments. I need to read them tonight. Noticed that all four books use the same image to introduce the topic; I need to discuss it in my paper, but maybe I want to find a new one for my introduction.

You might also want to keep a running list of your sources by call number and title, or include printouts of relevant articles or database entries, such as Vivian Chang did for her research log on a project discussing the fantasy world of *The Lord of the Rings* (see Figure 5.15).

While databases, catalogs, and search engines provide indispensable tools for conducting your research, don't overlook the resource you have in your peers. As colleagues in the research journey, your peers will have discovered helpful print sources, databases, and indexes. Ask others who are working on similar topics, share your research logs, and help each other along the route of your research.

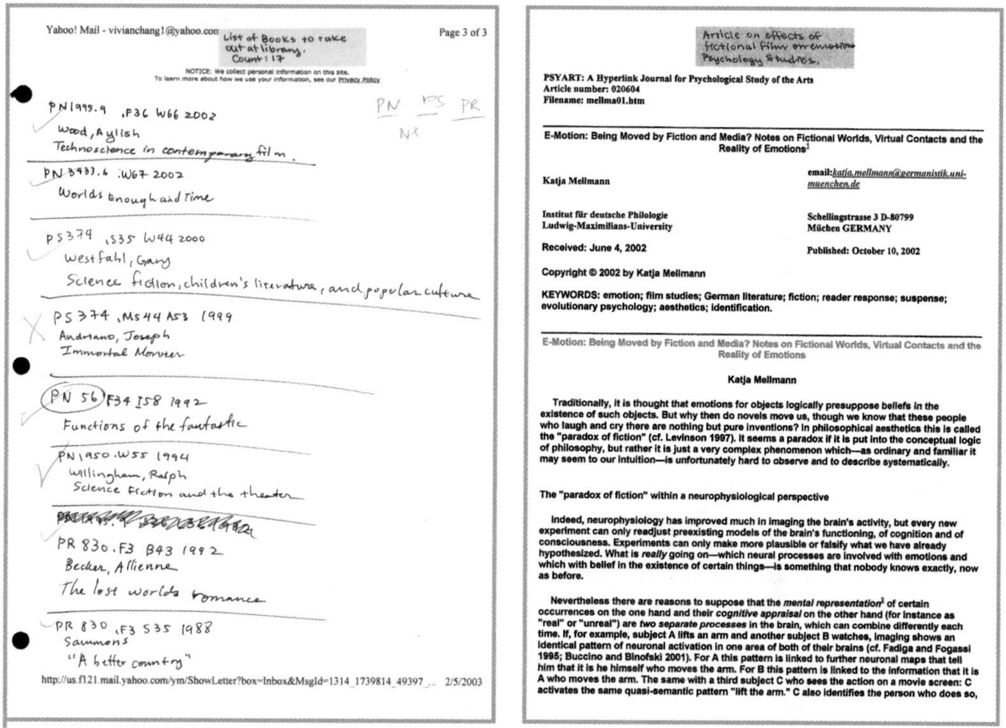

Yahoo! Mail - vivianchang1@yahoo.com — Page 3 of 3

List of Books to take out at library. Count: 17

NOTICE: We collect personal information on this site.
To learn more about how we use your information, see our Privacy Policy

PN PS PR

PN1995.9 .F36 W66 2002
Wood, Aylish
Technoscience in contemporary film.

PN 3433.6 .W67 2002
Worlds Enough and Time

PS374 .S35 W44 2000
Westfahl, Gary
Science fiction, children's literature, and popular culture

PS374 .M544 A53 1999
Andriano, Joseph
Immortal Monster

PN 56 F34 I58 1992
Functions of the fantastic

PN1950 .W55 1994
Willingham, Ralph
Science fiction and the theater

PR 830 .F3 B43 1992
Becker, Allienne
The lost worlds romance

PR 830 .F3 S35 1988
Sammons
"A better country"

http://us.f121.mail.yahoo.com/ym/ShowLetter?box=Inbox&MsgId=1314_1739814_49397_... 2/5/2003

Article on effects of fictional film Psychology Studies.

PSYART: A Hyperlink Journal for Psychological Study of the Arts
Article number: 020604
Filename: mellma01.htm

E-Motion: Being Moved by Fiction and Media? Notes on Fictional Worlds, Virtual Contacts and the Reality of Emotions[1]

Katja Mellmann — email: katja.mellmann@germanistik.uni-muenchen.de

Institut für deutsche Philologie
Ludwig-Maximilians-University
Schellingstrasse 3 D-80799
Müchen GERMANY

Received: June 4, 2002 — Published: October 10, 2002

Copyright © 2002 by Katja Mellmann

KEYWORDS: emotion; film studies; German literature; fiction; reader response; suspense; evolutionary psychology; aesthetics; identification.

E-Motion: Being Moved by Fiction and Media? Notes on Fictional Worlds, Virtual Contacts and the Reality of Emotions

Katja Mellmann

Traditionally, it is thought that emotions for objects logically presuppose beliefs in the existence of such objects. But why then do novels move us, though we know that these people who laugh and cry there are nothing but pure inventions? In philosophical aesthetics this is called the "paradox of fiction" (cf. Levinson 1997). It seems a paradox if it is put into the conceptual logic of philosophy, but rather it is just a very complex phenomenon which—as ordinary and familiar it may seem to our intuition—is unfortunately hard to observe and to describe systematically.

The "paradox of fiction" within a neurophysiological perspective

Indeed, neurophysiology has improved much in imaging the brain's activity, but every new experiment can only readjust preexisting models of the brain's functioning, of cognition and of consciousness. Experiments can only make more plausible or falsify what we have already hypothesized. What is *really* going on—which neural processes are involved with emotions and which with belief in the existence of certain things—is something that nobody knows exactly, now as before.

Nevertheless there are reasons to suppose that the *mental representation*[2] of certain occurrences on the one hand and their *cognitive appraisal* on the other hand (for instance as "real" or "unreal") are *two separate processes* in the brain, which can combine differently each time. If, for example, subject A lifts an arm and another subject B watches, imaging shows an identical pattern of neuronal activation in one area of both of their brains (cf. Fadiga and Fogassi 1995; Buccino and Binofski 2001). For A this pattern is linked to further neuronal maps that tell him that it is he himself who moves the arm. For B this pattern is linked to the information that it is A who moves the arm. The same with a third subject C who sees the action on a movie screen: C activates the same quasi-semantic pattern "lift the arm." C also identifies the person who does so,

FIGURE 5.15. Vivian Chang's research log includes both handwritten notes and annotated article printouts.

CREATIVE PRACTICE

Come up with three to six keywords as well as Library of Congress headings about your topic, and perform a search for both primary and secondary sources. Explore print sources through the library catalog as well as online texts through databases and e-journals. Then produce a **Preliminary Bibliography** for your research project—a list of 8–10 potential sources.

Next, form into groups of three or four and share your preliminary bibliographies. Each person in the group should spend five minutes presenting a narrative of the research process: What sources have you found so far? Which databases were unexpectedly fruitful to your search? What journals hold the most helpful secondary sources? How are you formatting your research log? Then, have each person in the group lend another person a particularly useful source. Broaden the base of your research argument by incorporating more sources.

"Research is never completed. . . . Around the corner lurks another possibility of interview, another book to read, a courthouse to explore, a document to verify."

—Catherine Drinker Bowen

Thinking about Field Research

Depending on your project, you might decide that you want to use not only print and electronic sources, but also **field research** in the form of interviews or surveys. Collecting these sources often involves fieldwork, gathering and collecting your own evidence and data. Imagine for a minute that you were writing a research paper on murals and the Chicano community. The photograph of the mural featured in Figure 5.16 would be a useful primary source as it reproduces the image in rich color and detail. However, think about how much more powerful a source this same wall would be if you were to visit it in person. Such *field research* would allow you perspective beyond the cropped edges of the photo: you could view the urban

FIGURE 5.16. The *Song of Unity* mural depicts a celebration of music and specific cultural groups.

context to better understand the mural's place among community structures; you could perhaps talk with members of the community to get a sense of the local significance of the painting (for instance, who created it, when it was painted, and what the community response was); you could observe at close range detail that might have escaped the photographer's image. Such first-hand field research adds depth to your argument by allowing you to learn from experts about the visual rhetoric of the mural.

Not all fieldwork involves trips to local sites: some involves gathering your own primary data about your topic from carefully determined sample groups or individuals. If you were interested in the impact of students' political campaign posters on a given campus population, for instance, you might do a survey of a sample of students; if you were studying the layout and impact of a new proposed park in your community, you might interview a city planner or the landscape architect involved in the project. One student, Sean Bruich, writing on recent marketing strategies used by the Oakland Athletics baseball team, wrote a letter to the team's marketing coordinator. Consult his letter to learn how to begin your field research.

You also can take advantage of resources closer to home by interviewing faculty members from your own university who have written or lectured on subjects related to your topic. This is a great way to make contacts and develop your iceberg of research, for, in addition to interviewing the faculty member as another secondary source, you can usually ask him or her to recommend two or three key books in the field that you might consult as you continue on your research journey.

COLLABORATIVE CHALLENGE

Brainstorm different kinds of field research you could conduct on your topic. Now, together with your group partners, come up with concrete strategies for contacting, setting up, and carrying out field research through letters, emails, phone calls, and interviews. What preliminary steps do you need to take? Should you read any of the interviewee's books or articles before the meeting? What three questions are most important for you to ask? How will you take notes during the interview? What follow-up techniques will you use after the field research is complete?

April 7, 2003

Lynne Tibbet
Sales & Marketing Coordinator
Oakland Athletics

Dear Ms. Tibbet,

My name is Sean Bruich and I am a freshman at Stanford University. As part of Stanford's required courses in writing, I am enrolled in Dr. Alyssa O'Brien's course on Visual Rhetoric. Writing a sizeable research paper that focuses on visual rhetoric is a required portion of this class. As a long time fan of the Oakland Athletics, I was hoping to write my paper on the marketing strategies employed by the Athletics over the course of the last few years (specifically, I'm hoping to focus on your "Baseball Country" and "Baseball: A's Style" ads since they are so memorable).

At this point, I'd like to request some materials from the Athletics. Specifically, if the A's could send me, either by email or by mail, the print materials from these campaigns, I would be really appreciative. In addition, if possible, I would love to also get copies of some of the commercial spots that are shown on TV. I will reimburse your office for any and all expenses incurred, including materials and mailing costs.

At some point, I'd like also to discuss with you or one of your colleagues how the A's create and direct their marketing campaigns if you have the time available.

I only need ads that are now or have been in the marketplace -- I'm not in any way requesting unpublished work. I will talk to my professor to ensure that none of these materials extend beyond this project, and are not republished or retransmitted in any way without prior permissions from the Athletics. In addition, if the A's need me to sign any confidentiality agreements, I would be happy to do so.

Basically, I'm going to start working on this term paper in the course of the next week or so, although I do have several smaller writing assignments that could be aided greatly by these materials if I can get a hold of them sooner.

Please do not hesitate to contact me if you have questions or want to discuss this situation further.

Thank you very much for your time!

Regards,

Sean

Sean Bruich
P.O. Box 12345
Stanford, CA 54321
(650) 555-1878 (dorm)
(650) 555-7694 (cell)

Sean writes a formal letter to the contact he has found for his field research.

He introduces himself and his project fully, relying on *ethos* and stating the purpose of his letter early.

He makes his request specific and feasible, taking into account any potential obstacles.

He ends politely, with an invitation for the person to contact him.

He lists his full contact information (you could also include email).

Evaluating Fieldwork and Statistics

When you conduct interviews and surveys, you are looking for materials to use in your paper as supporting arguments, evidence, or statistical data. But as you pursue your interviews and surveys, keep in mind the need to evaluate your field research sources as carefully as you assess your print and electronic sources. If you interview a professor, a marketing executive, a witness, or a roommate, consider the rhetorical stance of that person. What kind of bias does the person have concerning the topic of your project? Similarly, if you conduct a survey of your peers or in your dorm, remember to assess the value and credibility of your results as rigorously as you would evaluate the data of a published study. It's easy to fall into the trap of misusing statistics when making claims if you haven't taken into account the need for **statistical significance,** or, to use the words of famous social psychologist Philip Zimbardo, the measure by which a number obtains meaning in scientific fields. To reach this number, you need to design the survey carefully, conduct what's called a *random sample,* interview a *large enough* number of people, and ask a *range of different* people. These are complex parameters to follow, but you can learn about them by asking a statistics or psychology professor to talk you through the concepts.

It's important to appoint statistics carefully so that you don't misread information and so that you know how to create and incorporate statistical evidence accurately into your research paper. Professor Zimbardo's explanation of the difference between an occurrence

> "In normal English 'significant' means important while in statistics 'significant' means probably true (not due to chance). A research finding may be true without being important. When statisticians say a result is 'highly significant' they mean it is very probably true. They do not (necessarily) mean it is highly important."
> —Creative Research Systems

🔲 A Closer Look
Explore the meaning of these terms online through Creative Research Systems and the Internet Glossary of Statistical Terms. www.ablongman.com/envision050

> By common agreement, psychologists accept a difference between the groups [in a study] as "real" [and not open to chance] when the probability that it might be due to chance is less than 5 in 100 (indicated by the notation $p<.05$). A **significant difference** is one that meets this criterion. . . . That is, there is only a very slim possibility—less than 5 in 100 ($p< .05$) of the difference between groups shown in our data being merely due to a chance. Therefore, we can feel more confident that the difference is real. . . . Any conclusion, however, is only a statement of the *probable* relationship between the events that were investigated; it is never one of absolute certainty. Truth in science is provisional, always open to revision by later data from better studies, developed from better hypotheses.
> —Philip Zimbardo

due to chance and one *due to cause and effect* is a crucial one to remember not only when you are conducting your own surveys, but also when you assess a secondary source that relies on scientific studies and statistics. As Zimbardo argues, "Statistics are the backbone of psychological research. They are used to understand observations and to determine whether findings are, in fact, correct and significant. . . . But, statistics can also be used poorly or deceptively, misleading those who do not understand them" (595). The point here is that statistics also function as a rhetorical device, a mode of persuasion. You need to be especially vigilant about this ostensibly "objective" resource when using such materials as part of your iceberg of research, especially if you plan to depend on surveys or statistics in your argument.

Creating a Dialogue with Your Sources

"Create a dialogue with your sources, in script format, to get the research conversation started."

—Marvin Diogenes

Seeing Connections
For specific guidance and strategies for integrating sources, see Chapter 6.

Throughout this chapter, we are emphasizing the point that research is social, a relationship with the people whose ideas and writing comes before you. You are contributing to this conversation, building on the work of others, and adding a new perspective. Indeed, this notion of writing as communal is the reason why we use the author's name when citing a quotation or an idea; remember that all your sources are authored sources. From the "DoNoHarm" stem cell debate Website in Figure 5.7, to an article on the 1936 *Time* magazine person of the year in Figure 5.12, each one of these sources was composed by a person or group of people. If you think of these texts as written *by people such as yourself,* you will have an easier time remembering to acknowledge their ideas and integrate their quotations into your essay. You can begin contributing to this conversation through an exercise we call a **dialogue of sources,** or a fictional conversation among the primary and secondary sources of your research paper as a means to identify each one's central argument and main idea.

You can find a visual equivalent for the dialogue of sources in comedian Jon Stewart's video sketch from *The Daily Show,* "Bush v. Bush," in which he moderated a "debate" between President George W. Bush and his younger self, the Governor of Texas, George W. Bush on matters of foreign policy (see Figure 5.17). In reality, the debate was composed of carefully edited excerpts from speeches from different points in President Bush's career; the result was a provocative look into Bush's own changing opinion on U.S. foreign intervention. Although the video dialogue was comic, the premise was a sound one: many news commentary shows feature "round-table" discussions between a diverse group of people, with the idea of promoting a conversation about a relevant social or political topic.

You may find it helpful to create your own, literal *dialogue of sources* through which you can actively play out the diverse opinions that you encounter in your research process:

FIGURE 5.17. Screenshot from "Bush v. Bush," a debate staged by Jon Stewart on *The Daily Show*. Still courtesy of COMEDY CENTRAL.

- First, identify the key players from your potential of sources. Which ones have the most influential or important arguments?
- Then, create a cast of characters list in which you create a short "bio" for each speaker, including yourself, describing each person's credentials and rhetorical stance—their ethos and their argument. You may even want to create identifying icons or pictures to give "faces" to the participants.
- Now, draft the script. Begin by writing out key questions; ask your sources crucial questions about your topic. As they articulate their positions, put them in dialogue with one another. Use quotes from your sources where possible and include page numbers.
- Don't just play the "objective" moderator. Respond to the sources, and, in the process, start to develop your own argument.

A Closer Look

- Watch the "Bush v. Bush" debate in its entirety. Note how Stewart does not act as an "objective" interviewer but includes his own position through strategic questions, comments, facial expressions, and gestures.

- For a more serious version of the research dialogue, examine the Beckman Symposium from April 14–15, 2003 entitled, "Stem Cells, Regenerative Medicine and Cancer" and analyze the videos of talks, the discussion, and the dialogue among experts.
www.ablongman.com/envision051

Student Writing

See the dialogue of sources by Andrew Timmons's dialogue on PetCo Park and by Amanda Johnson on tobacco advertisements.
www.ablongman.com/envision052

Amanda Johnson: Dialogue of Sources, Excerpt

Amanda's dialogue actually begins with a list of speakers and their bios. Then she introduces the topic of her research project.

AJ: I would like to thank the panel for joining us this afternoon. We have quite a diverse group of writers, researchers, spokespeople, and a professor here to discuss the focus and objectives of current tobacco advertising. Since I know your comments on this subject vary widely, I suppose I will start off by asking you to talk about what you believe to be the focus of tobacco advertising as it exists today.

She reproduces the argument of each source, both print and interview, through paraphrase.

RJRT: RJ Reynolds tobacco products are among the best advertised in the industry and we take pride in our commitment to maintaining honest advertising to the public. We do not intend for our advertising to manipulate non-smokers into trying our products, nor do we choose to target these audiences. Advertising is simply a method by which we are able to maintain our share of the market and compete with other tobacco manufacturers.

By allowing debate to evolve, Amanda develops the complexity of her research project.

LW: How can you possibly claim to avoid targeting specific audiences and replenishing your older dwindling population with new younger smokers!?! The whole point of advertising is to get more people to buy your product and since market shares don't change all that much for large companies like yourself, the best way to get more people to buy your product is to increase the number of overall smokers. Youth are your best option because if you can get them hooked now, you will have a steady flow of income for several decades to come.

HH: Mr. White, you make a good point about general economic objectives. However, studies show that advertising does very little to change the number of new smokers. Countries that have banned advertising for tobacco-related products have seen very little decline in the number of consumers that buy their product. As RJRT stated previously, advertising is only successful at making adjustments within the market concerning the relative amounts each company is able to sell.

Most importantly, Amanda participates by questioning the responses, adding facts from her research, and moving the argument forward as she will need to do in her paper.

AJ: I recently reviewed a chart concerning the prevalence of smoking among U.S. adults and found that over the past 40 years since the Surgeon General first warned about cigarettes' cancerous effects the steady decline in smokers has slowed to rest around 25 percent of the population over the age of 18. With the number of people dying each day, it is surprising that this number does not continue to go down. How would you account for the slowed change?

Amanda Johnson, excerpted dialogue of sources on advertising and the tobacco industry; see the "bios" and the complete dialogue through the *Envision* Website.
www.ablongman.com/envision053

As you can tell from Amanda Johnson's dialogue of sources, this process of literally responding to the main arguments in your texts can produce a very helpful interchange about the research topic and help move you toward the refinement of your own main argument.

Note-Taking as a Prelude to Drafting

You can use the dialogue of sources as a note-taking strategy while you work through your research sources. Indeed, many students find this approach to note-taking to be the best way to create a thorough research log for their projects, one that keeps their own thesis evident. However, there are many methods of note-taking, and, at this point in your research process you probably have developed some techniques of your own: taking notes right in your research log, or on note cards, on loose-leaf paper, in a spiral notebook, or on your laptop. Realize that taking notes is much more than recording information: it is a chance for you to synthesize arguments and engage in a preliminary dialogue with your sources. For this reason, we advocate that you approach note-taking as an **interview** with your sources, one in which you both faithfully record their ideas and also respond to them and push them to elaborate further. We discussed interviewing as part of field research earlier in the chapter, when we talked about consulting the opinions of others as secondary sources in the dialogue of sources.

It's helpful to continue thinking in terms of the "dialogue" when you take notes in your research log. Be sure to credit your sources as real people sharing their work and words with you. Indeed, you can engage in your research log in the same type of interactive dialogue with your sources as you might have with faculty or other interviewees.

Moreover, if you write your notes in the same style as an interview, using clear name prompts alternating on the page between direct quotes from your text and your own summaries or commentaries, then you can avoid potentially misquoting or plagiarizing sources later. Another way to demarcate clearly between your own ideas and those of your sources is to compose what we call a **visual annotated bibliography,** a working list of potential sources in which you provide a short description of the argument of each one and explain its relevance to your own paper. The annotated bibliography is *visual* because you should include

AT A GLANCE

Constructing a Visual Annotated Bibliography

- List your sources in alphabetical order; you can separate your list into primary and secondary sources or provide one complete list.

- Include images for your primary sources and the covers or Website images of secondary sources to show each source's stance through visual rhetoric.

- For each source, be sure to include all identifying information.

- Briefly state the argument of each source, the possible audience, the bias "or slant of the writer, and include any specific passages of particular interest.

- Most importantly, explain the relevance of this source to your own research project and even where and how you might use it in your paper.

Carly Geehr
Visually Annotated Bibliography

Dr. Alyssa O'Brien
May 13, 2003

The American Media and Swimming: Investigating the "Uphill Battle"

Booth, Douglas and Colin Tatz, One-Eyed: a View of Australian Sport. Australia: Allen and Unwin, 2000.

In order to make my argument that swimming could be a more popular sport in the United States, I will need to present strong evidence: this book provides it to me. Booth and Tatz chronicle the history of Australian sports in both society and in the media. From their descriptions of media coverage and the role of gender in sports, I can find out why, culturally and historically, swimming has been able to achieve such a high level of popularity in Australia. Of particular interest to me so far has been their focus on the traditional, accepted role of women in sports—it is drastically different in US history. By comparison to my sources about American sports culture, I will find out the key differences between the two countries and hopefully draw some concrete conclusions as to why swimming is not as popular in the United States as it is in Australia. This photo is the image of a female Australian swimmer whose look and demeanor demand respect, unlike her beautified American counterparts (212). I will be able to compare the Australian images of swimmers with the American images of swimmers, hopefully noting some key differences in visual rhetoric techniques employed—preliminarily, I suspect that the American images will focus much more on aesthetics while Australian images will focus on intensity and ruggedness (more pertinent to the sport itself).

"Duel in the Pool Advertisement." 3 Apr 2003. <http://www.usaswimming.org/Duel>.

[A little background: USA Swimming recently staged its first "made-for-TV" dual meet versus the Australian national team. The goal was to attract network attention and draw the people who would normally be watching sports on weekend afternoons into watching swimming for a change. According to Mary Wagner, the ratings were good but not exceptional.] This image is one of the advertisements put out by USA Swimming before the event to attract its target audience of teenagers and others (particularly males) who would be watching television on Saturday and Sunday afternoons. It appeals mostly to ethos, citing Michael Phelps as a world record holder, but also appeals more subtly to pathos in using the national colors and the national flag to create a sense of nationalism and passion for the event. However, this image helps me support my claim that USA Swimming's promotions have fallen short of successful in that it is not an exciting image—if the intent was to attract teenagers and adults who typically watch traditional, exciting American sports, then this image fails to create sufficient energy to generate interest or a desire to deviate from watching normal weekend sports on TV.

FIGURE 5.18. Well-chosen images and detailed annotations show Carly Geehr's progress on her research project.

Student Writing
See samples of visual annotated bibliographies on a wide range of topics.
www.ablongman.com/envision054

visual images—primary sources you will analyze in your paper and the covers or Website of secondary sources that indicate the source's stance. Consider, for instance, Carly Geehr's visual annotated bibliography for her research project on the representations of swimming as a gendered sport in the American media throughout history (see Figure 5.18).

Both the image of a swimmer from the early 1920s in the secondary source by Douglas Booth and Colin Tatz, as well as the more recent advertising from *U.S.A. Swimming* eventually found their way into Carly's paper. The images in her bibliography therefore helped Carly refine her ambitious research project to concentrate on specific issues. In addition, Carly could begin to focus her own argument by responding rigorously to these sources in her visual annotated bibliography. As you write the annotated bibliography, remember that effective annotations and note-taking practices can help you develop the strategies of a careful scholar, and that these practices will move you toward finalizing your own argument about the topic. You might also want to begin

> [T]he writing that takes place in the *middle* of the research process—the note-taking stage—may be as important, if not more so, than the writing that takes place at the end—composing the draft. Writing in the middle helps you take possession of your source and establish your presence in the draft. It sharpens your thinking about your topic. And it is the best cure for unintentional plagiarism.
>
> —Bruce Ballenger

composing a preliminary draft of your paper from the annotations in your bibliography. Use the technique that Professor Bruce Ballenger calls "writing in the middle" of the research process to get you off to a solid start on actually writing out the argument of your project.

Implementing Your Research Skills

As you begin to articulate your contribution to the scholarly dialogue about your topic, utilize the strategies that you've learned in this chapter. These include visualizing research as a conversation that you are joining and understanding the process of researching your argument as a movement from surface to depth. As you learn to search and locate both primary and secondary sources, you can engage in critical evaluation of these texts in your research log. You can also engage in innovative fieldwork of your own to generate original resource material to use in your argument. As you move from covers to contents, you will watch your iceberg of research take shape and you will begin to let your own voice be heard.

PREWRITING CHECKLIST
Websites, Magazines, and Journals

❏ What images are featured on the cover? Do the images lend themselves to an appeal to logic? To an appeal to emotion? To an appeal to authority?

❏ Do the words included as headings and subheads on the cover contribute to any of these appeals?

❏ What do the cover images suggest about the contents of the larger text? Do they suggest a specific rhetorical stance or point of view? For instance, if the topic of a journal issue is animal testing, does the cover feature a prominent scientist who has made an important scientific discovery based on research work with mice, or does it feature a picture of those mice, hooked up to wires inside a small metal cage? What is the effect of each visual choice?   *(continued)*

Seeing Connections
For additional prewriting checklists on Websites, see Chapter 8.

❑ How do the words or copy work in conjunction with the image to suggest the entire text's rhetorical stance? Do the words complement the image? Do they offer a contrast to the image?

❑ What argument is generated by the interrelationship between word and image? What strategies do they use to motivate the reader to move beyond the cover and into the text's contents?

❑ How does the layout of the cover create a visual path, leading the reader through a series of visual and verbal cues designed to represent the stance of the text as a whole?

❑ Does the cover participate in any larger cultural conversations or make reference, implicitly or explicitly, to broader social issues? Consider how it might do this through both word and image.

❑ Consider the design elements of the cover. How do features such as use of color, font, layout, and image selection (photograph vs. illustration) work as persuasive elements in this text? What do they suggest about the text's larger contents or argument?

❑ Evaluate the contents based on the cover; now consider the rhetorical effectiveness of the cover as a precursor to the contents. Is it appropriate and well-matched? Would you use this source based solely on the cover, or can you think of a way to revise the cover to make it seem more useful to your research purposes?

WRITING PROJECTS

Visit the *Envision* Website for expanded assignment guidelines and student projects.

1. Continue to write in your *research log*; keep a running commentary/ assessment of potential research sources for your project. Realize that careful research notes are a crucial part of the process and they will help you avoid unintentional plagiarism of material. Include in your log a combination of typed notes, highlighted photocopies, emails to yourself, a CD-ROM of sources from databases, note cards, scanned in images, and other means of processing all the information you encounter.

2. Create a *visual annotated bibliography* of your sources to showcase the primary and secondary sources you'll employ in the major paper. Be sure that your working bibliography provides a range of primary and secondary sources—both print and electronic—and include images for your primary sources wherever possible to demonstrate the kinds of material you'll be analyzing in the project. Then, choose the most

significant, important, or useful sources and provide brief annotations for each one. See the Envision Website for students' work, a model entry, and more guidelines.

FOR ADDED CHALLENGE

Visit the *Envision* Website for expanded assignment guidelines and student projects.

1. Web-based Annotated Bibliography
Compose your annotated bibliography in a multimedia or Web-writing program such as Dreamweaver, Flash, or PowerPoint. Create links to your online sources and include scanned in images of the covers of your texts. You can also package your bibliography as a book.

2. Presentation and Collaboration: Workshop on Research
In groups of three or four, present your Web-based annotated bibliography to one another. Pull the "greatest hits" from your research log, create a multimedia annotated bibliography, and tell the class about how your research is going. In other words, *present a discussion of your work in progress.* You should identify your thesis, key points, obstacles, and successes so far. You'll get feedback from the class about your developing research project.

CHAPTER 5 ON THE WEB

Resources and Reading	Exercises and Assignments	Student Writing
• Closer Look links	• Source evaluation exercises	• Diagrams of the research process
• Writing and research tools for library and Web searches, note-taking, and constructing bibliographies	• Maintaining your research log	• Icebergs of Research
	• Interview and field research guidelines	• Research logs in various formats
• Links to sources for evaluating Websites	• Detailed directions for the visual annotated bibliography	• Preliminary and Annotated Bibliographies
• Links to magazine cover collections	• Peer Review forms	• Examples of the Dialogue of Sources
• Annotated readings	• Focus on diverse learners	• Visual Annotated Bibliographies
		• Student reflections on research

CHAPTER 6

Organizing and Writing Research Arguments

Taking a break from gathering and evaluating sources for your research argument, you pop a film into a DVD player. As you watch, you may be struck by the complex arrangement of materials into one fluid narrative or visual text. When the film ends, you click on the Scene Selection function and see the outline of the movie in small, visual chunks; each segment has a title and contributes to the meaning of the whole film.

Consider the graphic depiction of the PBS film "The Library Burns" in Figure 6.1. Here, several scenes are mapped visually like selections on a DVD scene sequence. We notice the central characters and main conflict, the development of the idea, and the key scenes in the progression of the film.

In many ways, the process of writing is much like film production, for both endeavors have many small steps, a dedication to a grounding vision or main idea, a carefully planned structure, and a rigorous editing process, among many other parallels. Since the processes of producing a film and producing a visually based research argument share such rich similarities, we'll use the medium of film throughout this chapter to explore various aspects of the research paper writing process: from constructing a visual map and formal outline to integrating sources, key quotations, dialogue, and evidence.

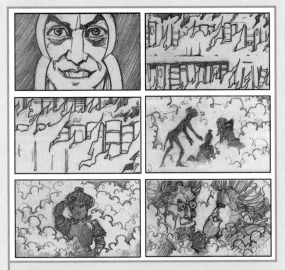

FIGURE 6.1. In the scene selection for "The Library Burns," graphic boxes lead the reader through key scenes, charting the development of the film as a whole.

Chapter Preview Questions

- What are my choices for visually representing my argument?
- How can I transform my visual map into a detailed outline?
- What strategies of organization will work best for my paper?
- How can I avoid plagiarism?
- How do I know when to quote, paraphrase, or summarize?
- Can I integrate visual texts as evidence in my paper?
- What techniques can I use to produce that first draft?
- How can collaboration and peer review help me revise?
- What is the best way to format my completed work?

We'll talk about incorporating sources responsibly in a way that sustains the conversation you began in the previous chapter, and we'll walk through the drafting and revision process. Just as many film scenes end up on the cutting room floor, so too will drafts and paragraphs of your research paper be written, edited, and cut from the final draft. You'll find that the process of completing your research argument is as collaborative as film production. Additionally, in both film and writing, there are parameters of length, cost, and time that you need to contend with in order to produce the best possible text. Finally, just as most film scenes are shot with a careful eye to composition, layout, location, and meaning, so too will you need to think carefully about how to use different kinds of texts—visual and verbal, primary and secondary, written and field research—within your project. No matter what your topic, you can think of the way in which film works to help you visualize the end product and move from notes to final paper.

Keep in mind, however, that there is no definitive stage when you begin "writing" your paper. The fact is that you are writing all along: prewriting, the proposal, the research log, the annotated bibliography, the dialogue of sources, the detailed organizational charts, and the outline are all ways to develop your argument through writing. Recognizing the connection between these shorter writing activities and the ostensibly all-consuming task of "writing the research paper" can help you make the process more enjoyable and productive; it can help you avoid "writer's block" as you see that you've been making progress all along.

Sketching Your Draft in Visual Form

Seeing Connections
We used the bubble
web to brainstorm
topic ideas in
Chapter 4.

In film and documentary, ideas for scenes and plot progression are often mapped out visually. You can use various forms of visual mapping to organize your research notes and argumentative ideas in order to sort, arrange, and to make various connections between ideas.

Bubble Visual Maps

One method is through a **bubble web,** in which you arrange your ideas into categories using shapes and colors. Figure 6.2 shows student Lee-Ming Zen's visual map for his project on the video game Lara Croft Tomb Raider entitled "Finding the Woman Who Never Was: Gender Exploration through Lara Croft." As Lee's legend for the

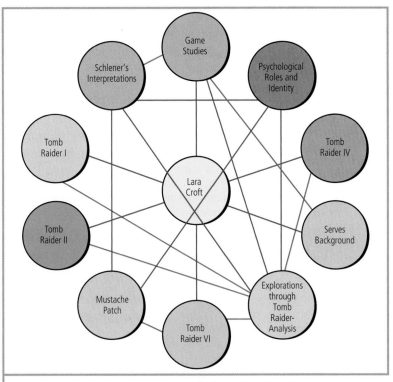

Legend:
Green = Content
(detail) related
Red = Idea/Broad
concept related
Blue = Requires
synthesis of ideas
and analysis

FIGURE 6.2. The Visual Map by Lee-Ming Zen facilitates the sorting of ideas.

visual map explains, each color adds a layer of meaning to the arrangements of shapes in the design. By grouping his research and his own ideas into categories contained within circles, and by drawing relationships between these categories through the use of colored lines, Lee can sort through the sources he has read, the ideas he has encountered, and the many points he wishes to cover in his research paper. Ultimately, Lee will need to create a formal outline, but for now, it is more important for him to make some sense of the wealth of materials from the research journey. He will then see exactly how he can begin to articulate his own argument on the video game.

Flowchart Visual Maps

In addition to such free-form visual maps, you could also try more hierarchical or linear *graphic flowcharts* as a means of organizing your materials. In **graphic flowcharts,** you can explore the relationships between items by listing one idea, then drawing an arrow to suggest cause and effect. As you continue to brainstorm and arrange your ideas, you find yourself with a linear web of ideas. Figure 6.3, for example, presents Ye Yuan's graphic flowchart of his ideas about war photography. Ye constructed this diagram by using the software program Inspiration to create bubbles of ideas in a sort

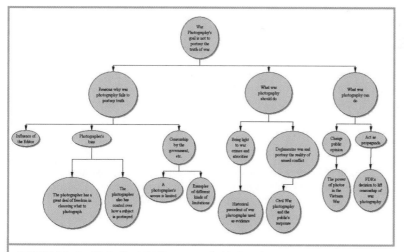

FIGURE 6.3. Graphic Outline by Ye Yuan, created with the software program Inspiration.

of brainstorming session. He then clicked on the "Arrange" button and reset his web into a hierarchal tree structure. This new visual hierarchy will help him assess how he is locating materials into his project. He can assess his work by asking questions:

- Is each point developed thoroughly?
- Do I have a balance among the sections?
- Is there a coherent whole?

Student Writing

Examine Jeff Lee's inspiration map on the gendered iconography of Egyptian rulers and Dylan Mark's bubble web on Disney World Theme Parks.
www.ablongman.com/envision055

Physical Maps of Sources

In addition to using software technology to visually map your ideas, you can reap the benefits of this process by physically making stacks out of your research books and materials. This organizational strategy functions as a concrete way of categorizing the resources you have and figuring out, visually, how they relate to one another. Additionally, you can produce the kinds of visual maps we've showcased above by using colored pens and paper or by cutting out shapes and constructing a three-dimensional model for your paper's organization. Finally, you can take your graphic web or flowchart and turn it into a sequence of scenes much like a DVD's scene selection through an organizational tool known as the *storyboard*.

A Closer Look

Explore a variety of dynamic storyboards categorized by Advertising, Commercial Production, and Film. www.ablongman.com/envision056

Storyboards as Visual Maps

The **storyboard** is actually a linear technique in which filmmakers chart the progression of ideas by chunking the film into smaller discrete units, much as you would in an outline. You might use this technique to begin arranging your ideas, sources, and points of argument into a clear sequence for your research paper. Figure 6.4 shows a widescreen storyboard, ready to be filled in both visually and verbally with your ideas.

> Storyboards are the visual equivalent of a rough draft of a written story. They allow filmmakers to see how the finished film might look before the laborious and costly processes of filming and editing begin. Storyboards are useful for deciding how to divide the script into shots, determining how to arrange the shots (a sort of pre-editing), and deciding camera placement.
>
> —Willam H. Phillips

FIGURE 6.4. Widescreen storyboard ready for content.

CREATIVE PRACTICE

Use any visual mapping technique and begin to arrange your ideas for the research paper. Create a web of ideas through a bubble web, or make a hierarchal flowchart of concepts. Alternatively, take your ideas for the trajectory of your paper and create a storyboard to visualize the progression of your argument. If you'd rather work with physical materials, gather colored pens, pencils, crayons, papers, scissors, tape, and glue, and then "create" relationships between ideas by arranging them visually on paper: cut out shapes, draw lines and links, glue pieces of paper together.

COLLABORATIVE CHALLENGE

When you are done constructing your visual map, present an overview of your graphic design, flowchart, storyboard, or physical collage to your peer review partners. Ask for feedback on what areas seem underdeveloped, isolated, or extraneous. Use this feedback to think about the balance of materials in your potential essay and how the pieces work together.

Student Writing

Consult Bries Deerose's flow-chart for a project on the U.S. office of Global Communications as well as various other visual maps produced by students for their research projects.
www.ablongman.com/envision057

As you can see, visual maps are powerful prewriting strategies; they allow you to begin to organize your materials. It can be quite challenging to turn on the computer and try to crank out a complete draft without allowing yourself to arrange the materials into some kind of order first. Bubble webs, graphic clusters, flowcharts, and storyboards are a great way to prewrite through visual means.

Moving from Visual Maps to Outline Strategies

While visual maps can help you sort out your materials, there does come a moment in your prewriting process when you need to decide on a more linear organization. For longer, more complex papers such as a research-based argument, the detailed, written outline is an extremely useful method of arranging ideas and expediting the drafting process. With outlining, as with some of the other techniques that we've discussed there are many ways to do it. The key is to recognize that outlines comprise a promise or plan for your paper and they show the relationship between sections. If you simply provide a list of topics, then you won't be able to see the argument of the whole paper, nor will you be able to check for connections and progression between points of your argument. In other words, the secret to producing a successful outline—and by extension a successful paper—is to pay special attention to the flow or development of ideas.

"An outline will help you to get an overall view of your paper and, perhaps more important, to figure out how each section of the paper relates to others."

—Joseph Gibaldi

It's often hard to know for certain what the best way of organizing your paper will be without some trial and error. We can learn a lot from films about the ways in which different texts are organized. Consider how a film's **trailer,** or short prerelease video, provides a brief outline of the key scenes, the main conflict, the crucial characters, and the message of the movie. In Figure 6.5, we see still shots from the theatrical trailer of *Kill Bill: Volume 1*.

A Closer Look

Visit the Apple movie trailer site to view an impressive range of recent movie trailers.
www.ablongman.com/envision058

Structured loosely as a narrative, this segment of the trailer suggests an outline of the film: Figure 6.5 moves from an identification of conflict, to defining the main character's central nemesis, to a scene of confrontation and physical combat. In doing so, the trailer reproduces one of the central themes of the *Kill Bill* series: the identification of evil and the quest for revenge through violence. But there are many ways to arrange these elements, each of which suggests a different argument for the film. The power of the trailer as an organizational tool is that it allows filmmakers or writers to experiment with order and meaning.

FIGURE 6.5. Still Shots from the trailer for *Kill Bill: Volume 1.*

COLLABORATIVE CHALLENGE

In groups of three or four, visit *The Matrix Revolutions* online and view two or three of the alternative television trailers, including "Give Anything" or "Power." Write down the main features of each trailer. How does each one function as an outline of the film's key scenes, characters, conflict, and message? What different tone or style is conveyed through the selection of imagery, the choice of music, and the emphasis on a particular plotline or character? What can you apply to your own outline strategies of arrangement? www.ablongman.com/envision059

Crafting Detailed Outlines

Avoid empty headers when creating your research outline.

Keeping the idea of the trailer in mind, take your ideas from the visual map you have created and craft them into a **formal outline,** a detailed chronological list that uses numbers and letters to indicate subsections of your argument. In doing so, try to avoid empty labels that serve no rhetorical function, such as "Introduction, Body, Conclusion." Instead, create several points within the "body" to show the development of your argument. Try using **argumentative subtitles** for each section of your outline by repeating the words of your thesis and by indicating what your rhetorical stance will be concerning each point in your outline. Finally, insert your primary source images in the outline to show how your essay will analyze an issue through a visual rhetoric lens. Lee-Ming Zen, for example, developed a formal outline from his visual map on video game character Lara Croft.

Student Writing

Anthony Bertrand's detailed outline on *The Matrix* provides a strong example to follow.
www.ablongman.com/envision060

Experimenting with Order in Outlines

As you might expect, there is no one way to order the materials into sections of your outline. Think about how most films follow a roughly chronological format: the opening scenes represent the temporal beginning of the plot, while the conclusion represents the temporal end. From *Gladiator* (2000) to the Wachowski brothers' *The Matrix Revolutions* (2003), we follow the same linear trajectory: we start at the "beginning" and end at the "end." However, some filmmakers opt for other modes of organization. In creating his film, *Memento* (2001), writer/director Christopher Nolan inverted conventional linear format

Lee-Ming Zen
Research Paper Outline
April 23, 2003
Dr. Alyssa O'Brien

Finding the Woman Who Never Was: Gender Role Exploration Through Lara Croft

I.   Introduction
    A. "Hook" line
    B. Background
    C. Thesis: By examining the various expressions of Lara Croft and the evolu-
        tion of her aesthetic character, we are offered a chance to explore the
        various cultural and sociological aspects of our understanding of gender,
        especially in relation to videogames. In particular, her evolution parallels
        the different stages of gender exploration that adolescents experience
        and struggle through. Yet, at the same time, Lara Croft is a paradox act-
        ing as an objectification of women that both stereotypes and empowers
        women by allowing anyone to explore gender through her body.
    D. Organizational hints

II. The Woman Who Never Was
    A. Origins of Lara Croft
        1. concept
        2. reasons
    B. Tomb Raider Series
        1. general information
        2. statistics to show the import and impact
    C. Schleiner's role interpretations of Lara Croft
        1. female Frankenstein
        2. drag queen
        3. dominatrix/femme fatale
        4. female role model
        5. lesbian idol
    D. University of Michigan's proposed stages of gender-role development
    E. Ideas and concepts of masculinity/femininity
        1. Girls
        2. Boys

III. Evolution of Lara Croft
    A. Version 1.0
        1. *Tomb Raider* box cover
        2. Lara Croft's features
        3. Schleiner's analysis's applications to this image
        4. Relation to Stage I in Parsons and Bryan

                                                        (continued)

Lee drafted a working title on his outline to help him focus the argument.

Lee includes a complete, detailed statement of his working thesis to guide and shape his outline.

Lee lists his argument points briefly in the body sections of his outline. If you prepare a more detailed outline, you may want to identify sources you will use to support your claims. Include quotations and page numbers.

B. Version 2.0
   1. Moustache patch image
   2. Moustache patch background and information
   3. Schleiner's analysis's applications to this image
   4. Relation to Stage II and especially Stage III in Parsons and Bryan
C. Explorative Analysis
   1. Flanagan's take
   2. Gender role exploration in Stages I-III through Lara Croft versions 1 and 2
   3. Game concept relation in gender exploration
      a) Game immersion
      b) Character identity
D. Version 4.0
   1. Version 3.0 is the same as the 2.0 engine but tweaked
      a) brief explanation of game engines
      b) lack of major change in her image
   2. A sexier Lara Croft – image analysis
   3. Analysis of changes in her image since versions 1 and 2
   4. Schleiner's analysis's applications to this image
   5. Relation to Stage III and IV in Parsons and Bryan
E. Version 6.0
   1. Concept art and the new 'realistic' look
      a) The new 'Gen-X' Lara Croft
   2. Changes since versions 1, 2, and 4
   3. Comparative analysis in regards to Schleiner and Flanagan (hopefully in order to begin tying everything back together)
   4. Relation to Stage IV and V in Parsons and Bryan
F. Explorative Analysis
   1. Gender role exploration in Stages III-V through Lara Croft versions 4 and 6
   2. Change in the trend of Lara as a parallel to the adolescent development
      a) Significance of this trend
      b) Applications of this trend to other research on gender identity, roles
   3. Game concept relation in gender exploration
      a) Game spaces
      b) Gender difference in technology use

IV. Conclusion
   A. Quick look back
   B. Overall import of these findings
   C. Further reaching impacts of this study

Indicate where your argument will lead to in your conclusion. Rather than just restate your thesis and summarize your argument, discuss the significance of your points.

by organizing his film in reverse chronological order: the opening scenes feature the chronological end of the narrative, with each consecutive scene taking one step further back in time. The audience experiences the events of the film in reverse order (from conclusion to beginning), replicating the experience of protagonist Leonard Shelby (Guy Pearce), who relies on a system of visual cues—tattoos and Polaroid photos—to chart his story (see Figure 6.6). This unique structure serves an important rhetorical purpose: as *Memento* moves viewers backward in time, it refuses to allow them any "memory" of earlier events and thereby encourages identification between the audience and the main character, a man without a memory.

FIGURE 6.6. *Memento* experiments with narrative order by creating a film that is told exclusively through a series of flashbacks.

Thematic Rather than Chronological Arrangement

Film documentaries offer us many examples of nonchronological organization which you may wish to use in your outline if you want to arrange your materials around thematic issues. For instance, if you were to visit the PBS Frontline Website to view the documentary "The Merchants of Cool," you would find the film chunked into segments. There is no chronological beginning-to-end ordering of information here; instead, the images are arranged by theme. The documentary moves from background into argument, into a complication of that argument, and then into a final example. In the initial segment, "hunting for cool," the film establishes a definition for "cool-hunting" and sets up the general research problem: how do advertisers successfully market products to teens? The next segment, "under-the-radar marketing," shifts the focus from advertising to company image, while "the mtv machine" narrows this focus to look closely at the example of MTV as a marketing tool.

Seeing Connections
For a detailed discussion of formal strategies of arrangement in papers, see Chapter 3.

Once the film has established how companies market to teens, it then complicates its research question in "the giant feedback loop," considering whether advertising creates or rather just mirrors teen culture. Finally, in "teen rebellion," the documentary reinforces its thesis, ending with the example of the band Limp Bizkit to demonstrate how even extreme materials can be successfully marketed to a mass audience. In this way, the organization functions as part of the film's argument. Structure (*form*) fits the argument (*content*).

A Closer Look
Watch Frontline's "The Merchants of Cool," paying close attention to how the argument as a whole is organized.
www.ablongman.com/envision061

AT A GLANCE

Useful Organization Strategies

- **Chronological** (relevant for historical discussions)
- **Thematic** (helps with diverse case studies)
- **Cause and effect** (focuses on consequences)
- **Illustrative** (emphasizes examples of a pattern)
- **Macro to micro** (moves from the general to the specific)
- **Micro to macro** (moves from the specific to the general)
- **Narrative** (employs the personal experience)

Organizing Your Argument

One of the benefits of outlining is that it provides the opportunity to experiment with different types of organizational structures in order to discover which one works best for your paper. Depending on your topic, you can try a variety of approaches, just as filmmakers rearrange a film in different *trailers*. Do you want to start your paper with a question, move through evidence, and then arrive at a declarative thesis statement? Or do you feel that your argument is best served by a firm thesis statement upfront, followed by an accumulation of supporting evidence that ultimately gestures toward larger, related issues? The key in organizing your paper is to consider the relationship between *form* and *content,* or the way in which your structure can facilitate your argument.

"Then you take it all—the chronology, the letters, the interviews, your own knowledge, the newspaper cuttings, the history books, the diary, the thousand hours of contemplation, and you try to make a whole of it, not a chronicle but a drama, with a beginning and an end."

—Alan Paton, on completing his biography of South African statesman Jan Hofmeyr

COLLABORATIVE CHALLENGE

Take your own outline, and, using scissors, cut it into pieces so that each main subject heading (together with its related subcategories) is on a separate piece of paper. For example, for a five-paragraph essay, you would end up with five pieces: an introduction, a piece for your first section, a piece for your second section, a piece for your third section, and a conclusion; for a research outline, you should have at least eight pieces. Be sure to cut *off* the heading numbers from each piece of paper so that there is no sense of the way the headings were originally arranged on your outline. Now shuffle your pieces so they are out of order, and give them to your collaboration partners. Have your partners reassemble the pieces in the order that they feel is most appropriate for your argument and then describe to you the reasons they ordered the information in that way. Now discuss your original organization and the rationale behind it.

You can use your formal outline to begin to experiment with the best possible ways of including research materials; it will save you a lot of time as you approach the writing process itself to insert sources right into the outline. This technique can help you troubleshoot areas where you might need to do supplemental research or expand your argument.

Working with Subheads and Transitions

Subheads are a terrific way to structure your outline and eventual essay into discrete units to show the progression of your argument and help your reader make sense of a complex argument. Subheads work particularly well for longer, research-based essays. You can transform the key parts of your outline into a short list of argumentative subheads. But don't hesitate to get creative by connecting your subheads thematically or by using a single metaphor to add a rich layer of vivid words to your essay. After you write a list of working subheads, exchange them with a partner. Suggest modifications and new ideas to each other; keep focused on using subheads as you use transitions: to advance the argument of the essay.

If you find yourself using metaphoric language in each of your subheads, then you have seen how consistency in language can help the flow of your writing. When creating **transitions,** those phrases that provide the connective tissue between paragraphs of your paper, think about how you can signal the next idea, build on the previous idea, or reiterate the key terms of your thesis as you advance your argument. Many students like to think of the game of dominos when composing transitions: each domino can only touch another domino with a matching number; two connects with two, three with three. Using this notion of progressive, connecting terms, incorporate transitions within sections of your paper to give it overall structure and flow.

AT A GLANCE

Assessing Outlines

- *Thesis:* Is it complex, contentious, and interesting?

- *Argument:* Is there a fluid progression of ideas? Does each one relate back to the thesis? Is there extraneous information that can be cut? Do more points need to be developed?

- *Sources:* Are primary sources identified for analysis in the paper? Are secondary sources listed to provide support and authority for the argument? Are there sufficient sources listed for each point? Are visual texts included as argumentative evidence?

- *Format:* Are there argumentative and interesting subtitles?

Student Writing

See creative and argumentative *subheads* inserted right in Dexian's formal outline for his project on McDonald's advertising in Asia. www.ablongman.com/envision062

Transitions work like a game of dominos.

Avoiding Plagiarism

Seeing Connections
For more discussion
on research as a con-
versation or dialogue
of sources, see
Chapter 5.

As you develop subheads and additional structuring devices for your argument, it is crucial to keep in mind the concept that you are contributing to an ongoing conversation with other scholars, critics, and people concerned about your topic. Every single one of your sources is an important participant, and when you are writing a research-based argument using a large number of texts, you need to know how to work with those sources appropriately and effectively. We like to think of working with sources as responding to people whose work we **cite**—or quote—as a way of including them in the dialogue. Think to yourself, "I speak my part, I refer to another person's view, and I provide a citation of the statement." With research papers, you are having a conversation with an entire room of people, introducing each person in turn, and serving as the moderator.

"The term 'plagiarism' came from the word *plagiarius,* which literally meant 'kidnapper.'"

—Peter Morgan and Glenn Reynolds

This notion of including your sources as people, as the cast of characters for your research paper, can help you avoid **plagiarism,** or using another person's idea as your own. The etymological origin of *plagiarism,* according to scholars Peter Morgan and Glenn Reynolds, concerns stealing someone's work. In classical times, imitation was not a crime. But with the invention of printing technology, copyright law, and a cultural emphasis on intellectual property as profitable came a concern about taking someone else's ideas—and hence their earning potential—whether intentionally or unintentionally. The consequent demand for originality in writing, which continues in academic and professional circles today, is linked to profit margins, and explains why plagiarism remains a punishable act. Understanding the history and significance of using other ideas as your own, you can better avoid the danger of taking someone's work as your own.

A Closer Look

Purdue's Online Writing Lab's page on plagiarism offers not only definitions but exercises designed to help writers identify and avoid citation problems.
www.ablongman.com/envision063

In addition to watching out for plagiarism for historical, economically based reasons, there is also an even more compelling, ethical reason for keeping the conversation model in mind. As you work with sources, realize that the claims you are able to make are in fact based on the foundation provided by others. Identifying your sources thus becomes a writing strategy that you need to implement out of respect for those who

> The writing of history is a rich process of building on the work of the past with the hope that others will build on what you have done. Through footnotes you point the way to future historians.
>
> —Doris Kearns Goodwin

have come before you. By acknowledging their names, ideas, and words, you contribute to a body of knowledge by graciously thanking those who have paved the way. So while there are legal issues related to intellectual property, copyright law, and "fair use" that you need to know about, if you keep the *respect principle* in mind, it is unlikely that you'll fall into the trap of inadvertently "stealing" someone's work.

You can get started on including your sources by name in your research paper by listing them right in your detailed outline at appropriate places. Include direct quotations where possible; don't forget to cite your sources for both paraphrase and quotations. Make sure you include the full names of your sources; cite them as people and put in page numbers wherever possible to practice responsible and respectful writing strategies.

Student Writing

Look at Matt Niles's detailed research outline including sources and quotations for his project on Abercrombie and Fitch.
www.ablongman.com/envision064

COLLABORATIVE CHALLENGE

Watch Michael Moore's *Bowling for Columbine* (2002). Together with two or three peers, create an outline for one section of the film. In other words, compose your best approximation of the outline that the film editors used, so that you can show Moore's strategic insertion of "primary" or "secondary" sources. Once you have finished, look at your outline and consider the following questions: Where does the film use primary sources? Where does it use secondary sources? How does Moore convey his own opinion? How does he respond to the secondary sources and then assert his own point of view? Have each person in the group play the role of a different character in the film in order to see the way in which the sources are real, live people.

Spotlight on Your Argument

In *Bowling for Columbine,* Michael Moore is careful to introduce and acknowledge his sources. The film relies on research in a variety of ways: as background contextual material or flashbacks, offering a context for the narrator's comments or for dramatic recreations; as actual interview segments, where a primary or secondary authority speaks directly to the reader about the issue at hand; and as quotations read from the narrator, either directly or through voice-over. But, as the promotional movie poster in Figure 6.7 suggests, he also openly voices his opinion in the film, making his rhetorical stance a prominent part of the overall text. That is, Moore emphasizes his own argument even while he includes many other voices in his film.

As you approach the writing of your paper, you will want to think about diverse ways to present your argument. To a certain degree, while your argument is at center stage, you as the writer may remain behind the scenes and still create a text that captures your unique perspective on a subject. Think of the power of a casting director on a film set. In a film such as Franco Zeffirelli's version of *Hamlet* (1990), for instance, the entire sexual politics of the narrative was influenced by the decision to cast Glenn Close (age 43 at the time) as Queen Gertrude, mother to Mel Gibson's Hamlet (Gibson was 34). Their close proximity in age set in relief an incest plot at which Shakespeare himself had only hinted. In essence, what audiences watched in the movie theater was less Shakespeare's *Hamlet* and more Zeffirelli's interpretation of it. In your own writing, you have a comparable power; the way in which you "cast" your sources can influence your reader's understanding of your argument.

FIGURE 6.7. The visual rhetoric of the promotional movie poster for *Bowling for Columbine* reveals the way Michael Moore emphasizes his own argument in the film.

In fact, your treatment of your sources will define your approach to your topic. Consider the "objectivity" of a celebrity biography on A&E; while the text purports to offer no explicit argument, the selection of quotations used, the identities of people interviewed, and the emphasis given to certain stages of the artist's career all collaborate to produce not some objective *truth,* but a single *version* of that artist's life. Or think about

Oliver Stone's *JFK* (1991) and the controversy it stirred. The film was in fact an argument: Stone built on primary and secondary evidence to create his own interpretation of the events surrounding President John Kennedy's assassination. For years after its release, *JFK* has sparked heated debate; many of the film's most vocal critics continue to argue over the validity of Stone's version of events.

Sometimes, you will want to step out of the shadows and articulate your argument more explicitly to the audience. We see this happen in "The Merchants of Cool," when narrator Douglas Rushkoff interjects his own questions at key points, designed to facilitate the audience's own understanding of the issues contained in the film, or in Moore's *Bowling for Columbine.* Whichever way you go—whether you serve as the director behind the scenes or as a character on center stage— you should decide what role you, the writer, will play in your paper. The key is to choose the role that will produce the most effective argument on your topic, one that fits the needs of your rhetorical situation. Your voice is your spotlight on your argument; it should have rhetorical purpose and complement the content of your project.

CREATIVE PRACTICE

Watch *Protesting the Protesters* through the *Envision* Website. How does the filmmaker convey his own opinion about the subject of war protest? More specifically, how does he use the interplay between image and spoken word to reproduce his argument? How does his voice-over commentary function as a spotlight developing his research argument?
www.ablongman.com/envision065

Working with Sources

After you decide on your approach to working with sources—as a strong explicit narrator or as the synthesizer of information—you need to get started actually putting this plan into complete sentences as you turn your outline into a rough draft. But how will you actually introduce and weave these other voices—your sources—into your written prose?

As you work on the balance between your sources and your own argument, you will need to include your sources not only appropriately (to avoid plagiarism) and strategically (to decide on how much of a presence you will have in the paper) but also purposefully (to provide a range of quotations and supporting evidence for your paper). We call this process **integrating sources,** and it's a complex process that occurs in three basic ways:

- **Summary** (synthesizing a great deal of information from a source)
- **Paraphrase** (putting a source quotation into your own words)
- **Direct quotation** (excerpting a specific passage from a source, enclosing it in quotation marks)

AT A GLANCE

Reasons to Use Direct Quotation

- *Evidence:* The quotation provides tangible evidence for part of your argument.
- *Ethos:* The original author is a primary source or an expert on the subject, and including a direct quotation would increase the ethos of your argument.
- *Language:* The original author used memorable phrasing or a has a particular voice that would be lost in paraphrase.

You'll want to alternate between methods while incorporating your sources with stylistic variety. This means knowing your options as a writer and selecting the best method for each rhetorical situation within your research essay. There is no single "correct" way to integrate sources. Instead, to accomplish the goal of purposeful citation with variation, you'll need to make some important choices. When should you paraphrase? Insert a direct quote? Summarize material? Your decisions will be dictated by the specific needs of each part of your argument, but there are some guidelines that you should follow.

If a quotation does not fit into any of the categories above, then consider paraphrasing or summarizing it. What you want to avoid is a paper dominated by unnecessary quotations: in such a case, your own voice—what the reader expects most in your paper—gets buried. It's sort of what happens in film when you splice together too many different scenes. The reader becomes lost in the montage and can no longer follow the narrative. If you are worried that you have integrated too many sources (and lost your own voice), then spend some time reviewing the drafts and ask yourself:

- Am I still the moderator of this conversation?
- Is my voice clear, compelling, and original?
- Do I allow my own argument to emerge as foremost in this piece?

It is possible to integrate too many sources. Ask yourself: "How much is too much?"

Ultimately, source material should *support and supplement* your own argument, not supplant it.

Integrating, Not Inserting Quotations

But how, practically, do you go about integrating sources appropriately and effectively rather than simply inserting them? To work successfully with quotations, try using the three Rs: *read, record, relate.*

While a direct splice may be a successful film technique, in argumentative writing, we need clearer signposts of transition and context. Consider the stylistic options available to you to integrate sources by reading through the quotation examples for a paper on *The Lord of the Rings.*

- **Using an introductory clause/phrase:** When you use this technique, you formally introduce the quote with a clause or phrase, one which often—but not always—refers to the author and/or the original text title. For instance:

  > Speaking of the underlying homoerotic tensions in *The Return of the King,* cultural critic Zoe Harper suggests, "*The Lord of the Rings*'s narrative climax parallels an increasing anxiety about the intimacy of Frodo and Sam's relationship, which it defuses through its recuperative emphasis on Sam's marriage and children at the end of the film" (88).

- **Using an incorporated structure:** Writers using this strategy meld the quotation into their own sentence seamlessly so that it flows smoothly with the rest of their prose. For example:

  > As *The Return of the King* moves to its conclusion, the relationship between Frodo and Sam comes increasingly to resemble a romantic one—from the

AT A GLANCE

How to Integrate Sources Appropriately and Effectively

- *Read.* Read a text carefully and actively, underlining passages that move you or suggest moments of deep meaning, or passages that might contribute to your argument/interpretation. If you are working with online texts, cut and paste the citation into a word document, noting the paragraph number (for Websites) or page number (for regular texts) in parentheses. Always keep track of the page number and source information if you transcribe citations as you read.

  You'll need this part in order to provide the citation in your writing.

- *Record.* Keep a notebook or an annotated computer file of quotes in which you *record* your reactions to a particular passage you've read. Does this passage move you? How so? Does it reveal the theme of the text, the climax of the scene, the point of the argument, the purpose of the passage? Always engage critically with a citation, developing your reason for including it later.

  You'll need this part in order to provide your interpretation of the citation.

- *Relate.* Place the citation, and your interpretation, in an appropriate place in your essay. Where in the paragraph should the quotation and the comment appear? What is around it, above it, after it? Make sure that you *relate* the inserted text to the material which precedes and follows your citation + integration. Never just "stick in a quote" without explanation and strategic placement.

  You'll need this part in order to achieve the most successful quotation integration.

hobbits' obvious affection for one another to Sam's rivalry with Gollum for Frodo's affections—a resemblance that the film ultimately "defuses through its recuperative emphasis on Sam's marriage and children at the end of the film" (Harper 88).

■ **Using an interrupted structure:** In this variation on the above models, the writer breaks the quote into two halves, embedding information regarding the author and/or the original text in the middle of the quotation itself. Here is an illustration of this technique:

> "*The Lord of the Rings*'s narrative climax parallels an increasing anxiety about the intimacy of Frodo and Sam's relationship," cultural critic Zoe Harper suggests, "which it defuses through its recuperative emphasis on Sam's marriage and children at the end of the film" (88).

■ **Using an end comment:** In this technique, writers insert the quotation and then provide an interpretation, or closing comment, in order to advance the argument:

> Cultural critic Zoe Harper's claim that *The Return of the King*'s "narrative climax parallels an increasing anxiety about the intimacy of Frodo and Sam's relationship" (88) has added relevance when considered in context of the larger genre of male "buddy" movies designed to appeal to a predominantly male, heterosexual audience.

Notice that in this case, you place the page number at the end of the quotation and before your own argument begins in order to distinguish between Harper's ideas and your own. In this way, you build on the work of others, advancing knowledge and giving credit, but also emphasizing your own unique contribution.

Experiment with these different strategies in your own writing to determine which best serves your rhetorical purpose. For instance, if you wanted to draw attention to the *author* of a quotation, to add ethos to your argument, you might opt to integrate using an introductory clause such as the one above; however, if you wanted to emphasize *information*, rather than

AT A GLANCE

Final Check for Integrating Sources

• Did you . . . introduce the quote in various ways?

• Did you . . . link the reference to your argument to show the relevance?

• Did you . . . comment on it afterwards to advance your argument?

• Did you . . . cite it properly using the appropriate documentation style for your subject area?

authorship, an incorporated structure might be more effective. One key to remember is to avoid overusing any one type of integration strategy; otherwise your writing style might become too monotonous, like a film that relies too heavily on the same types of shots.

Documentation During Integration

As you incorporate sources into your draft, be sure to include correct parenthetical citations for each quotation or paraphrase. This would also be a good time to begin drafting your works cited list or bibliography, to save time later. While you might be tempted to view the construction of such a list as an imposition or a waste of time, realize that the purpose is not only to provide a "list of credits" for your references, but also to provide interested readers the resources to continue learning about your topic. Just as you undoubtedly found certain articles inspiring while investigating your topic and used them as springboards for more focused research, so too might your paper serve as a similar means of leading your readers to intriguing ideas and articles.

Use a recent handbook, such as the *MLA Handbook for the Writers of Research Papers* or *The Penguin Handbook,* to help you format both your parenthetical citations and your source lists according to the method specified in your assignment.

COLLABORATIVE CHALLENGE

To check if you need to cite information you've paraphrased, or if you are worried about citing information that is "common knowledge," ask your roommate or your peer reviewer to assess your outline or draft. Any passage that stands out as unfamiliar should be marked with a highlighter. Then, return the favor by examining your reader's work-in-progress with highlighter in hand. You can help point out to your peers what knowledge is most probably not readily available to you (or other readers) without the help of sources. Your peer reviewers can also point out material that *is* "common knowledge" and doesn't need to be cited.

Effective Arrangement of Visual Evidence

Since you are using visual material as a crucial component of your argument—whether as the subject of analysis or as supporting evidence for your claims—it is important that you incorporate visuals into your essay in a rhetorically effective manner. Give careful consideration to issues of arrangement and style as you decide how to

A Closer Look

Michael Goldberg's Website "Some Suggestions on 'How to Read a Film,'" offers an extremely useful overview of specific terminology involved in film criticism as well as a bibliography and a list of links.

www.ablongman.com/envision066

integrate your visual evidence. How do the placement and presentation of images affect your overall persuasiveness? How does your strategic use of visuals shape the force of your own argument about the power of visual rhetoric? These questions are constantly on the minds of filmmakers as they splice and edit their work. Their arrangement of images directly determines the nature of the message conveyed to the audience and transforms the nature of the cinematic experience.

If in a crime drama, for instance, you insert an image identifying a murderer at the *end* of the film, you create a mystery, such as in *The Usual Suspects* (1995), where the viewers' experience is one of suspense and finally gratification as the narrative carries them through the story to a final moment of visual revelation. However, think about what a different film *The Usual Suspects* would have been had the question *"Who Is Keyser Soze?"* been answered early in the movie, perhaps by a well-placed flashback. In that case, the filmmaker could have produced a very different type of suspense and a different type of movie (a thriller), where the viewer, allowed the privileged "who-dunnit" information early on, could have watched the film with greater attention, anxiety, and appreciation. But it was precisely Bryan Singer's decision to delay the visual revelation to the film's conclusion that created such an impression with the cinematic audiences across the United States. We, as viewers, encounter the suspects seen in Figure 6.8 at the beginning of the movie and need to wrestle through the narrative alongside U.S. Customs Special Agents (see Figure 6.9).

FIGURE 6.8. The line-up from *The Usual Suspects* (1995), an image which confronts the viewer from the beginning, creating a sense of suspense in the audience.

FIGURE 6.9. This image prompts viewer identification with U.S. Customs Agent Dave Kujan (Chazz Palminteri) and Police Officer Sergeant Jeffrey Rabin (Dan Hedaya) as they try to solve the murder mystery.

Visually, the film holds back information until the end, when the cinematography itself uncovers the truth of the "thriller."

Placing Images in a Paper

As a writer, you can take the lead from film and increase the persuasive power of your own images by *arranging* and *integrating* them deliberately, or with **rhetorical purpose.** In academic writing, we accomplish this through strategic placement of visual evidence and through use of effective signposts and captions. First of all, think about the *placement* of your images: Will you put them in an appendix? on your title page? on a separate page? on the same page as your general exposition? Each decision is both a stylistic and rhetorical choice. An image placed in an appendix tends to be viewed as supplementary, not as integral to an argument; an image on a title page might act as an epigraph to set a mood for a paper, but it is less effective as a specific visual example. If you want to use your images as *argumentative evidence,* you need to show them to your reader as you analyze them; placing them beside the words of your argument will be the most successful strategy.

Once you have determined the placement that best serves your rhetorical purpose, you need to insert the image effectively. Like a quotation, an image cannot be dropped into a text without comment; it needs to be connected to your argument through deliberate textual markers. You can accomplish this through making *explicit references* to the image and even taking the time to explain the visual rhetoric for the reader. Your analysis of its meaning will advance your own argument by persuading readers to see the image as you do, rather than make alternative interpretations which might conflict with the point of your paper. You should also include a **textual reference** to the image within your prose, such as "see Figure 1." Moreover, it's necessary to draft a **caption** for the image that reiterates the relationship between the point you are making in the paper and the visual evidence you include. Most important, however, is your analysis of the image in the actual writing

> Be careful not to assume that an image "speaks for itself." Be sure to analyze it for the reader.

AT A GLANCE

Integrating Images

- *Placement and Arrangement:* Where should you position the image in your paper to achieve your rhetorical purpose? In the text, side by side with your argument, or with another image? as part of an appendix? on a cover page?

- *Textual Reference:* Have you referred to the image in the prose of your argument and drawn out your interpretation of the text? Just as you would explicate the lines of a poem for your reader, make sure to explain the significance and details of an image that you use as evidence in your essay.

- *Captions:* Have you included the key elements: figure number, descriptive or argumentative explanation, and complete source information for the image?

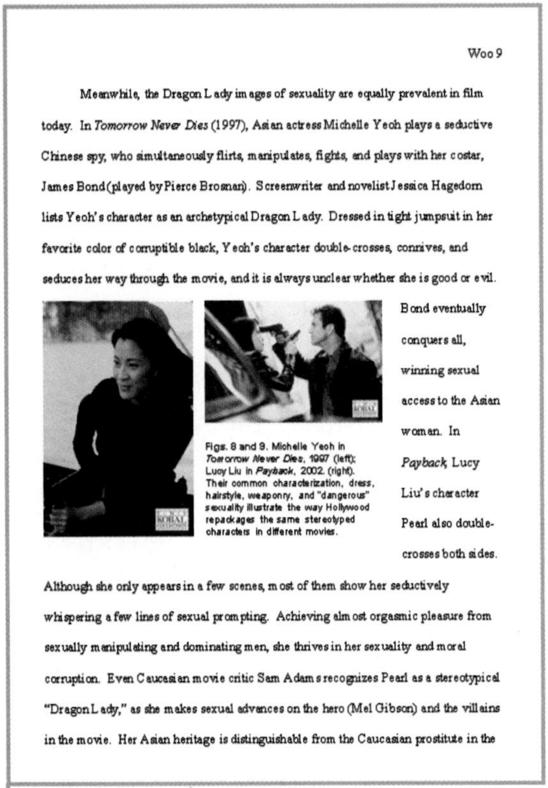

Woo 9

Meanwhile, the Dragon Lady images of sexuality are equally prevalent in film today. In *Tomorrow Never Dies* (1997), Asian actress Michelle Yeoh plays a seductive Chinese spy, who simultaneously flirts, manipulates, fights, and plays with her costar, James Bond (played by Pierce Brosnan). Screenwriter and novelist Jessica Hagedorn lists Yeoh's character as an archetypical Dragon Lady. Dressed in tight jumpsuit in her favorite color of corruptible black, Yeoh's character double-crosses, connives, and seduces her way through the movie, and it is always unclear whether she is good or evil.

Figs. 8 and 9. Michelle Yeoh in *Tomorrow Never Dies*, 1997 (left); Lucy Liu in *Payback*, 2002 (right). Their common characterization, dress, hairstyle, weaponry, and "dangerous" sexuality illustrate the way Hollywood repackages the same stereotyped characters in different movies.

Bond eventually conquers all, winning sexual access to the Asian woman. In *Payback*, Lucy Liu's character Pearl also double-crosses both sides.

Although she only appears in a few scenes, most of them show her seductively whispering a few lines of sexual prompting. Achieving almost orgasmic pleasure from sexually manipulating and dominating men, she thrives in her sexuality and moral corruption. Even Caucasian movie critic Sam Adams recognizes Pearl as a stereotypical "Dragon Lady," as she makes sexual advances on the hero (Mel Gibson) and the villains in the movie. Her Asian heritage is distinguishable from the Caucasian prostitute in the

FIGURE 6.10. Allison Woo, "Slaying the Dragon: The Struggle to Reconcile Modern Asian Identity with Depictions of Asian Women in Past and Present American Film," page 9, showcases visual and verbal arguments working together.

of your paper; don't hide the meaning of the image in the caption. The visual and verbal need to work together as a strategy of persuasion.

A page from student Allison Woo's paper on Asian-American female stereotypes in contemporary cinema provides an example of effective placement and captioning of visuals (see Figure 6.10). Allison has inserted two images into a paragraph in which she analyzes female stereotypes in two films: *Tomorrow Never Dies* (1997) and *Payback* (1999). Notice how, rather than relegating these images to an appendix, Allison made the most of their rhetorical force by positioning the images into the paragraph itself and, therefore, making the visual an integral part of the argument. Furthermore, she has arranged the visuals so that they are in dialogue with one another, reproducing the comparison that is the purpose of her paragraph. In this way, the two figures function effectively as visual evidence for her argument: the striking similarity in pose, costume, and demeanor between actresses Lucy Liu and Michelle Yeoh substantiate Allison's points about the prominence of the "Dragon Lady" stereotype in popular American films.

Allison's caption is also worth noting: she lists the necessary information (figure numbers, descriptive titles, names of the actresses and films, and the year of release), and sources for the images. She comments on the relevance of the images to her larger argument, explaining the relationship between specific and more general cinematic trends that the paragraph itself explores. The caption, without directly paraphrasing part of the argument, reinforces its central point. Through this successful union of word and image, Allison greatly increases the persuasiveness of her argument.

COLLABORATIVE CHALLENGE

Working with a new group of peer reviewers, exchange drafts that include visuals without captions. Have each group member suggest different captions for the pictures. Discuss how they differ and which one works best rhetorically in relation to the surrounding paragraph and also to your larger argument.

Citing Sources of Visual Images

When you decide to integrate visuals in your writing, you need to spend a few moments thinking about issues of copyright and permissions whether you are dealing with images or print quotations, you are using materials produced or prepared by another person and you must give that person credit for the work. In some cases—particularly if you plan to publish your work—you also need to obtain permission to use it.

As you read (or browse through catalogs of images), you need to record the source of the image. If you have copied an image from the Web (by right clicking and choosing "Save Picture As"), you need to include as much of the full source information as you can find: the Website author, the title, the sponsoring organization, the date. If you have found visuals (photographs, charts, ads) from print sources and scanned them into a computer in order to insert them into your essay, then you need to list the print source in full as well as information about the original image (the name of the photographer, the image title, and the date). Keep careful track as you locate images, give appropriate credit when you use them in your essay, and ask for permission if necessary.

To document images, include full source information in the caption itself or prepare a list of figures for the Works Cited list.

Seeing Connections
For specific suggestions on ways to begin a research log, see Chapter 4.

"Information graphics—tables, charts, graphs, and maps—use our powerful abilities of visual discrimination to compare, notice trends, and understand complex relationships among parts."
—Susan Hilligoss

Graphs, Charts, and Statistical Data

Depending on the topic of your research paper, you may also find it necessary to include informational graphics—tables, graphs or charts—as visual evidence. While you should select, place, and cite them with as much care as you would visual images, also take some time to consider their power as seemingly objective arguments. Such texts are in fact ways of

A Closer Look

Edward Tufte's many books explore through visually stimulating pages the way in information graphics can be conveyed effectively and responsibly; see *The Visual Display of Quantitative Information* (Graphics Press, 2001) and *Visual Explanations: Images and Quantities, Evidence and Narrative* (Graphics Press, 1997).

Seeing Connections
Consult Chapter 5 for guidance on using data properly from social psychology professors who work with statistics.

graphically interpreting statistics and other data. Whether you are inserting an information graphic from one of your sources or designing your own, keep in mind the ways in which your choice of selection or design will contribute to the kind of argument the information graphic will make.

Moreover, as you insert information graphics, keep in mind the need to present the data itself clearly and without too much distraction from the visual presentation strategies of your graphics. As Edward Tufte, the contemporary document design guru, reminds us in his book, *The Visual Display of Quantitative Information,* a little design goes a long way; the image should impart the information and not overshadow the meaning of any statistics or data that you might use as evidence for your argument.

Student Writing

For a rigorous examination of the way in which charts, graphics, and visual representations of financial data function rhetorically, read student Eric Adamson's prize-winning essay, "Malleability, Misrepresentation, Manipulation: The Rhetoric of Images in Economic Forecasting."
www.ablongman.com/envision067

Drafting Your Research Argument

As you continue to forge ahead with your research argument, turning from an outline to a full draft or composing sections of your argument in separate time blocks, realize that there are many strategies for getting it done.

Keeping Your Passion

As you move deeper into the writing process, integrating quotations and working out the flow of your argument, don't lose sight of your enthusiasm for your subject. Reread your earliest freewrites and your entries in your research log. What goals, what motivations prompted you to begin the project? What aspects of your topic excited you, angered you, or inspired you? What contribution did you imagine yourself making to this discussion? As you begin synthesizing your information and creating a unified argument, you are in effect realizing that initial vision. Remember, your reader will be reading your paper in order to learn *your* particular point of view on the subject. Your drafts are your shooting scripts, if you will, the versions of your paper that ultimately you will transform through careful review, editing, and revision, into your "release" of the text into final form.

You should also allow yourself well-needed energy breaks. Brief time periods away from the writing process can often recharge and

"Almost all writers are familiar with the experience of feeling stuck, blocked, overwhelmed, or behind schedule in their writing."

—David Rasch

AT A GLANCE

Strategies for Drafting

- *Following the linear path:* Start at the beginning, writing the introduction and then moving sequentially through the first draft of the paper.

- *Fleshing out the outline:* Gradually transform the outline into a full draft, moving from a keyword outline to a prose outline by systematically expanding each of the sections; as you add more detail, the keywords fall away, leaving behind drafted paragraphs.

- *Writing from the middle:* Start writing from a point of greatest strength or start with a section you can complete easily. Then write around it and fill out sections as you go.

- *Freewrite then reverse outline:* First, produce pages of freewriting; then compose a detailed **reverse outline** where you record the point of every paragraph to assess the argument's flow and structure; finally, reorder and rewrite the paper multiple times until it begins to take the proper form for the argument.

For each of these ways of working, the key is to start, and keep writing.

reinvigorate your approach to the paper and help you think through difficult points in the argument. Ironically, a pause in drafting can also help you avoid writer's block by allowing you to remember what interests you about this project in the first place. Finally, if you are having trouble getting through the draft process, allow yourself to write what Anne Lamott author of *Bird by Bird,* famously calls the "shitty first draft." This first version is by no means perfect or even close to what the final paper will look like. It is instead a written attempt at getting your ideas on paper. Freeing yourself to write something—anything—can help you escape from the weight of perfectionism or the fear of failure that often paralyzes writers. You will have plenty of opportunities to rework the material, show your draft to others, and move forward with the writing process.

> " . . . shitty first drafts. All good writers write them. This is how they end up with good second drafts and terrific third drafts."
>
> —Anne Lamott

Making the Most of Collaboration

As you work through your draft, take advantage of the community of writers in your class to talk through your ideas and share work in progress. You might find your organizational plan confirmed by your peers, or you might be pleasantly surprised by their ideas for alternative structures, ways of integrating sources, or suggestions for images

"Each episode of the *The Simpsons* is a collaborative process. We work on every script in teams of 11 to 19 people."

—John Collier, Greg Daniels, and Paul Lieberstein

to include in the paper. Such discussions can help you get back your fire for your project as well as give you extremely useful advice to implement in the writing of the draft. Moreover, your peers' responses to your work in progress can help you determine if your writing is effectively persuasive or not.

Consider how collaboration works in the film industry. Even though a film is generally recognized as a unified expression of a single idea, in actuality it is the product of the collaborative effort of dozens of individuals, from the screenwriter and actors, to the key grips and camera operators. But there is another, often less recognized collaborator: the audience. Think about how novels are adapted to the large screen: whether by adding a romantic subplot or substituting a "Hollywood ending" for a less palatable one, many scriptwriters deliberately revise original texts to accommodate the perceived desires of a mass audience. Sometimes an entire narrative is recast to make it more marketable; the 1995 hit, *Clueless*, is a good example of film in which an early nineteenth-century classic—*Emma* by Jane Austen—was updated to appeal to a mainstream twentieth-century audience.

A Closer Look

On the *Envision* Website, you'll find peer review forms designed to guide your writing group partners through key questions in response to your draft.
www.ablongman.com/envision068

Seeing Connections
For a detailed discussion and visual representation of the rhetorical situation, see Chapter 1.

A Closer Look

In "Mass Marketing Jane Austen: Men, Women, and Courtship in Two Film Adaptations," literary critic Deborah Kaplan analyzes the way two recent film adaptations of *Emma* and *Sense and Sensibility* modified the plot out of consideration for the perceived desires of the twentieth-century mass audience.

Sometimes the audience's intervention is more direct. It is common practice for many filmmakers to hold "advance screenings" of major releases, designed to gauge audience reaction. In 1986, a preview audience's reaction to the ending of the film *Fatal Attraction* was so negative that director Adrian Lyne reshot the final scenes. When the film was released in the following year, it featured a markedly different conclusion. Similarly, the version of *BladeRunner* released in 1982 was significantly edited in an attempt to increase its box-office appeal; however, in this case, director Ridley Scott changed the ending yet again years later, releasing his *BladeRunner—The Director's Cut* eleven years after the movie first appeared. In each case, collaboration shaped the final version and made evident the rhetorical triangle between audience, writer, and text. Similarly, writing needs to take into consideration the audience's expectations; we write or make films to show an audience our work, so we need to respond to audience needs when we write and revise our texts.

CREATIVE PRACTICE

Watch *BladeRunner (1982)* and *BladeRunner—The Director's Cut* (1993). Take notes to record the differences between the two films. Then consider how the differences in editing changed the underlying message of "the film." If you are familiar with the original novel, Philip K. Dick's *When Androids Dream of Electric Sheep* (1968), you might explore how the plot of that novel was adapted to accommodate the demands of a 1980s viewing audience. If you were directing a new version today, how might you change the ending for a twenty-first-century audience? Now, consider how a research-based argument on these texts would need to discuss such differences in audience as well as attend to the paper's own audience. What if you were writing your essay for an academic audience? for a circle of film critics? for a scientific forum on robotics? Brainstorm about differences you'd make in style, use of evidence, and argument.

"A rhetorician, I take it, is like one voice in a dialogue. Put several such voices together, with each voicing its own special assertion, let them act upon one another in cooperative competition, and you get a dialectic that, properly developed, can lead to the views transcending the limitations of each."
—Kenneth Burke

As the Creative Practice suggests, as a writer you can also benefit from "advance screenings" of your work; the collaborative work you do on the structure and content of your outlines and drafts should guide you to a revised product that satisfies both you and your audience. But to do so, you need feedback from your audience in the form of peer review; then you will need to revise your draft to accommodate the suggestions you receive.

Revising Your Draft

As many professional writers can attest, a text goes through numerous drafts on its way to becoming a polished final product. Even filmmakers produce multiple drafts of their movies before they release their film, experimenting with different sequencing, camera shots, and pacing to create what they consider to be the fulfillment of their artistic vision. We've all seen the by-products of this process: **outtakes** from popular film or television programs. What these segments represent are moments of work (writing, producing, and shooting) which, after review and editing, were removed to streamline the film.

"If writing must be a precise form of communication, it should be treated like a precision instrument. It should be sharpened, and it should not be used carelessly."
—Theodore M. Bernstein

Sometimes it's difficult to reshape your work during revision; it's hard to leave some of your writing behind on the cutting room floor. However, as your project develops, its focus may change: sources or ideas that seemed important to you during the early stages of research may become less relevant, even tangential; a promising strategy of argumentation may turn out to be less suitable to your project; a key transition may be no longer necessary once you reorganize the argument. As you turn to your draft with a critical eye, what you should find is that in order to transform your paper into the best possible written product, you'll need to move beyond proofreading or editing, and into the realm of macro changes, or **revision.**

That's not to suggest that proofreading is not a necessary part of the revision process; it is. Careless grammatical and punctuation errors and spelling mistakes can damage your ethos as an author, and they need to be corrected. It is very probable that you've been doing such microrevision throughout the drafting process—editing for style, grammar, punctuation, and spelling. However, sometimes it's difficult to do *broader revisions* until you have a substantial part of your paper written. It is only once your argument starts coming together that you can recognize the most productive ways to modify it in order to optimize its effectiveness. This is the key to successful revision: you have to be open *both* to microediting and to large-scale, multiple revisions. It is probable that you will go through two or three different cycles of revision; it also is quite probable that your finished product may look substantially different from your first version. What you need to do as a writer is to evaluate the strengths and weaknesses of your essay and revise accordingly. Think of this process as **re-vision,** or seeing it again with new eyes, seeing it in a new light.

In addition to your own assessment of your writing, you also should take into account **peer evaluation** of your drafts; consider your peer review ses-

> "Writing and rewriting are a constant search for what one is saying."
>
> —John Updike

AT A GLANCE

Questions for Assessing Your Draft

- *Argument consistency:* Are your introduction and conclusion arguing the same points, or have you changed your argument by the end? Either revise the end to be consistent with your original thinking, or embrace your new vision and rework the beginning.

- *Organization and progression:* Does your paper flow logically, developing one idea seamlessly into the next? Do you provide important theoretical foundations, definitions, or background at the beginning of the paper to guide the audience through the rest of your argument?

- *Your voice versus sources:* Do you foreground your own argument in your paper or do you focus primarily on your sources' arguments, locating your point of view primarily in the conclusion? If the latter is true, bring your voice out more in commentaries on the quotations.

- *Information:* Are there any holes in your research? Do you need to supplement your evidence with additional research, interviews, surveys, or other source materials?

- *Opposition and concession:* Do you adequately address opposing arguments? Do you integrate your opposition into your argument (i.e., deal with them as they arise), or have you constructed a single paragraph in which you deal with opposing opinion?

sions "advance screenings" with your audience. Sometimes you'll find that your peer reviewers vocalize ideas that echo your own concerns about your draft; other times, you may be surprised by their reactions. Do keep in mind that their comments are informed *suggestions,* not mandates; your task, as the writer, is to assess the feedback you receive and implement those changes that seem to best address the needs of both your argument and your audience. As with any filmmaker looking to transform a creative vision into a box-office hit, you want to reach your audience, but not sacrifice your own voice or argument in doing so.

One way to facilitate a productive peer session is to use directed peer review questions for one-on-one discussions of your draft, rather than to rely exclusively on oral comments. When exchanging drafts with a peer group, you also may find it helpful to attach a covering memo that points your readers to specific questions you have about your draft so that they can customize their responses to address the particular issues that concern you as a writer.

COLLABORATIVE CHALLENGE

Form peer review groups to exchange the drafts of your research papers. Read your peer review partners' papers carefully, annotating them with **constructive feedback,** or positively framed suggestions about what might be changed and why. You might also complete the questions from the Checklist for Peer-editing the First Draft on the *Envision* Website. Then, meet with your group and talk about both the strengths in the papers and suggestions for improvement. Next, go back to your computer and revise your paper. Bring a new version to class and exchange your second draft with a group composed of one new reader and one reader who was part of your group for the first draft. Again, read the drafts and write comments on them. This time, complete the questions on *Envision's* Website for the Checklist for Peer-editing the Second Draft. Meet with your group and consider carefully the responses from both your new reader and your repeat reviewer. What do the suggestions have in common? How has your revision strengthened your argument? What further revisions do your peers suggest? Finally, discuss the extent to which audience feedback factors into your revision process.

www.ablongman.com/envision069

AT A GLANCE

Revising Your Own Draft

1. *Read your essay out loud* or have someone read it to you. You can hear mistakes and inconsistencies that you unknowingly skipped over when reading silently.

2. *Gain critical distance.* Put your essay away for a few hours, or even a few days, so that you can come back to it fresh.

3. *Answer peer review questions* for your own essay.

4. *Don't be chained to your monitor.* Print out your draft, making revisions by hand. We conceptualize information differently on paper vs. on a screen.

5. *Use your computer* to help you look at your writing in different ways. Take a paragraph and divide it into distinct sentences, which you line up one under another. Look for patterns (repetition: deliberate or accidental?), style issues (variety in sentence structure?), and fluidity of transitions between sentences.

6. *Take into account feedback* even if it initially doesn't seem significant. You might not decide to act on the advice, but at least consider it before dismissing it.

7. *Revise out of order.* Choose paragraphs at random and look at them individually, or, begin at the end. Sometimes our conclusions are the weakest simply because we always get to them last, when we're tired; start revisions with your conclusion first.

8. *Look at the whole of revision.* As you correct mistakes or prose problems, consider the impact that the revision makes on the rest of the essay. Sometimes it is possible just to add a missing comma or substitute in a more precise verb, but often you need to revise more than just the isolated problem so that the sentence/paragraph/ essay as a whole continues to "fit" and flow together.

Revision as a Continual Process

Sometimes, we may continue to revise our paper even after we have "finished." Think back to our earlier *BladeRunner* example and how Ridley Scott revised the film for re-release years after its first showing. Similarly, while you may be satisfied with your final research product when you turn it in, it is possible that you have set the groundwork for a longer research project that you may return to later in your college career. Or, you may decide to seek publication for your essay in a school newspaper, magazine, or a national journal. In such cases, you may need to modify or expand on your argument for this new rhetorical situation; you may produce your own "director's cut," a paper identical in topic to the original but developed in a significantly different fashion. Keep in mind that revision is indeed "re-vision," and that *all writing is re-writing.*

All work is
work-in-progress.

Focusing on Your Project

In this chapter, you have learned strategies for visual mapping, organizing, outlining, drafting, and revising your research paper. You have explored ways of casting your argument and acquired concrete methods for integrating both written sources and visual texts as evidence for your argument. Chances are you have written the first full draft of your paper. Feel free to approach these writer's tasks creatively, such as creating a hypertext outline or packaging your research paper electronically on a CD-ROM with links to visual material such as film clips, advertisement videos, or audio files. Your work as a writer has only just started, and the "premiere" of your project awaits.

PREWRITING CHECKLIST
Analyzing Film and Documentary

❏ Assess the genre of the film (comedy? horror? drama? film noire? documentary?) and how this affects the audience's response to its content. Does the film combine elements of different genres? What is the rhetorical effect of this hybridization?

❏ What is the plot of the film—what is the organizational structure?

❏ How is this plot arranged? chronologically? in parallel sequences? thematically? What is the rhetorical significance of arrangement?

❏ What is the message conveyed to the reader? Is it persuasive or informative? Is this message conveyed through reliance on pathos, logos, or ethos?

❏ How is the ethos of the filmmaker conveyed to the audience?

❏ What notable types of shots does the filmmaker use? Jot down one or two instances where cinematic technique (zoom-in, cuts between scenes, fade in/fade out, montage) are used for rhetorical effect.

❏ Is there a narrator in the film? voice-over? What is the effect on the audience?

❏ Is there any framing, a way of setting the beginning and end in context?

❏ How is time handled? Does the film move in chronological order? reverse chronological order? What is the significance of such rhetorical choices on the meaning and power of the film? Are flashbacks used in the film? What effect is achieved through use of flashbacks?

❏ How are pathos, ethos, and logos produced by the different cinematic techniques? For instance, is pathos created through close-ups of characters? Is ethos created through allusions to famous film or filmmaking techniques? Is logos constructed through the insertion of a narrator's viewpoint?

❏ What is the audience's point of identification in the film? Is the audience supposed to identify with a single narrator? Does the film negotiate the audience's reaction in any specific ways? How?

❏ How is setting used to construct a specific mood that affects the impact of the message of the film?

(continued)

❏ Is the film an adaptation of another work, a play or a novel? To the best of your knowledge, what modifications where made to customize the narrative for a cinematic audience? Does the text-as-film differ in content or message from the text in its original form? Can you see traces of revision and rewriting?

WRITING PROJECTS

Visit the *Envision* Website for expanded assignment guidelines and student projects.

1. **Visual representation of your research materials**

   Create a visual representation of your argument. This can be in the form of a bubble map, a flowchart, a hierarchal set of bubbles, a storyboard, or a handmade construction paper model. Give your ideas some kind of shape before turning to the outline. Try to write an annotation for each part of your drawing, model, or storyboard in order to help you move from mass of material to coherent research-based essay.

2. **Detailed formal outline with images and sources**

   Working with your research materials and notes, create a written outline of your ideas, using numbers and letters to indicate subsections of your argument. Avoid the following: *I. Introduction, II. Body, III. Conclusion.* Instead, create several points within the "body" to show the development of your argument. You may want to start with a topic outline, but ideally you should aim for argumentative headings. Include your working thesis statement at an appropriate place in your outline and include visuals that you will analyze in the essay itself. After you draft the outline once, go back and insert your primary source images in the outline to show how your research paper will analyze an issue through a visual rhetoric lens. Finally, add material from your sources at appropriate places. Include direct quotations where possible; don't forget to cite your sources for both paraphrase and quotations. Make sure you include the full names and page numbers for your sources wherever you can.

3. **The visual research-based argument paper**

   Write a 12-15-page argumentative research paper on a visual rhetoric-oriented topic. Consider the images that shape a debate, tell a certain history, or persuade an audience in a certain way. In other words, address an issue through a visual rhetoric lens. You should integrate visuals as well as research materials that can include articles, books, interviews, field research, surveys (either published or that you conduct yourself), TV programs, Internet texts, and other primary and secondary sources. Keep in mind that, since this is a research paper, you need a balance between both primary and secondary materials. In addition, you should use both electronic and paper sources. Ultimately, your goal should be prove a thesis statement with apt evidence, integrating visuals and using appropriate rhetorical and argumentative strategies.

FOR ADDED CHALLENGE

 Visit the *Envision* Website for expanded assignment guidelines and student projects.

1. **Annotated visual outline with source quotations**
   Take the formal outline with images described in Writing Project 2 one step further and insert actual quotations (with page numbers) from your research sources. Additionally, write captions with argumentative blurbs for each of your images. This annotated outline might easily turn into the prose outline or even the paper itself. Use it to check the balance of sources, the progression of ideas, and the complexity of your argument.

2. **Electronic research paper with active links, film, clips, multimedia**
   Transform the visual research-based argument paper (Writing Project 3) into electronic format, taking advantage of the rhetorical possibilities of this medium. Create either a Microsoft word document or a Web page with active embedded links, or film clips, audio, use of color, graphics, etc. as appropriate to your topic. Turn this paper in on CD-ROM or in the form of a Website on the World Wide Web.

3. **Cover page and self-reflection cover letter**
   After you have completed your essay, create a cover page for your research paper with a title, a key image, a one-paragraph abstract, and a "bio" of yourself as a writer. Then, attach to the back of the essay a one-page reflection letter that serves as a self-evaluation. Reflect back on your research process and the development of your argument through research and revision. Include comments on the strengths of the essay, the types of revisions you made throughout your writing process, and how the collaborative process of peer review improved your essay. Your might want to close by looking ahead to how you can continue to write about this issue in future projects and in future academic or professional situations.

CHAPTER 6 ON THE WEB

Resources and Readings	Exercises and Assignments	Student Writing
• Closer Look links	• Outlining and peer review exercises	• Detailed research outlines
• Tools for visual mapping, outlining, citing sources	• Detailed outline guidelines	• Visual outlines
• Links to sources for avoiding plagiarism	• Directions for the visual research-based argument	• Research papers on variety of topics
• Links to film, trailer, and storyboard galleries	• Peer Review forms	• Cover pages and "bios" of completed research papers
• Annotated readings	• Focus on diverse learners	• Self-reflection letters
• Visual mapping exercises	• Visual maps, cluster webs, graphic brainstorms	

Alternative Energy for W[?]

25% of U.S. power will be produced from 75 million lbs. of **uranium** taken[...]

However, most homes on the Navajo Reservation are withou[...]

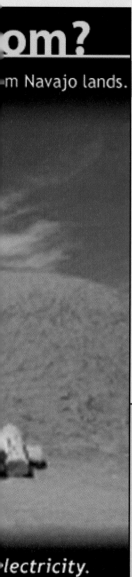

om?

m Navajo lands.

lectricity.

g our Environment

To use multimedia technologies effectively, writers
have to use practices that are not just verbal but visual,
spatial, aural, and gestural to make meaning.

—Mary Hocks

Composing Presentations

R hetoric evolved as a technique in classical Greece for teaching people how to speak both eloquently and persuasively in public. Today, we turn to rhetoric to learn how to shape any text, including verbal, visual, or written communication. But there does come a point when these different ways of communicating intersect. Think of the famous "I Have a Dream" speech delivered by Dr. Martin Luther King, Jr. This powerful rhetorical moment did not derive solely from the written script. As the image in Figure 7.1 demonstrates, it was the convergence of well-crafted language, passionate delivery, and deliberate gesture and posture that combined to produce that landmark articulation of the civil rights movement. You might look to King and other powerful orators as models for effective presentation strategies as you consider sharing your ideas with a broader audience. At the end of a class, for instance, you may be asked to create a speech or visual presentation to communicate your research argument to the entire class. Alternatively, you may wish to communicate your argument to a public audience of concerned citizens, student activists, or community professionals. To do so, you'll need to develop strategies for designing, delivering, and documenting effective oral and multimedia presentations.

FIGURE 7.1. Martin Luther King, Jr. acknowledges the crowd at the Lincoln Memorial with a gesture during his "I Have a Dream" speech in Washington, DC, August 28, 1963.

Chapter Preview Questions

- What are my presentation options?
- How do audience and purpose shape my choices?
- What multimedia texts can I use?
- How can I transform a written argument into a visual, spoken presentation?
- When should I use a speech, a poster session, a PowerPoint show, or a live performance?
- What strategies of design and delivery will help me?
- How can I include the rhetoric of gesture and embodied rhetoric?
- How can the canons of memory and delivery help my presentation?

Possibilities for Presentations

We see presentations all the time—from a professor's PowerPoint lecture to a sorority's campaign for new recruits—and they can take all sorts of forms, from formal "pitches" aimed at executives in a business meeting to carefully staged performance art in community centers. A doctor sharing the results of a ground-breaking study will not only write a paper for publication, but he or she will present those findings at a national conference. A politician will not only help create a television commercial, but he or she will communicate core values during scheduled talks on the election trail. A designer will not only write up a memo detailing the rationale and features of a new building or a new clothing line, but he or she will present those ideas in oral, written, and visual form to a particular audience.

As you begin to brainstorm ways that you can present your ideas to a specific audience, do some field research. Consider the many kinds of presentations you encounter as part of your academic experience. Do you attend lectures on specific topics, where a single speaker stands at a podium and delivers a verbal argument? Have you been an audience member for a formal academic panel, where multiple speakers take turns presenting arguments, sometimes providing handouts to the audience or using a projection screen to convey their ideas? Or is your most frequent experience with presentations the PowerPoint lecture, a favorite means of instruction in university classes, where lecturers provide a point-by-point map of their

Seeing Connections
See one student's encounter with visual rhetoric, from dorm posters to Power-Point lectures, by reading about Alex in Chapter 1.

materials, include images related to the subject matter, and sometimes post a copy of the slides on a Website for future reading? In all these cases, while the speaker may or may not use visual evidence to convey the argument, there are nevertheless important visual rhetoric strategies at work as well as both written and oral rhetoric strategies such as the writing of the script and the delivery of the message. Different ways of speaking, using visual media, and addressing an audience are part of the visual component of the complex process that goes into a public presentation.

Presentations with Embodied Rhetoric

How many times have you seen a presentation in which the speaker dressed up to make a point, or used the rhetoric of his or her body to persuade the audience? This form of presentation is a genre we call **embodied rhetoric,** a presentation whereby the body becomes a visual means of communicating the message. The most famous example of using embodied rhetoric in public presentations probably belongs to the Guerrilla Girls, a feminist grass-roots movement dedicated to raising awareness about gender discrimination in the art world. As you can see from Figure 7.2, they actually embody their message of "guerrilla warfare" against the art establishment by wearing gorilla masks that function as visual signs for their argument that they are at "war" with the art establishment. The incongruity of the masks and the clearly feminine bodies (indicated by stockings, dresses, and heeled shoes), provides a powerful presentation of their female guerrilla war against discrimination. In this way, the body—including the costume, stance, and way of speaking—performs a rhetorical act that carries the argumentative force of the presentation. You too use embodied rhetoric whenever you give a presentation: the clothes you wear, how you stand, the voice you choose, and even how you hold the materials you use to convey your argument—all these aspects contribute to the embodied rhetoric of your presentation. Therefore, there are important choices to make when designing and delivering a multimedia presentation.

FIGURE 7.2. The Guerrilla Girls present at a symposium on the feminist role in contemporary performance art.

CREATIVE PRACTICE

Keep a log of all the different kinds of presentations you encounter in one week at your university. Write up your reflections in the form of a short narrative. If possible, take a camera with you and document your observations of each kind of presentation. What are the differences between them? Write down as many details as possible and reflect on which type of presentation you would like to try.

Using Visual Rhetoric in Presentations

Now that we've opened our eyes to the great variety of presentation modes, we need to begin to think critically about their verbal, visual, and bodily elements. When we hear the word *presentation,* we often think of purely verbal communication: a speech, an oral presentation, a talk given in a dorm, a formal lecture by a famous person in the field. Yet more and more frequently, even the shortest talks are augmented by strategically chosen visual texts—what we used to call "visual aids"—that in fact perform a crucial rhetorical function: they collaborate with words to convey the speaker's message or argument. A photo of extensive crop damage can provide evidence in an environmental science lecture, and a chart can communicate economic trends to an audience quickly and effectively. Sometimes, moreover, visuals provide a stronger message or even contradict the verbal component of the speech. We might find that a presenter uses a visual text ironically—to show a slide listing statistics that refute an opponent's argument or to provide an emotional appeal while the speaker conveys information in a flat tone of voice. In these ways, visual texts communicate powerful arguments that you can use as part of your overall presentation.

Consider what kinds of visual material you might use, for example, to accompany a talk on gender norms and advertising. Jean Kilbourne, a famous media critic who writes about the way advertisements shape ideas

Student Writing
Read student reflections on presentations they have seen as part of their field research.
www.ablongman.com/envision070

A Closer Look
Watch Jean Kilbourne's presentation on media and body image, *Slim Hopes: Advertising and the Obsession with Thinness.* Dir. Sut Jhally. Northampton, MA: Media Education Foundation, 1995.

about gender in society, uses a number of visual rhetoric strategies in her public presentations. You can see some of these techniques in the filmed versions of her presentations, such as *Slim Hopes: Advertising and the Obsession with Thinness.*

At the beginning of her presentation, Kilbourne shows a single slide of a woman from a L'Oreal advertisement, and she provides a careful rhetorical analysis of its meaning and implications for ideas of beauty in society. This deliberate focus on one piece of visual evidence is only one strategy for using visual rhetoric in a presentation. Kilbourne then moves to a *close-up comparative analysis* of two contrasting images in order to add more of her argument into her presentation. Kilbourne then switches to a third strategy. She uses a **montage**—or rapid series of images—of ads in order to reproduce for the audience the way in which images of "ideal beauty" bombard us from every corner. The images themselves reproduce her argument, and the audience sees the evidence while experiencing the argument.

Because of her carefully designed presentations, Kilbourne has won a number of awards and been lauded as one of the most powerful public speakers today. Her presentation style is clearly very different from that of the Guerrilla Girls; she doesn't dress up in a costume that shocks audiences, but instead presents herself in professional, formal attire (see Figure 7.3). Thus while the research topics of Jean Kilbourne and the Guerrilla Girls might be similar—both are concerned with gender and social equality—their strategies of presentation and visual rhetoric differ significantly. Why is this so? Much of it depends on audience, purpose, and persona. These key rhetorical concepts, already discussed in depth in this book, must be kept in mind as you begin to craft your own verbal and visual presentations.

FIGURE 7.3. Jean Kilbourne, award-winning public lecturer.

Attention to Purpose, Audience, Possibilities

As you can tell, every presentation meets the needs of a particular *audience,* and the design of the presentation will be closely related to the needs and expectations of a specific audience. The Guerrilla

Girls, creating public art about gender and equality, seek to shake up the audience of museum administrators and public officials, hence their choice of visual "Gorilla tactics" that work through pathos; Kilbourne, in contrast, seeks to inform and persuade an academic and popular audience, hence her logical appeal through formal language, conservative or business attire, and a chronological series of images. Because their purposes and their audiences are different, they pursue different possibilities for their presentations. The Guerrilla Girls' presentation leans more toward a performance; their personas are shocking and they use nontraditional means (costumes) to communicate their argument against discrimination. Jean Kilbourne's persona is more traditional, academic, and ethos-based and, consequently, her presentation consists of a public lecture.

Seeing Connections
For techniques to use in your own rhetorical analysis, see the discussion on analyzing visual rhetoric in Chapter 1; on the uses of pathos, logos, and ethos, in Chapter 2; and on constructing effective thesis statements in Chapter 3.

FIGURE 7.4. Woman standing next to a flipchart.

Consider other kinds of purposes, audiences, personas, and possibilities shown in Figures 7.4–7.6. What kind of audience might each of the speakers be facing? How does each one need to design a presentation, select

FIGURE 7.5. A collaborative presentation in which speakers take turns.

FIGURE 7.6. Ray Hanania, stand-up comic, engages audiences on his own.

words and visual material, and practice a form of delivery that is specific to the rhetorical situation?

COLLABORATIVE CHALLENGE

In teams of two or three, assess Figures 7.4 to 7.6 in terms of choice of audience, persona, purpose, and presentation strategies. Then, go exploring and find a parallel presentation outside this textbook. You can pursue any of the following leads:

- Compare Figure 7.4 or 7.5 to the presentations given at a formal board meeting (you might watch a film scene from a recent movie).
- Compare Figure 7.4 or 7.5 to an academic conference at your university; what are the differences between a business and academic audience?
- Compare Figure 7.6 to a stand-up comic by watching a recording or live show (you might choose from Ellen Degeneris, Chris Rock, or Robin Williams).
- Compare any of the figures to one of the presentations you noted in your field research from the Creative Practice earlier in this chapter (p. 201).

Together, write a brief comparison. Try to highlight three or four shared strategies used by each presenter. When you share your findings with the class, explain how the *expectations and expertise* of the audience shape the choice of presentation style.

Once you have determined your audience and your purpose, then you can begin to transform your research argument into a written script, a series of note cards, a short memorized blurb, or a piece of performance art that you will use to communicate your point. Whether you will be presenting to your class, to a larger academic audience as part of a conference panel, to a university forum, or to a public audience, you have many choices to make. Be innovative and purposeful; *think rhetorically.* Once you have some possibilities in mind for the overall presentation, it's time to turn to the text. You need to plan, draft, and prepare the script to accompany your visual and embodied rhetoric. This is especially important if you are trying to change a dense

15-page research paper into a 10-minute speech or multimedia presentation.

Transforming Your Research Argument into a Presentation

The process of transforming your research-based argument into a presentation can be quite challenging, for you need to take into account scope, content, and style. If you have 15 written pages of argument, this would probably take 40 minutes or more to read out loud. But of course, you would certainly not choose to simply read your written paper, for writing is often different when meant to be read silently versus when meant to be read out loud. Only in certain academic circles is there a preference for complex, written prose as a formal presentation style. In most cases, audiences desire clear, conversational speech, with *pauses, varied intonations,* and *colloquial language* that is easy to follow. In order to achieve this goal, you need to think about transforming your research argument from one kind of writing to another—from writing for readers to writing for listeners. You'll also need to cut down the sheer amount of material you can convey and think about ways to present it in an interesting, memorable way.

AT A GLANCE

Questions for Determining Your Presentation's Possibilities

- Who is my audience? What are the expectations and expertise of this audience?
- What is my purpose? What do I hope to accomplish? What is my ultimate goal with this presentation?
- Who is my persona for this presentation? Do I want to approach my audience as an authority or as a peer?
- What kind of tone do I want to use in my presentation? (fun, serious, informative, sarcastic, concerned, alarmed, practical, or any other tone)
- What kinds of verbal examples, visual materials, and embodied rhetoric do I want to use as part of this presentation?

KEY STEPS FOR TRANSFORMING YOUR RESEARCH ARGUMENT INTO A PRESENTATION

Scope	Content	Style
How do you convert 10, 15, or even 20 pages of argument into a 5-, 10- or 15-minute oral presentation? *Answer: Selection*	How do you reframe the content so that it makes sense to your audience? *Answer: Organization*	How do you change the written word to a spoken, visual, and digital medium? *Answer: Translation*

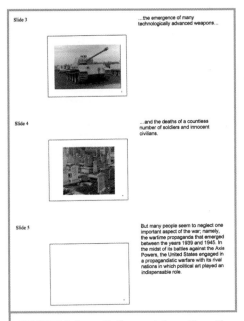

FIGURE 7.7. Tommy Tsai's presentation outline with images includes a blank slide.

Seeing Connections
To facilitate re-ordering your written argument into a presentation, use the brainstorming techniques in Chapter 4.

Selection

Keep in mind as you consider what materials to select, that you should always plan for a shorter presentation time than what you actually have allotted. Most of us speak for longer than we realize; so if you are planning material for a 10-minute presentation, aim for 8; a 15-minute presentation, aim for 12; a 5-minute presentation, aim for 3. One way to keep your time frame manageable is to select a subset of material to present. That is, if you cover three main areas in your written argument, aim to cover only one. Also, if you plan on speaking extemporaneously (or improvising), be sure that you build this into your schedule for your presentation as well.

Organization

You have an opportunity to **reorder** your written argument to meet the needs and expectations of a listening audience. You might, for instance, begin with your conclusion and then convey the narrative of your research. Or, you might want to show your visual evidence first, ask questions, and then provide your thesis at the end. In other words, you don't need to create your presentation as a miniature version of your written talk. Be innovative in your choice of organization. Make a flowchart, outline, or block graphic of each element of your presentation. Don't forget your opening "hook" and closing message as you work on organizing your presentation. Try matching each component to a minute-by-minute schedule in order to make sure that you are within time limits. And finally, don't hesitate to draw or paste in images right on your **visual outline** to show how and when you will use visual rhetoric as a part of your presentation (see Figure 7.7). The key is to see the presentation as its own genre of writing and draft a text that meets the needs of your audience *and* your own purpose.

Translation

Most audience members resist being lectured in dry, boring ways. Think about presentations you've attended where the speaker read from a script without looking up, changing inflection, or using shorter sentences that would be easy to process. More often than not, listeners need more explicit **sign-posting**—*indicating the steps in an argu-ment*—than do readers of papers. Use specific language, transitional phrases, or prose structures to help your reader understand the structure and progress of your argument. Moreover, you might want to examine the length of your sentences, the complexity of your prose, and the sophistication of your diction as you rewrite your research argument for a verbal presentation.

AT A GLANCE

Signposting

Help listeners by including these terms to structure your argument:

- first
- second
- third
- on one hand
- on the other hand

- for example
- consider
- but
- yet
- in conclusion

CREATIVE PRACTICE

Visit the *Envision* Website to compare the writing in Martin Luther King, Jr.'s "Letter from Birmingham Jail" with the transcript of his famous speech, "I've Been to the Mountain Top." How does each one indicate either a reader or a listener as the primary audience? Now work on writing for different audiences: translate the letter into a speech and the speech into a written argument. What did you change? What rhetorical techniques work best for each form of writing? What can you apply from this exercise to your own process of translation?

www.ablongman.com/envision071

The Transformation in Action

Let's take a look at how several students transformed written research papers into multimedia research presentations. Jessica Luo, for example, wrote her paper on the media coverage of the Tiananmen Square Incident in 1989; for her research paper, she decided to select a significant number of photographs from both the Chinese press and the European press. She organized them into pairs to demonstrate the different persuasive arguments made through the

AT A GLANCE

The Focusing Questions

1. What matters most about this project?
2. What two or three points can I make to convey my answer to the above question?
3. What do I want my audience to walk away thinking about when I am done?

photos by each media. Then, she wrote a script explaining her project to the class. As Jessica worked on the transformation of her paper into a presentation, she used the questions in the At A Glance box to help her with the steps of *selection, organization,* and *translation.*

Before getting back to Jessica's project, let's discuss the significance of the focusing questions in the At A Glance box. Question 1 will help you identify the crux of your presentation. This may be your thesis, but it may also *not* be your thesis. That is, in the course of writing your paper, you may have found that what really matters most is the need to raise awareness about an issue, the need to publicize potential solutions to a problem, or the need to advocate for a particular research agenda. Question 2 will help you select material from your research paper in order to convey this crux. Question 3 will help you confirm your purpose and begin to translate your main point into a medium that will persuade your audience: do you want to raise awareness, rally support, propose a change, offer new insights, or suggest avenues of future research? You need to design your presentation accordingly.

Jessica Luo decided that she wanted to raise awareness about the diverse media treatments and, moreover, that she wanted to teach students about the larger context in which the massacre occurred. She also wanted to move a mainly American student audience into caring about an incident that happened in China over 15 years ago. Thus, she decided to transform her "objective" writer's voice into a personal narrative and used rhythmic, repetitive terms that explained the rhetorical significance of each image.

Student Writing
See Jessica Luo's complex two-part presentation.
www.ablongman.com/envision072

Considering Strategies of Design

The term *multimedia* can be taken quite literally to mean any media text, from illustrations on a chalk board to the most advanced technological graphic, from a prop or handout to a sound-enhanced documentary montage.

Designing your presentation opens the door to creativity. As you can tell from Jessica Luo's presentation, often an unconventional approach can be the most persuasive, powerful, and effective in communicating your argument to the class. Jessica's combination of personal narrative, careful rhetorical analysis of contrasting images, mesmerizing script, strong voice, and solid delivery, all combined in a creative and compelling presentation. Let's discuss some other examples to get your ideas flowing about the possibilities available to you for your presentation. These designs include *multimedia, media components,* and even *embodied rhetoric* in a variety of ways.

- For a project on land mines, Stewart Dorsey decided to show two separate PowerPoint presentations side by side on two large projection screens. You could do this with slides or even overheads. He placed himself in the middle of the two screens in order to suggest that his argument offered a feasible compromise between polarized camps.

- Max Echtemendy used a hands-on approach to design for his research presentation on fantasy violence. First, he set up a table showing horror novels, DVD boxes, articles in magazines, music videos, and many other examples of "fantasy violence all around us." Then, he asked the students to complete a brief questionnaire, and he worked with their answers as he discussed the key elements of his argument. He ended by showing a clip from *The Lord of the Rings* and asking for audience response.

- Tom Hurlbutt, exploring the implications of Internet surveillance, created a dynamic PowerPoint presentation that linked to Websites, asked students to log onto Amazon, and revealed code that showed their search history from previous class sessions. In this way he integrated graphic effects in a rhetorically purposeful way.

- Ben Rosenbrough not only used embodied rhetoric by dressing up like Marilyn Manson to demonstrate the visual rhetoric at the center of his research paper; he also showed video clips and gave out an annotated bibliography of rock history and censorship. But most impressively, he facilitated a successful question-and-answer session by making a passing reference comparing Elvis and Manson. When a student asked him about this parallel, he advanced his PowerPoint show to present a slide documenting the connections in a powerful way. His surprise preparation for the question-and-answer session made his presentation design exceptionally successful.

- Eric Jung, for a presentation on art and technology, transformed the classroom into a twenty-second-century museum, complete with "exhibits" of technologically produced art. He assumed the role of museum guide and gave the class a "tour" of the exhibit, concluding with a "retrospective" lecture about the early twenty-first-century debate over how digital media changed popular conceptions of art.

As you can tell from these innovative projects, there are many effective ways to use strategies of selection, organization, and translation to design the most intriguing, powerful, and appropriate presentation for your purposes.

Take ten minutes to brainstorm the design possibilities for your presentation. Complete the following questions:

1. What format will your presentation take?

2. What materials do you plan to use in your presentation?

3. What might be a potential outline for your presentation?

Now, peer review your responses with a partner. Have each person suggest changes, new ideas, and alternative ways of designing the presentation. You might also use this time to begin to practice the presentation. Finally, in order to get a sense of how your presentation will change according to your audience, consider how your answers would change depending on whether you presented to a class audience or a group of friends in the door, a review panel at a company or a potential employer. Experiment to find the most effective ways to design your presentation.

Ways of Writing for Diverse Presentations

As we've discussed so far, there are many ways to produce an effective and compelling presentation of your research argument. After you have thought creatively about your options, made innovative choices, and designed your presentation, you need to write out some kind of guideline for you to follow when speaking to your audience. We've stressed the importance of reshaping your written argument through the process of selection, organization, and translation; now we want to go over specific kinds of writing that might fit your needs.

"You persuade a man only insofar as you can talk his language by speech, gesture, tonality, order, image, attitude, idea, identifying your ways with his."

—Burke

Writing for Oral Presentations

If you decide to convey your research argument through primarily verbal means, without much in the way of visual rhetoric, you still need to work through the process of *selection, organization,* and *translation.* Your writing, in this case, will probably take the form of a **script.** You'll want to incorporate signposting, pauses, colloquial language, and concrete examples. And you'll want to engage your audience through humor, pathos, solid evidence, and even questions. You might listen to several MP3 files of famous speeches in order to discern the ways in which orators over time use specific strategies to engage their audiences.

A Closer Look

Browse the American Rhetoric Website's Online Speech Bank for oral rhetoric drawn from historical sources as well as from films. www.ablongman.com/envision073

CREATIVE PRACTICE

Compare the very different styles of two speeches, both given by women, both concerning human rights, but presented to very different audiences and by very different personas: Eleanor Roosevelt's speech entitled "Adoption of the Declaration of Human Rights," delivered December 9, 1948, in Paris, France, and a speech by Cher (played by Alicia Silverstone) from the movie *Clueless* (1995) on "Whether all oppressed people should be allowed refuge in America." Look at the written versions of their speeches as you listen to them talk. What characteristics of spoken word does each piece of writing share? How are they different?

www.ablongman.com/envision074

Seeing Connections
To facilitate writing your script, refer back to the section on brainstorming in Chapter 4, and on drafting in Chapter 6.

As you write out your own script, annotate your written copy with places where you can pause, emphasize words, look up, or laugh. Also include reminders of when to point to visuals.

Writing for Poster Sessions

In contrast to developing a purely verbal speech, you may decide to use a more hybrid presentation that communicates an argument both through visual texts. This mode is used most frequently in the sciences, where information is presented through the format of the **poster session.** That is, science conferences often consist of giant halls showcasing hundreds of these posters. Visitors walk past the posters, reading the ones of interest and often requesting a copy of the paper on which the poster is based. If you plan on pursuing a science major, you might want to use this presentation format to practice writing in that medium. Angela Chen, for instance, decided to present her research paper on the ethics of animal testing as a poster session since she planned to major in biology and wanted practice in communicating through a format specific to her future career plans. You, too, might try out this method and develop your skills in writing for poster sessions.

FIGURE 7.8. A poster session in the Biological Sciences, Drake University.

To write for a poster session, scientists take material from their larger research projects, select salient points, organize the material into shorter written summaries with complementary charts and illustrations, and then attach the materials to a poster board. The ultimate goal of a poster session is that every student or group of students produces a visual-verbal display that conveys the research accurately, concisely, and in an engaging way. In Figure 7.8, we see a poster session in the Biological Sciences Department of Drake University. Here the students have created a smaller version of the professional conference model by offering their university audience a chance to examine all the projects from their particular classes.

When you turn to create your own poster session, keep in mind the fundamental elements for writing this kind of presentation described in the At A Glance box. There is a deliberate way to write effective writing poster presentations; you need to create visual-verbal texts that are consistent in format and easily understood by the audience members.

AT A GLANCE

Guidelines for Creating Posters for a Poster Session

- Make sure your poster is readable for a distance; size your fonts accordingly.
- Put the poster's title, authors, and academic affiliation at the top.
- Avoid visual clutter; use white space effectively to offset different elements, including tables, figures, and written texts.
- Arrange materials in columns rather than rows.
- Avoid long passages of texts; rely primarily on visual persuasion.
- Always check with the conference organizers for their specific guidelines.

For more detailed advice, see
www.ablongman.com/envision075

Writing for PowerPoint or Slide-Based Presentations

In addition to poster sessions, PowerPoint presentations have become very popular in both academic and professional contexts. The software itself is just a tool, but it's an incredibly helpful and time-saving one that can organize and display your key points of argument and your visual materials into a series of slides. The more you become familiar with PowerPoint as a tool, the more you can use it effectively to offer a

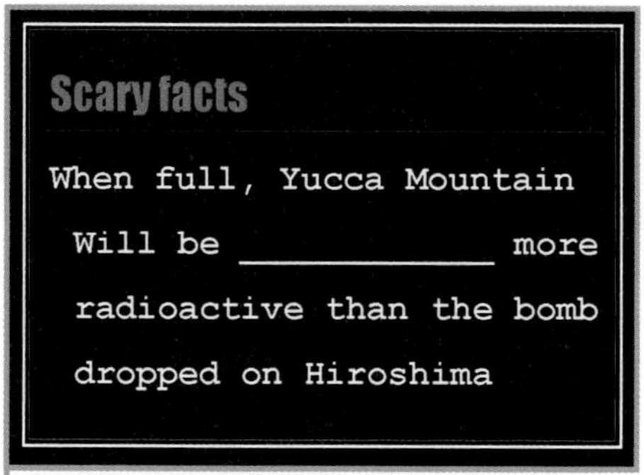

FIGURE 7.9. Natalie Farrell: Yucca Mountain and Nuclear Waste: Gambling with the Future of the Human Race, December 2002; slide 5.

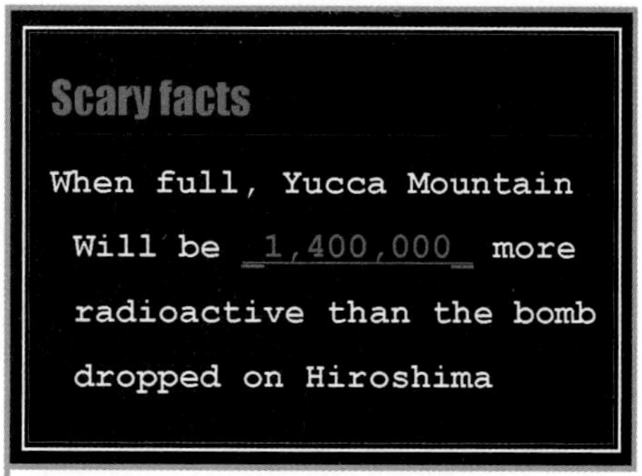

FIGURE 7.10. Natalie Farrell's presentation, slide 6.

timed slide show of images, to emphasize points through visual design (highlighting text, blowing up images, sliding across a picture, engaging the audience by filling in blanks as you speak, and much more). Alex Bleyleben, for instance, used PowerPoint to project slides of endangered rhinos for a paper on global activism. In one dramatic move, he included a black slide to shift the audience's attention from the gruesome images back to his own presence at the podium as he delivered the key points of his argument. Then, he concluded with an impressive image. Another student, Natalie Farrell, taught herself PowerPoint in one evening for her presentation on Yucca Mountain. She included slides with deliberate blanks in order to engage the class and ask them to calculate the projected environmental risk of a nuclear disaster (see Figures 7.9 and 7.10).

As Natalie clicked forward in her presentation, she elicited the class to guess at the power of radiation in Yucca Mountain before shocking the audience with the actual numbers. She succeeded in what cultural critic Stephen Shugart deems is the necessity of "transforming the concept of PowerPoint from 'presenting at' into 'a way of promoting discussion' or to use it in unconventional ways to create more effective learning situations." One way to think about writing with PowerPoint as a discussion tool is to return to our model of research as a conversation or dialogue. How can you engage your audience, as Natalie did, rather than throw data at them or run through a list of ideas?

Include a blank or black slide in the middle of your PowerPoint presentation to refocus your audience's attention on you, the speaker.

A Closer Look

Read different perspectives in the debate over the value of PowerPoint in two different essays: Ian Parker's "Absolute Power-Point," *The New Yorker* (28 May 2001: 76-87) and Stephen Shugart, "Beyond PowerPoint" *The Educator's Voice*.

www.ablongman.com/envision076

When writing for PowerPoint, keep in mind the way you want your audience to respond. Remember that before this software was developed, a speaker needed to use slides to share visual material. If you think of using PowerPoint the way you would use slides in a presentation, then you may be less likely to fill each slide with bulleted lists of information or large amounts of writing. Consider exactly how you plan to use each slide and then craft your presentation around your answers:

- Do you want to show photographs, cartoons, or other visual images?
- Do you want to raise questions and then fill in answers?
- Do you want to show an interactive map or link to a Website?
- Do you want a blank slide for emphasis or use other creative methods of presentations?

AT A GLANCE

Writing an Effective PowerPoint Presentation

- Use purposeful visuals rather than clip art.
- Spend time discussing the images on each slide.
- Don't put too much text on each slide or rely too heavily on bullet lists.
- Keep fonts consistent in style, size, and color to avoid distracting the audience.
- Break complex ideas into multiple slides.
- Give a handout with full quotations as necessary.
- Include sound effects and animation rhetorically rather than for flair or flash.

For more detailed advice, see
www.ablongman.com/envision077

These are all purposeful, rhetorical ways of writing for a PowerPoint presentation. Again, begin with your purpose and your audience, and then design your presentation to meet your needs. The guidelines presented here cover some of the more common techniques you should incorporate in your presentation. But realize that you can modify these "rules" to suit your own needs. Some students have told us that they find it helpful to use PowerPoint rather than create a poster session or present a purely oral speech because the program provides a structure that they can use to help pace their presentations or keep them on track. This seems to be particularly true for students presenting in a second language or for students who experience a great deal of anxiety when speaking. PowerPoint's timed slide function and ease for creating placeholders serve a *double rhetorical purpose* for such students: they actually find it helpful to read information off the slides, and in this way the presentation tool helps convey information and facilitate delivery. Consider your own needs as a speaker when you select your mode of presentation. Slide-based presentations in PowerPoint can be very compelling for an audience and very rewarding for you as a presenter.

Possibilities for PowerPoint

Using a conventional PowerPoint format, Tracy Hadnott created five slides to serve as placeholders for her research-based presentation on the ethics of stem cell research. As shown in Figure 7.11, she used a classic design, preventing the paper from being too cluttered. In the colored line on the left side of the slide, the mosaic colors replicate strands of DNA, so the image serves a double purpose: it conveyed the content of her argument visually while she presented it orally.

Similarly, Sarah Trube designed her slides with careful attention to the visual argument made by the slide background. For her presentation on global warming, humorously titled "Escaping the Frying Pan: The Media Fire and the Scrambled Egg of Global Climate Change," she used a background template which showed a watery image of the earth and sky in order to create the right mood (see Figure 7.12) After giv-

FIGURE 7.11. Tracy Hadnott, "Stem Cell Research through a Visual Lens," slide 2.

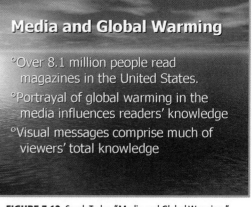

FIGURE 7.12. Sarah Trube, "Media and Global Warming," slide 9.

ing the audience a brief outline of her talk, she then identified her terms and shared her survey research into the ignorance of the American public on questions of climate. Then, she led the class through a rhetorical analysis of a series of political cartoons and over-simplified media visual representations. The design of the presentation served as a visual component of her argument to save the earth.

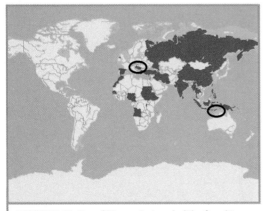

FIGURE 7.13. One of Morgan Springer's slides from his dynamic map in a PowerPoint presentation on self-determination in Kosovo and East Timor.

Morgan Springer created a dynamic map on PowerPoint that filled in with red color the countries that are experiencing political wars and military dictatorship (see Figure 7.13). He then showed images of genocide that many Americans have yet to see and concluded with a bold quote from a leading expert whom he interviewed for his research paper on self-determination in Kosovo and East Timor.

Using a more humorous and interactive approach for his presentation on the visual strategies of political campaigns, Kavi Vyas got the audience thinking about his argument by pretending to hold an election for the new governor of California. He announced the election in the first slide, and then gave everyone a handout of his second slide that showed himself ostensibly dressed up as different candidates. After taking a class "vote," he delved into his argument that often voters respond to effective visual appeals rather than the substantive platforms of any given candidate. Figures 7.14 and 7.15 show two consecutive slides from his presentation. The obvious use of humor made his presentation quite engaging while also effective in communicating his critique of the two-party system.

Student Writing
See Morgan Springer's dynamic map in motion from his PowerPoint presentation. www.ablongman.con/envision078

CREATIVE PRACTICE

Experiment with designing slides for your research presentation, either using PowerPoint or transparencies for overhead projection. First, create a title slide. Then, try making slides that show only images, enlarged to fit the whole screen. Next, experiment with text slides. Should you use a bulleted list? A question, then an answer? A blank to be filled in with the click of a mouse or an impromptu over heard notation? Finally, try some interactive or dynamic features, such as links to Web pages, images that cascade and change, or even audio recordings. Avoid using sounds as mere decoration; make every slide a rhetorical part of your persuasive presentation.

FIGURE 7.14. Kavi Vyas, presentation slide 1.

FIGURE 7.15. Kavi Vyas, presentation slide 2.

Choosing Methods of Delivery

Seeing Connections
To review the canons of rhetoric—invention, arrangement, style, memory, and delivery—refer back to Chapter 3.

As you can tell, the way in which you present your visual materials is just as crucial as drafting content for that presentation. In other words, after *selection, arrangement,* and *design* of materials, you need to think about ways of *delivering* the presentation. But why is delivery so important? Won't the content carry the persuasiveness of the presentation? If the writing is good, then won't the delivery be good? Indeed, the writing must be good; the selection, organization, and translation of your argument into an appropriate, audience-centered design are crucial for your success. But you also need to attend to *how* you communicate your argument to your audience. In other words, you need to involve those last two canons of rhetoric, *memory* and *delivery.* In brief, **memory** entails memorizing one's argument to communicate it to the audience, while **delivery** entails combining a wide range of strategies for best effect.

A Closer Look

Learn more about Book 11 of Quintilian's classic treatise, *Institutio Oritoria,* which focuses on the last two canons of rhetoric: memory and delivery.
www.ablongman.com/envision079

AT A GLANCE

Some Fundamental Elements of Delivery

- **Stance or posture** (or embodied rhetoric)
- **Gesture** (use of hands to communicate information)
- **Voice** (pitch, tone, loudness, softness, and enunciation)
- **Pacing** (of words, visuals, and argument)
- **Rhetorical appeals** (use of logos, pathos, ethos)
- **Visuals** (slides, posters, graphics, handouts)
- **Embodied visuals** (not only stance but dress, appearance, mannerisms)
- **Style** (elements such as repetition, allusion, metaphor, stories, personal narrative, jokes, and pauses)

We know that memory was crucial for rhetoricians before the invention of the printing press. Speakers would memorize phrases, stories, and histories to pass down from generation to generation. Significantly, this process occurred through a form of visual organization called an **architectural mnemonic technique,** a method in which you associate a phrase to a room or a part of a house so that as you look around during your presentation you receive visual clues to trigger your memory. Scholars William Covino and David Jolliffe explain that the rhetorician Cicero described this technique as "a set of visual images like the rooms of a house, which can be associated with the items in a long speech" (67). As you think about strategies of presentation, you might want to try and memorize key parts of your speech through this technique by creating a visual map of your script. Also, attend to the way in which your audience will remember your words, and choose your examples, your diction, your pacing accordingly. In this way, memory leads naturally into delivery, the last canon of rhetoric.

For many speakers, the most important canon is delivery. The ancient Greek orator Demosthenes, for example, when asked which three of the five canons of rhetoric he considered most significant, replied, "Delivery, Delivery, Delivery." In other words, so crucial is this fifth canon of rhetoric that it can supercede the rest. Consider the two different models (see Figures 7.16 and 7.17). Does Figure 7.16 suggest a confident and approachable speaker who leans casually against a lectern while gesturing and making eye contact with his audience? To some, this may be effective public speaking, body language, and communication style; many students appreciate a more casual form of delivery. In business settings, however, this delivery may be viewed as sloppy, disrespectful, and not quite formal enough. While the man in Figure 7.17 may appear pedantic, overly formal, and rigid to a casual audience, in a different context, he might seem extremely professional, competent, and appropriately unemotional. It is all a matter of matching delivery strategy to purpose and audience. Remember that the *entire* body—from body language to clothes, posture, expression, and gestures—participates in the communication of ideas and information. These are aspects of delivery—embodied rhetoric, voice, and eye contact—to choose carefully and practice in front of a trial audience.

"Delivery, the last of the five *canons of rhetoric*, concerns itself (as does style) with *how* something is said, rather than *what* is said (the province of *Invention*)."

—Dr. Gideon Burton

FIGURE 7.16. One form of delivery.

FIGURE 7.17. Another form of delivery.

Delivery, as one of the five canons of rhetoric, deals primarily with the effectiveness of a speech's presentation. Oral communication, combined with variations in the presenter's voice and body movements, comprises the delivery of speech. The speaker's ability to manipulate auditory and visual techniques enables him/her to effectively convey his/her argument to the audience.

—Kelly Ingleman

COLLABORATIVE CHALLENGE

With a partner from class, conduct field research on the delivery strategies of three different speakers. Write down your impressions using the elements in the At A Glance box. Then, assess each speaker in terms of the effectiveness and appropriateness of delivery strategies based on the needs of the audience. For example: Does a formal speaker put an entire lecture hall to sleep through monotone voice, lack of gestures, and a formal body language, or does the speaker use humor, vivid expressions, and clear pauses to keep the audience engaged? Does a teacher in a small seminar use direct eye contact and open body language to invite participation, or does the speaker stand towering over the group and silence others? Finally, identify key techniques that you can apply from each speaker in terms of excellent strategies of delivery and try to use them in your own presentation.

Student Writing

Read reports on delivery styles from field research conducted by students in preparation for their own presentations.

www.ablongman.com/envision080

As you can tell, there is much to consider, select, and experiment with in the delivery of your presentation. Try different modes—diverse postures, tones, metaphoric phrases, stories, and expressions. Pay attention to how you use humor or pathos, logical persuasion, or storytelling. Always, keep your audience and purpose in mind. And finally, consider, what message are you sending with your gestures?

The Rhetoric of Gesture

Going all the way back to classical rhetoric, *gestures* have performed a crucial role in communication and were considered an integral part of a speaker's delivery. Today, gestures are used in a variety of ways to convey ideas to an audience. Keep in mind that your **gestures**—hand and body movements—perform rhetorically as acts of persuasion in your presentation. Often, when we think about the term *gesture* in relation to public speaking, we think of very overt or deliberate gestures that public speakers make for emphasis, such as the one in Figure 7.18, where a woman uses her pencil to direct the audience's attention. Our eyes will follow her pencil and we will focus on the chart or slide

FIGURE 7.18. The hand, pointing sharply, moves the audience's attention away from the body and to the visual text or graphic.

she has chosen to use as visual material in her presentation. The gesture is a careful rhetorical move: it has purpose and works effectively as a strategy of communication. But often, gestures in public speaking seem less carefully composed, such as the one in Figure 7.19. Here, we see the speaker in mid-sentence, his hands raised as if in an involuntary accompaniment to his words. Perhaps he is emphasizing some point, or maybe he is explaining a process to the audience. Either way, the rhetoric of gesture is less effective here than in Figure 7.18. While we all use gestures without realizing that we do, it is in fact possible to train ourselves to use the visual rhetoric of the body more carefully, and even strategically, as an integral part of our overall presentation design.

In Figure 7.20, for instance, a man stands looking at the audience and holding a yellow card in his hand. His gesture, the open palm extended toward the audience, seems quite natural and even unplanned. But, it is in fact very composed: the open palm invites the audience to listen; it is tilted down to allow words to travel and open the space between speaker and audience. The rest of the body is very controlled so that gesture takes on great rhetorical force. It is an effective, if subtle, use of the rhetoric of gesture in public speaking. Similarly, your purpose in using gestures as part of a presentation should be to harness the power of the body effectively to communicate ideas.

A Closer Look

To examine an example of the power of the rhetoric of gesture, view the three different cover images of Condoleezza Rice on the front page of the April 9, 2004 *San Francisco Chronicle* and other prominent newspapers. Compare the strategic use of hand motions by studying these images through the *Envision* Website.

www.ablongman.com/envision081

FIGURE 7.19. Radio personality Dennis Prager delivers a speech entitled "The Pathology of Anti-Americanism and Anti-Zionism" using gestures with both hands.

FIGURE 7.20. A man uses an open-palm gesture.

CREATIVE PRACTICE

Analyze the gestures used by one of the most famous public speakers, Martin Luther King, Jr. (see Figures 7.21 and 7.22). Write a brief analysis of the suggested meaning and purpose of each gesture, describing each of the images below as you make your argument. Then, select the words you might match to the gesture. This exercise will help you explore strategies to use in your own presentations.

FIGURE 7.22. Martin Luther King, Jr., emphasizes his point at a mass rally in Philadelphia, August 4, 1965.

FIGURE 7.21. Martin Luther King, Jr. gesturing at a Press Conference.

COLLABORATIVE CHALLENGE

Now, get into small groups and compare your responses to the Creative Practice. Then, find images of other public speakers—past and present—that either recall or offer different strategies from the ones that King used. You might look at photographs of the president, study archival footage of previous leaders (Hitler, Churchill, Clinton), or take photographs of a public speaker at your school or place of worship. Write up your analyses of these gestures to share with the class. Consider enacting them in your presentation to the class as a whole.

Practicing Your Presentation

Speakers like Martin Luther King, Jr. dedicate much of their time to practicing their delivery. Similarly, two ideologically opposed political figures, Adolf Hitler and Winston Churchill, relied extensively on practice to develop their delivery. First-person testimonies about Hitler suggest that he incessantly recorded himself speaking and using hand gestures. Then, he would watch the films over and over again, selecting the motions that he felt were most powerful. Next, he would practice that form of delivery—the tone of voice, the pacing, the bodily stance, and the hand gestures—until he felt it was perfect. Finally, he would destroy the recordings so that no one would know how carefully he practiced. The practice made his delivery seem natural and his power seem real. At the opposite end of the spectrum, Winston Churchill used voice alone to persuade the British public to withstand the waves of Nazi attacks night after night in the bombing of Britain. Over the radio wires, his practiced and powerful words—delivered with the perfect amount of confidence and encouragement—helped the British prevail in such dark days. These examples reveal the power of practice in strengthening delivery and its capacity to persuade audiences.

Student Writing
Vince Gonzales's research project explores the methods Hitler used to prepare for his speeches. www.ablongman.com/envision082

> Winston Churchill could never have stirred the British public as he did were it not for the grave, serious, and controlled tone of voice that he employed in his radio speeches. His faith in the allied powers rang out in stentorian cadences that by their very vibrations instilled belief in the masses. His message was often cliché, but his delivery was never anything but spell-binding. Had he had a feeble voice, perhaps Germany would have fared better.
>
> —Dr. Gideon Burton

Other national leaders have also seized on the importance of the visual rhetoric of the body and the power of voice as part of their delivery strategies. Consider the characteristic pitch, word choice, expression, and body language of the past three presidents, offered so consistently to the press that comedy shows such as *Saturday Night Live* can use these forms of delivery to represent the entire person in a mocking way. A more recent—and less political—example of practice making for effective delivery occurs in the movie *Catch Me If You Can,* a film inspired by the real-life story of Frank Abagnale, a man who impersonated a teacher, a pilot, a doctor, and a lawyer. Throughout the film, Abagnale repeats the conventional modes of speaking, dressing, standing, and presenting used by these diverse professionals by changing his clothing, body language, hand gestures, and eye contact in each scene. Most significantly, Abagnale perfected these professional presentations by watching television shows and films that taught him how to act in each "performance." He practiced in hotel rooms and then enacted his part without anyone suspecting that he was a fraud.

As you can see from Figures 7.23 and 7.24, Abagnale uses the visual materials of dress—the doctor's coat, the lawyer's suit—as well as props such as the legal briefs as additional strategies of delivery. He practiced with these elements and then put them into play for his performance. Your presentation gives you an opportunity to persuade in the same way.

FIGURE 7.23. Passing himself off as an Emergency Room doctor, Frank Abagnale (Leonardo Dicaprio) confers with two residents in *Catch Me If You Can.*

FIGURE 7.24. Abagnale performs as a lawyer in another scene from this movie.

COLLABORATIVE CHALLENGE

Have someone digitally record or film you while you practice your presentation to find out if you make any involuntary movements (such as rubbing your chin, clicking a pen, or twirling your hair) or verbal tics (such as saying "umm" too many times). Select two or three strong expressions, gestures, and verbal phrases that you can use with rhetorical purpose and effectiveness. Then, practice these again on film until you feel completely confident. In addition to practicing your delivery, work on the canon of memory by trying to memorize some key points of your presentation in order to deliver them without having to look at your notes or script.

Anticipating Problems and the Question-and-Answer Session

As you practice your presentation, don't forget to consider problems that might arise, such as faulty technology, a bored or confused audience, or even hostile hecklers. To troubleshoot technology issues, visit your room and test out your equipment in advance if possible. Make sure you have backup for the technology: a CD-ROM of your presentation or an extra copy on your email account. But remember, even if your practice session goes smoothly, bring handouts or overheads in case your PowerPoint slides don't work and be prepared to talk without technology if necessary. Also, be ready to cut down or extend the length of your talk by indicating on your speech where you could stop, or points you might discuss in more detail. Realize that the more comfortable you are with your material, the more you can adapt on the spot to the needs of your audience.

This includes handling the question-and-answer session well. Think in advance about what kinds of questions you might be asked so that you can prepare some answers. You might practice trial responses with a peer group member. Consider having some new evidence, a stunning visual, or even a handout prepared to answer a question that you hope might be asked after your presentation.

Student Writing

Read Ben Rosebrough's presentation script to see how he planned a "surprise slide" for the question-and-answer session.

www.ablongman.com/envision083

Documenting Your Presentation

Design. Delivery. Practice. What is left? After all your hard work on your presentation, you probably want to leave some kind of trace, a written artifact, or a form of textual memory of the presentation. **Documentation**—*some form of written or visual evidence of your presentation's argument*—is the answer. Documentation serves an important rhetorical function, to inform and persuade. This might take the form of a **handout** which provides additional information in the form of an annotated bibliography, a summary of your key points and thesis, visual rhetoric from your presentation, references for further reading, or a printout of your PowerPoint presentation. You should put your contact information on it so the audience can ask you further questions. Documentation might also consist of a **text** or **script** for your presentation. This can either be the annotated printout of your PowerPoint presentation, a full speech, or a typed-up set of notes in outline form with placemarkers for your slides or media aids such as shown in Tommy Tsai's visual outline (see Figure 7.7 on page 206). More innovatively, you might forge documentation in the form of a **creative take-away** that reflects a key aspect of your presentation. Consider Wendy Hagenmaier's handout for her project on media coverage of the bombing of Hiroshima and Nagasaki (see Figure 7.25). The cover of the *New York Times* from August 1945 is attached to a small candle; Wendy's caption reads, "Light this candle in remembrance of how the August 1945 atomic bombings of Hiroshima and Nagasaki have been remembered by Japanese and American photojournalists. The 'flashes' of its flame will serve to remind you that photojournalistic coverage is often an attempt to shape collective national memory and that remembrance is subjective." Another student, Falco Pichler, presenting his research finding on Nike marketing strategies, created a "backstage pass" to what he called the "Nike Show" and invited students to read his paper online. Aaron Johnson, presenting his research

Seeing Connections
For further discussion of visual annotated bibliographies, see Chapter 5. To explore more possibilities for different forms of visual arguments, refer to Chapter 8.

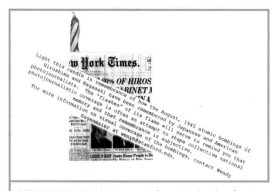

FIGURE 7.25. Wendy Hagenmaier's creative handout for the class audience.

on media representation of athletes who take performance-enhancing drugs, made a mock subscription card with the distorted title, "Sport Exaggerated" as creative documentation for his presentation (see Figure 7.26). Through Photoshop, he was able to embed a cover of *Sports Illustrated* into the subscription card and list the main points of his argument as "advertising points" for his presentation. Notice his complete contact information at the bottom of the card.

These different examples begin to show the range of creative documentation strategies you might pursue as the final part of your presentation.

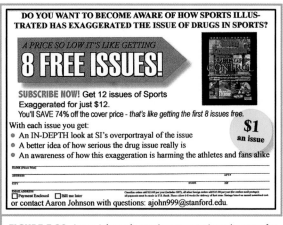

FIGURE 7.26. Aaron Johnson's creative presentation take-away for his research project on *Sports Illustrated*.

Taking the lead from Aaron, you might even craft an interactive visual take-away such as a graphic montage, a minibook, or other forms of visual argument. The importance of such texts—whether conventional prose handouts or compelling visual creations—lies in their power to make your presentation memorable, convincing, and engaging. So consider your strategies for documentation as carefully as you design your entire presentation.

Student Writing

See examples of creative take-aways including a minibook on war photography, Saddam Hussein trading cards, a lollipop favor, and a choose-your-own-adventure book. www.ablongman.com/envision085

Creating Your Own Presentation

In this chapter, you have explored possibilities for presentations; learned how to convert a written argument into a spoken, visual, multimedia presentation or performance; and worked through the different ways of writing for oral, poster, and PowerPoint presentations. Recall the strategies of design, arrangement, and delivery you have learned, and keep in mind the importance of both gesture and embodied rhetoric as ways of communicating your message and your purpose to your particular audience. Finally, as you begin to craft your own presentation, remember the old adage, "practice makes perfect"; we need to peer review and revise our presentations as much as we need to collaborate on drafts and revise our written work. In these ways, you can anticipate problems and harness your creativity as you shape your ideas into a memorable, moving, and persuasive form of rhetorical communication.

PREWRITING CHECKLIST
Analyzing Presentations

❑ What is the presenter's purpose? To inform? persuade? instruct? motivate? initiate discussion? Did the presentation successfully accomplish that purpose?

❑ What is the presenter's own relationship to the topic he or she discussed? Is the presenter an expert? a novice? fairly well-informed?

❑ Was the presentation appropriate for the audience? Consider language, organization, explanation of technical or specialized concepts.

❑ Did the speaker present him- or herself as an authority, instructing the audience? as a peer sharing information? Did the presenter make eye contact (indicating a direct relationship with the audience) or simply read from a prepared text (indicating a focus on the material rather than the audience)? How did this affect the structure and style of the presentation?

❑ How was the presentation structured? Was an outline or summary provided for the audience to follow? Was this done orally, on the board, in a handout, or on a slide? Was the development of the argument clear? Did it follow the designated structure?

❑ Did the presenter take into account the audience's reaction? For instance, did he or she notice some confusion in the audience and pause to explain a difficult point?

❑ How did the presentation begin? Did the presenter use any effective oral or visual devices to "hook" the audience? Was there a clear conclusion?

❑ Were the main points clearly developed? How was the scope of the presentation? Was there too much information? too little?

❑ Did the presenter use word choice appropriate to the occasion, audience, and subject matter? Were the sentence structures too complex (as if to be read silently) or more colloquial (as if to be read aloud)? Did the presenter project his or her voice enough? Did he or she speak slowly and clearly or rush through the material?

❑ Did the presenter use any formal devices—figurative language, deliberate repetition, literary allusions?

❑ Consider the presenter's embodied rhetoric. Did he or she stand or sit? Remain stationary, or move around? Did the presenter use gestures, facial expression, or even costume to add to the rhetorical effect of the argument?

❑ How did the presenter use visuals? Did he or she show slides, bring in posters, write on a blackboard, distribute handouts, engage in role-playing, pass around books, bring in material evidence for the presentation? Were the visual components rhetorically purposeful or did they seem an afterthought?

❑ If the presenter used posters: Were they clear and accessible to the audience? Did they stand alone as arguments, or was their meaning only clear in conjunction with the oral presentation? Were the words large enough to read from a distance? Did the poster avoid visual clutter? Did it contain a clear title and use information graphics effectively?

❑ If the presenter used a slide program such as PowerPoint: Was the visual design of the slides effective? Did they have a unity of theme, color, and layout? Did the presenter avoid visual clutter on the slides? How much text was on each slide? Were placeholders used for emphasis or pacing? Were there innovations in the slideshow, such as using dual screens, animation, or embedded clips or Internet links? Were these effective or distracting? Did the presenter speak to the computer screen, rather than the audience? Was the screen blocked by the presenter's body, obscuring the slides?

❑ If the presenter used the blackboard or whiteboard: Did he or she write clearly and legibly? Were the notations on the board purposeful? Did the presenter block the board, making it difficult to read?

❑ If the presenter used technology: Were there any technical difficulties? Did the presenter: overcome them smoothly (for instance, having a backup plan), or have a difficult time recovering from the glitch, perhaps because of relying more heavily on technology than on the force of argument?

❑ Did the presenter finish within the allotted time? How did he or she handle the question-and-answer session?

WRITING PROJECTS

Visit the *Envision* Website for expanded assignment guidelines and student projects.

1. **Field Research as Preparation for Your Presentation**
   As part of the necessary preparation for writing your own presentation, conduct field research in the form of observing three public speeches, presentations, or oral/multi-media arguments, and type up a brief rhetorical analysis on the *delivery, rhetorical strategies,* and *effectiveness* of each one. These presentations can include lectures in any of your classes, speakers visiting campus or your dorms, or the practice presentation of a member of your class. Find three different speakers or presentations in order to expand the possibilities available to you. Write a brief analysis of each one; try to be as specific as possible in your observations and make sure that you indicate what strategies you plan to use in your own presentation.

2. **Write the Presentation**
   Create and deliver a timed presentation of your research argument for your class (ask your instructor for the precise time limit). You should include the appropriate media (visual rhetoric, PowerPoint slides, Websites, movie clips, performative or interactive aspects). In addition, the oral delivery of your presentation might include a handout that you distribute to the class to provide information in the form of an annotated bibliography, a summary of your key points and thesis, visual rhetoric from your presentation, references for further reading, a printout of your PowerPoint presentation, etc., formatted in the proper manner (or in a creative way if that works for your presentation) with your complete contact information on it.

FOR ADDED CHALLENGE

Visit the *Envision* Website for expanded assignment guidelines and student projects.

1. **Written Documentation**
   Take the assignment above (Writing Project 2) one step further by compiling a *script* for your presentation. This can either be the annotated printout of your PowerPoint presentation, a full speech, or notes in outline form (with placemarkers for your slides or multimedia). Include references in the text/script of your presentation to any materials you use (handouts and printouts of multimedia).

2. **Collaborative Presentation**
   Rather than work alone on your presentation, get into groups (two to four per group works best) to design, deliver, and document your presentation to the class. You might want to divide the tasks of selecting material, brainstorming strategies of presentation, and designing your visual materials. Will you take turns speaking

throughout the presentation or will each person be responsible for a distinct segment of the presentation? Will one person write the script, another person deliver it—perhaps from memory—while a third creates the slides or images? Take time to choose the strategy that best suits your audience and your purpose. And don't forget to practice together.

3. **Community Writing Presentation**
   Either in groups or individually, design your presentation for a specific community audience. What happens if you present your research project on performance art to a group of politicians, to school administrators, to the theater department? Think about how your message can reach a broader audience in this way. What if your project is on the educational poster campaign to prevent the spread of AIDS? After you design one presentation for your writing class, rewrite it to meet the audience expectations of a not-for-profit organization, an international amnesty meeting, or an urban center continuing education class.

CHAPTER 7 ON THE WEB

Resources and Readings	Exercises and Assignments	Student Writing
• Closer Look links • Tools for planning presentations, poster session production, PowerPoint, and more • Links to Websites and resources on memory and delivery • Online collections of speeches, commencement addresses, and PowerPoint models • Annotated readings	• Brainstorm exercises • Design possibilities worksheet • Detailed guidelines for creating presentation posters • Field Research Assignment • Directions for the speaking spot, the multimedia presentation, and collaborative work • Peer Review forms • Focus on diverse learners	• Field research on multiple speakers • Detailed design and content plans for presentations • Scripts and PowerPoint presentations • Visual outlines • Creative take-aways and handouts from presentations • Self-reflection letters

www.ablongman.com/envision

CHAPTER 8

Designing Visual Arguments and Websites

Writing in a visual culture entails not only writing about visual texts, but also producing compelling and compact multimedia texts that exist on their own as independent creations, such as photo essasys, Websites, brochures, and posters. Unlike oral presentations, which are often one-time live performances, these types of visual texts endure long after the speaker has finished and the audience has dispersed. Someone surfing the Web, browsing through departmental publications, or looking at an exhibit case in the hall of the library might see this work and find it a powerful piece of visual rhetoric. The provocative advertisement featured in Figure 8.1, for instance, is an innovative visual argument that communicates a powerful message about the contemporary definition of feminine beauty; here the image of the realistically proportioned doll, set in a confident, casual pose against a natural background of ivy, produces a strong argument about standards of body image in the mass media.

As you approach the process of constructing your own visual argu-

FIGURE 8.1. This Body Shop opinion advertisement shocks the reader into questioning concepts of beauty.

ment—whether based on your research project, drawn from your presentation, or related to a new topic altogether—you'll experiment with different media to make a powerful argument with images. Building on the work you've done in previous chapters, you'll learn new strategies for arranging, designing, and producing enduring and innovative visual arguments that persuade viewers to agree with your message.

Chapter Preview Questions

- How do I go about creating a visual argument?
- What forms of decorum should I employ?
- How might I produce an opinion advertisement?
- How can I craft a photo essay?
- What are my options for Web design?
- What other types of visual arguments might I create?

Approaching the Visual Argument

In order to understand the way in which you can craft your own visual argument, let's return to Alex, our hypothetical student from Chapter 1, whom we left sitting in the back row of her lecture class on Writing and Social Issues. An entire semester has passed since we last saw her, and in that time she has been developing her skills as a writer, researcher, and rhetorician. Her interest in a future Health and Society major has led her to write an analysis of anti-smoking advertisements, complete a 15-page research paper on the urban subculture of teenage runaways, and give a presentation on the effectiveness of AIDS-awareness posters. Now, for her final project, Alex needs to create a visual argument based on the topic of one of these past assignments and display it as part of a class exhibit. She has several choices of media for her visual argument: she can make an *opinion advertisement*, or *op-ad*, for her argument; she could produce a *photo essay* in either paper or electronic format; she could generate a *Web page* or Website devoted to her topic; or she could design a *brochure*, a *collage*, or even a *mural*. To create her project she has four key decisions to make: Alex must identify her **argument** (her main point), her **audience**

AT A GLANCE

Decisions about Visual Arguments

- Who is my audience? What are their concerns or needs?
- How do I want my audience to encounter my argument? (On the Web, as a movie, in a magazine, as part of an exhibition)
- How will my argument be best served by a specific medium and form?

(who she intends to reach with her argument), her **medium** (such as advertisement, photo essay, or Website), and the specific **form** (the layout and design) for her visual argument.

The first two elements—*argument* and *audience*—are foundational to any persuasive text; to create an effective argument, you must have a clear sense of your main point and your target audience. For most college assignments, your audience is usually your instructor and your classmates; however, when you use a visual medium for your argument, you are more likely to reach an audience beyond the classroom. An op-ad, published in a school newspaper, might reach the entire student body; a photo essay that becomes part of a department exhibit, can touch the entire campus community; a well-designed Website, linked to external sites, may be read by a national, or even international, audience. Yet despite the range of readers, you need to know which specific audience your argument is designed to persuade; keep this focus as you head into design strategies.

Once you know *what* your argument is and *whom* you are trying to persuade, then you can decide on the *medium* that would most effectively reach them. For instance, it would be ineffective to make a Website to argue the merits of technology to technophobes; a person who was apprehensive about the Internet would not be likely to go online to read it. Similarly, if you wanted to convince children to stay off drugs, which would be the most appropriate medium: a cartoon-based television commercial or a full-page print newspaper ad? Although both forms might contain the identical argument, the TV ad has the greater likelihood of reaching and, therefore, influencing your intended audience. In other words, the most appropriate medium is the one that will most powerfully convey your argument to your audience given the specifics of your rhetorical situation.

Seeing Connections
To read detailed instruction on the best strategies for working with Power-Point and other slide-based presentation tools, see Chapter 7.

Keep in mind that each medium structures information in very distinct and purposeful ways; for instance, a PowerPoint slide is set up differently than a Web page, just as a Web page is set up differently than a magazine advertisement. Therefore, part of creating a powerful visual argument lies in identifying your chosen medium's conventions of structure and style and in adjusting the form of your argument—its layout, design, style, and organization of information—to be the most appropriate choice for your project.

Consider, for instance, how the Guerrilla Girls, a set of activist artists well known for their powerful public performances, also convey their political and social messages through a variety of visual and print media—posters, postcards, flyers, presentations, protests, embodied rhetoric, and published books. In each case, their choice of medium and form depends on their argument and target audience. In Figure 8.2, they use the billboard to reach a broad segment of the population driving through Los Angeles in order to protest Hollywood's gender discrimination policies.

Here, the argument works through a combination of visual and verbal elements: the montage image of Trend Lott's head on top of a gold Oscar statue catches the driver's eye through pathos and distorted ethos, while the bold letters in blue and red accentuate the logical argument that the conservative Senate has more inclusive gender

Seeing Connections
For a discussion of the Guerrilla Girls' presentations as performances in embodied rhetoric, see Chapter 7.

FIGURE 8.2. The Guerrilla Girls billboard at Highland and Melrose in Hollywood protests gender inequality through visual argument.

practices than the movie indutry. In this way, through the specific lay-out, design, style, and organization of their billboard, the Guerrilla Girls successfully use the lights of Hollywood to spotlight their protest against the paucity of film directors. Their innovative way of shifting between media should demonstrate to you how your choices about audience, argument, medium, and form can work together to produce effective visual arguments.

Decorum in Contemporary Arguments

Seeing Connections
The concept of *kairos* is treated extensively in Chapter 2.

To use terms from classical rhetoric, the decisions you face when creating a visual argument are ones that have to do with **decorum**—a concept affiliated with the principle of ***kairos*** (appropriate time and place) that involves attention to audience, duration, and style. Decorum itself is sometimes defined as "appropriateness" and has been tied to the classical idea of *prepons,* "meaning to say or do whatever is fitting in a given situation" (Crowley 232). When practicing decorum, classical students of rhetoric were urged to adopt a style appropriate to their given situation, one that took into account the specific dictates of audience, topic, and context for that occasion.

Decorum: "A central rhetorical principle requiring one's words and subject matter be aptly fit to each other, to the circumstances and occasion *(kairos),* the audience, and the speaker."

—Dr. Gideon Burton

In modern rhetoric, the idea of decorum continues to direct choices of form. Just as you need to consider argument, audience, and format in order to arrive at an appropriate **style** for an oral or multimedia presentation, so too with visual arguments you will need to take into account the specific rules of your medium concerning the arrangement and delivery of information. One way to make such choices, as the ancient rhetoricians realized, is through evaluating your possibilities in terms of **purpose.** In the Roman rhetorical tradition, Cicero separated his discussion of decorum into three levels of style that he tied to different argumentative purposes.

Cicero defined the **grand style** as the most formal mode of discourse, employing sophisticated language, imagery, and rhetorical devices; its goal was to move the audience. He considered **middle style** less formal than grand style, but not completely colloquial; while it used some verbal ornamentation, it developed its argument more slowly and thoroughly in an attempt to persuade the audience by pleasing them. The final level, **plain style,** mimics conversation in its speech and rhythms, aiming to teach or instruct the audience in a clear and straightforward way. If we add *decorum* to our rhetorical tool kit, then we can begin to make decisions about how to create

LEVELS OF DECORUM

Level	Rhetorical Purpose	Characteristics	Example Topic: Anti-smoking Campaign
Grand or high style	To move	Ornate language; formal structures; many rhetorical devices	An anti-smoking advertisement
Middle style	To please	Some ornamentation, but less formal than grand style; argument is developed at a steady but leisurely pace	A photo essay or collage about effects of smoking or lung cancer
Plain or low style	To instruct	The least formal style; closest to spoken language; emphasis on clarity, simplicity, and directness	A Website devoted to the physiology and psychology of nicotine addiction

visual arguments. As demonstrated in the Levels of Decorum table, adapted from The Forest of Rhetoric, we can attend to argument, audience, medium, and form in terms of defining the *purpose* or *level of style* for an argument. Like our classical counterparts, we must decide if we intend to *move, please,* or *teach* our audience and adopt a style that best suits this goal.

For the rest of this chapter, we'll look at a variety of different models for visual arguments, examining the way in which we need to adjust our choice of style according to the formal and rhetorical demands of each.

> The most effective visual argument considers a combination of factors: audience, argument, medium, purpose, and form.

Crafting the Op-Ad as a Public Argument

When deciding on the medium and form for your visual argument, you might be drawn to one of the most concise and common types of visual rhetoric: the **opinion advertisement.** Most op-ads, such as the Body Shop example we saw in Figure 8.1 or the Guerrilla Girls billboard in Figure 8.2, are advertisements that promote an opinion more than an actual consumer product. Many nonprofit organizations, special interest groups, and political parties find the op-ad to

> *Seeing Connections*
> For detailed analysis of advertisements as persuasive visual rhetoric texts, see Chapter 2.

FIGURE 8.3. Anti-smoking op-ad produced by the Campaign for Tobacco-Free Kids.

Source: http://tobaccofreekids.org/actioncenter/printpostss.html. Accessed July 12, 2003.

be a particularly useful and effective way to reach their target audiences. Like all advertisements, the op-ad is a compact persuasive text, one that uses deliberate rhetorical strategies and appeals to convey its message. In addition, like other types of ads, an op-ad may rely partially on written text, but it tends to prioritize the visual components of its argument.

In Figure 8.3, for instance, the ad makes its point through a strategic combination of visual elements: a photograph of young girl, cigarette held casually in one hand with semblance of adult sophistication; a fragment of a Philip Morris report, seemingly ripped from an official document; a prominent header that accentuates key words in boldface type; and an effective layout that sets up a one-to-one correspondence between the two central objects—the teenager's cigarette and the Philip Morris memo. These visual elements create an argument based both on pathos (the girl's image) and on logos (the fragmentary document), designed to convince parents of the insidious practices of tobacco companies.

COLLABORATIVE CHALLENGE

The Campaign for Tobacco-Free Kids used the image of the girl with the cigarette in Figure 8.3 five years earlier in a different anti-smoking advertisement. With a partner, go to your library and find a copy of the *New York Times* for March 11, 1998, and locate the Tobacco-Free Kids ad with the heading "The Lives of Five Million Kids Could Go Up in Smoke." With your partner, discuss the different ways in which this image is used in the two advertisements. Consider layout, design, style, typeface, and, most importantly, how they work together to produce an overall argument. Now brainstorm a third ad, using the same picture as a starting point, but directed toward a teen audience. Share your ideas for the new op-ad with the class.

Seeing Connections
To consider the rhetorical strategies used in cigarette ad parodies, see the discussion of the Truth campaign's ad "Body-bags" in Chapter 2.

Parody in Visual Arguments

Anti-smoking ads also provide multiple examples of a specific type of rhetoric strategy: **parody,** the use of one text's formal properties to subvert the meaning of the original and make an independent argument. Parody is a particularly effective strategy for an opinion advertisement because it directly targets a particular product, brand, company or ideology when making an argument. Such

A Closer Look
To further explore the relationship between audience and argument in the op-ad, compare several different anti-drug ads (in both print and commercial form), aimed at different audiences, by visiting the National Youth Anti-Drug Media Campaign Website. www.ablongman.com/envision086

ads evoke and then subvert traditional advertising in order to make their own arguments about the product, the company, or the politics behind selling a brand. We see parody at work in Figure 8.4, a spoof ad from *Adbusters* magazine's Website.

FIGURE 8.4. This Joe Chemo ad derives its power from its parody of the well-known Joe Camel character.

Here, the iconic figure of Joe Camel has been transformed in an attempt to dramatize the link between cigarettes and lung cancer. In this ad, Joe Camel becomes Joe Chemo; notice the way in which even the mascot's trademark symbol of his "coolness"—his sunglasses—have found their way into this parody ad, transformed, as he gazes on them sorrowfully, into a symbol of loss. Held away from his face, exposing his ravaged eyes, they are a now mere reminder of the ostensibly "cool" life he once had with his cigarette-smoking ways.

CREATIVE PRACTICE

Visit the False Advertising Gallery, and select an ad that uses parody as a strategy of argument. Describe what claim you think the ad is making. Now, working with that claim, design a different op-ad that makes the same argument but does not use parody to do so. Write a brief analysis of the two ads, exploring the different form, content, and persuasiveness of each ad.

www.ablongman.com/envision087

Calls to Action

In each of these op-ads, the argument was shaped with attention not only to *audience,* but to *purpose.* While some ads aim to inform, others have a more pro-active agenda, trying to produce a certain behavior in their viewers—such as motivating them to actually take action against tobacco companies. The American Legacy Foundation offers us an example of the potentials for the op-ad form. During its 2002–2003 Infect Truth Campaign, this organization produced a series of advertisements designed to move the reader to action.

Student Writing
View Travis Skare's powerful call to action in his Flash animation op-ad on alternative fuel sources.
www.ablongman.com/envision088

One ad typical of this series featured a rather blurry photograph of a woman, seen through a window in conversation with friends (see Figure 8.5). There is nothing exceptional about the image itself, except perhaps for the vivid orange of her rather large earrings. The color complements the orange background of the facing page, where the reader finds the ad's main text, enclosed neatly in two perfect circles: "The $8.2 billion the tobacco industry spends per year in marketing should go in one ear . . . and out the other." A glance at the

FIGURE 8.5. This Truth ad encourages anti-smoking activism in its message and its design.

bottom of this page reveals a diagram showing hands cutting and modifying the circles. Suddenly it becomes clear: these are how-to instructions for turning the circular texts into the very earrings that the woman is wearing. The op-ad, therefore, presents both an argument against tobacco advertising and a template for grass-roots activism. The op-ad is interactive, with the reader literally drawn into the argument itself.

The ads in Figure 8.4 and Figure 8.5 present the same underlying argument: don't smoke. Yet, as we saw, the end products varied widely, largely due to differences in audience, style, and purpose. Yet we can draw certain generalizations about the op-ad that you might find helpful should you decide that would be an appropriate visual medium for your own argument. In the next sections, we'll discuss these features in terms of format, visual juxtaposition, and verbal elements.

> Consider working with the op-ad form if you want to present a strong, clear-cut argument (such as don't drink and drive, support Affirmative Action in schools, or eliminate corporate branding on campus) using either an individual image or a select group of images.

Attending to Page Format

As you design your op-ad, consider what part of the page viewers attend to most. According to research completed by the organization Adbusters, the visual part of any page is noticed significantly more than any text on the same page. As Adbusters points out, "the most

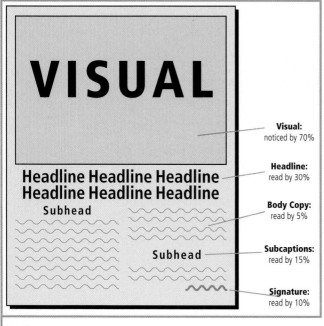

FIGURE 8.6. A visual representation of what readers notice most on a page.

important criteria is that image be the most interesting one possible and [constitute] at least half your ad whenever possible"; in other words, the image conveys the primary rhetorical force of your argument. See Figure 8.6 for a graphic interpretation of these research findings and a useful diagram for understanding the way readers process the information contained in an advertisement.

Figure 8.6 shows that 70% of viewers notice visuals most. After that, viewers attend to the headline next, and only slightly to the body copy, subcaption, and the signature. Knowing this, consider the visuals the most important elements in the op-ad design, with your headline second in importance. Follow a suggestion from Adbusters: "The most important thing to remember here is that your headline must be short, snappy and must touch the people that read it. Your headline must affect the readers emotionally, either by making them laugh, making them angry, making them curious or making them think." At issue here is rhetorical appeal: you need to think carefully about which appeal—pathos, ethos, or logos— would provide the most effective way to engage your audience.

Visual Juxtaposition in Op-Ads

Let's look at the process by which one student, Carrie Tsosie, constructed her op-ad. After writing an effective research paper that argued the dangers of allowing uranium mining on or near Navajo reservations, Carrie decided to reformulate her central points as an op-ad in order to reach a larger audience. Her initial considerations were her visual format and her headline—two elements of her ad that underwent some revision.

Carrie Tsosie, Reflection Letter
My first idea was to have an image of a deformed lamb because then the audience would see what radiation poisoning can do. I wanted to use the phrase "Stop mining before it starts," but it seemed like that phrase was overdone, and I don't think that my audience could really relate to the deformed lamb because they do not know how important it is to some Navajo people and their lives.

As shown in her completed op-ad (Figure 8.7), Carrie decided against the pathos-based image of a sick animal, and decided instead to visually feature different human environments. In addition, rather than base her ad on a strong imperative such as "Stop

Student Writing
See Flip Tanedo's op-ad on year-round school in the Los Angeles Public School System.
www.ablongman.com/envision089

Mining," she opted to soften her voice and reach her audience by asking them to reassess their assumptions about alternative energy.

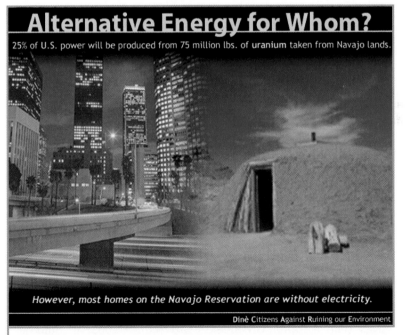

Alternative Energy for Whom?

25% of U.S. power will be produced from 75 million lbs. of **uranium** taken from Navajo lands.

However, most homes on the Navajo Reservation are without electricity.

Dinè Citizens Against Ruining our Environment

FIGURE 8.7. Carrie Tsosie's op-ad uses the power of visual juxtaposition to make its argument.

AT A GLANCE

Creating Op-Ads

- Decide on your argument and audience and the appeals (pathos, logos, ethos) that you want to implement in the ad
- Select a key image or images for your ad
- Consider the relationship between word and image: How much print text will you include? What will its function be?
- Draft text, including a short and snappy headline, to work in conjunction with your central image or images.
- Experiment with layout—arrangement, image size, organization of text—to arrive at the most powerful design.

She does so first by heading the ad with a provocative question—"Alternative Energy for Whom?"—and then following the words with a striking visual argument. It is here, in the image, that we find the main work of argumentation. Carrie combined an image from the urban landscape with a stereotypical image from the reservation to produce a striking effect, using **juxtaposition** as a rhetorical device to call attention to the discrepancy between these ways of life. This is an argument driven by the visual, where unique blended images establish the framework of comparison-contrast that informs her entire critique of U.S. mining practices.

Producing the Photo Essay as a Persuasive Document

Seeing Connections
For a detailed discussion on understanding and analyzing photos, see Chapter 3.

As we've seen, op-ads offer you the benefit of a concise, forceful argument. However, at times, you may want to develop your points more thoroughly than one page allows or, alternatively, use the visual space to show the range of material with which you've been working. If so, a photo essay might be a good option to choose for your class exhibit. In the most basic terms, a photo essay is an essay in which the images, rather than the print text, convey the central argument. This form is in many ways a variation on the conventional word-based essay where verbal texts take priority and images are often used as supplements. In a photo essay, by contrast, the visual collaborates equally with the verbal or, more often, the visual becomes the *primary mode* of representation and persuasion.

Within those parameters, the photo essay can assume many different forms: it could be a series of striking documentary photographs and an extended discussion of the life of southern share-croppers published together in book form, such as Walker Evans's and James Agee's *Let Us Now Praise Famous Men* (1941); it could be a book-length photo essay that juxtaposes images with first-person narratives, such as Lauren Greenfield's *Girl Culture* (2002); it could be a striking 14-page color spread in a magazine, such as Jennifer Steinberg

Holland and Anup and Manoj Shah's "Zebras" in the September 2003 issue of *National Geographic;* or it could even be an online arrangement of captioned photos, such as *A Rescue Worker's Chronicle,* created by paramedic Matthew Levy. In each case, the photographs and written text work together or the images themselves carry the primary weight of the argument.

COLLABORATIVE CHALLENGE

Just as with op-ads, the context of the photo essay can affect the reader's experience with your argument. For this collaborative challenge, you should work in pairs: one person will find the print form of Lauren Greenfield's *Girl Culture* (Chronicle Books, 2002) in your university library; the other partner should access the abbreviated electronic version online through the *Envision* Website.

Each person should take notes on how his or her text's argument is created through layout and design, rhetorical strategies, attention to audience, and the relationship between the verbal and the visual. After evaluating the photo essays individually, meet to discuss your observations and together generate a list of general features or guidelines for online versus print photo essays to share with the class as a whole.

www.ablongman.com/envision090

> "The photographs are not illustrative. They and the text are coequal, mutually independent, and fully collaborative."
>
> —James Agee

As a genre, the photo essay first emerged in 1936 with the launching of *Life* magazine, whose mission statement was "to see life; to see the world." Over the 63 years that it remained in print, *Life* hosted many of America's most famous photo essays, covering a range of topics from the space race, to the Vietnam War, the civil rights movement, and rock and roll. Some of the most famous early picture stories were created by photographer W. Eugene Smith, who offers us a good case study of the complexities of organization endemic to producing a well-crafted photo essay. In fact, the issue of organization, arrangement (the third canon of rhetoric), is a crucial one for any visual argument, if only because many of the relationships between words and ideas found in verbal discourse do not always translate easily into visual form. Smith wrestled with this issue of structure and arrangement for years in his quest to draft his epic photo essay, *Pittsburgh*. Between 1955 and 1957, Smith took over seventeen thousand pictures of Pittsburgh which he then attempted to group and order into a coherent

Seeing Connections Chapter 3 provides concrete examples of arrangement as the third canon of rhetoric.

AT A GLANCE

Strategies for Selecting and Arranging Images in a Photo Essay

- Decide on the scope of your project but be careful; it is possible to produce a well-developed photo essay that follows several interrelated ideas, yet it might be more productive to focus on a single theme.
- Categorize your images, ranking their effectiveness and arranging them within the theme groups according to similarities in point of view, subject, tone, or composition.
- Organize them into different configurations. Experiment by arranging them chronologically, by importance, by theme, and by subject.
- Draft some written text and consider the relationship between word and image.
- Experiment with layout, and different ways of formatting the words and images on pages.

argument about the city. While this process contains some similarities to writing, the task of organizing images puts different demands on the author as well.

Pictured in Figure 8.8 is one of the many bulletin boards that filled Smith's house at this time, so he could arrange the photos that he intended to use in different parts of his essay. Notice how Smith pinned the photographs on the boards; this technique allowed him the freedom to rearrange the essay as he experimented with the shape of his argument. As you can see, Smith's primary unit of meaning was the photograph itself; since he didn't rely on written text, the images themselves carry the full import of the argument. The *relationship* between the images therefore was the driving force of the overall work, a fact that is apparent even in the photo essay's final form (see Figure 8.9), where Smith juxtaposes images of children playing in the street, an emotional encounter between a bride and her mother, and a crowded parking lot in order to convey the various moods of the city.

FIGURE 8.8. One of Eugene Smith's bulletin boards on which he organized his photographs for his Pittsburgh project.

Untitled, ca. 1955-56. Photograph by W. Eugene Smith.

FIGURE 8.9. A page from "Labyrinthian Walk." Originally published in *Popular Photography*'s *Photography Annual, 1959.*

Photograph by W. Eugene Smith.

> The [photo]essay is relationships between photos. One must develop an awareness of the relationships, instead of just taking pictures. A person can go out and take pictures forever, and still never be able to unite, or bring together, these photos into a single theme, unless they have thought about the entire story or essay. The photos must be related—one photograph says something about the subject; the next may amplify on that subject, or may add its own dimension to the subject.
>
> —W. Eugene Smith, quoted in Cody.

What is useful for us about Smith's example is the way every aspect of a photo essay's design—from text, to photo selection, to arrangement—functions as a deliberate rhetorical act. As you construct your own photo essay, keep in mind that designing a photo essay is like drafting a research paper: you may take pages and pages of notes, but the task of actually crafting the argument involves an ongoing process of sifting through information, deciding between relevant and irrelevant material, and arranging the most powerful evidence in your finished product.

CREATIVE PRACTICE

Compose a photo essay about your university. First, decide on your thesis—that is, the main argument you wish to make about your school: is it an institution that prides itself on academic excellence? on student life? on tradition? on diversity? Then, using a digital or 35-millimeter camera, take pictures appropriate for this photo essay. You may find that you need to revise your thesis as you start taking the actual photographs: remember, any form of composition requires a continual process of reassessment and revision. Then, using at least eight photographs, construct a paper-based photo essay, using captions or print text as you feel appropriate.

Seeing Connections
You might want to review Chapter 3 for more insights about photographs as visual arguments.

The photo essay you created in the Creative Practice probably resembles one you might find in promotional material distributed by your university; however, for the most part, we rarely see the modern photo essay in paper form. Today, electronic photo essays are more numerous; they have become part of the way we understand important events and news, due in large part to Internet news sources such

A Closer Look

For a critical and theoretical discussion of the print photo essay and the relationship between word and image, read "Photography and Language" and "Spy and Counterspy" from W. J. T. Mitchell's "The Photographic Essay: Four Case Studies." *Picture Theory: Essays on Verbal and Visual Representation* (Chicago: University of Chicago Press, 1994).

as CNN.com, Time.com and MSNBC.com, which routinely publish hypertext photo essays and picture stories on their sites. These visual texts generally are composed of a series of sequential images and captions that work together to suggest a certain viewpoint or argument about a person, event, or story. What is interesting about these photo essays is how closely, in terms of arrangement, they model themselves on print texts, following a linear relationship between images.

"What happens when text moves from page to screen? First, the digital text becomes unfixed and interactive. The reader can change it, become writer."

—Richard Lanham

As Figure 8.10 demonstrates, each installment in the photo essay contains (1) a photo, (2) an accompanying caption, (3) an audio option, (4) and, a table of contents toolbar that allows the reader to navigate between images and, in this case, between "chapters." The result is an electronic text that maintains many structural similarities to print

FIGURE 8.10. "Hope at Heartbreak Motel" represents the modern photo essay: a sequential series of images with accompanying captions and audio option.

text: it offers the reader a clear sense of progression from beginning to end—while investing its argument with the rhetorical force of multiple media (word, image, sound). Organizations like *Time* and MSNBC undoubtedly are drawn to this format out of concern for their audience: in their reliance on both verbal and visual structures, their picture stories successfully appeal to both the novice and expert Web user.

Electronic photo essays often do not have to be as linear in their organization as that featured in Figure 8.10, however. One student, Ye Yuan, in creating a photo essay online, used a more dynamic format that gave the reader greater control over the way information was accessed and, relatedly, over the way in which the argument itself was assembled.

Figure 8.11 demonstrates this reader-oriented dynamic; the arrangement of information, though it follows a roughly left-to-right, top-to-bottom organization, also opens up the possibility by browsing this photo essay in a less rigidly determined fashion. As you might expect, clicking on the bolded titles takes you to a series of sequential images from that time period, offering structure to this broad discussion of war photography. At first glance, this arrangement might seem to rely on a traditional hierarchy of image and word, with the pictures serving as a secondary layer to the word-based introduction. Yet, as soon as the reader begins to interact with this photo essay, moving the mouse across the page, this illusion is dispelled. Each bolded title actually contains a roll-over graphic (see Figure 8.12), so that when the reader moves the mouse over the

> You might see a *photo essay* described as a *picture story* on many news Websites.

> Create your visual argument as a photo essay if you have a topic that can be effectively argued through an accumulation of visual arguments and evidence presented as a sequence of images.

FIGURE 8.11. Ye Yuan, "Looking Through the Lens," photo essay, page 1.

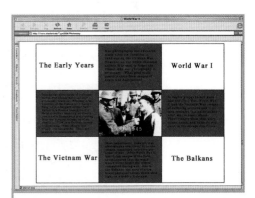

FIGURE 8.12. Page 1 of Ye Yuan's photo essay, with roll-over graphic activated.

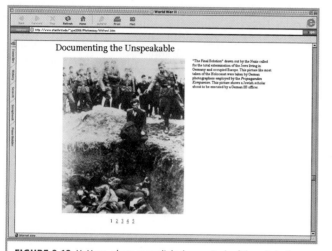

FIGURE 8.13. Ye Yuan, photo essay, linked page. Each of these linked pages contains a single photograph with an explanatory caption.

words, a representative image appears. This dynamic relationship between word and image suggests a conjunction of meaning between the two; cooperation between the visual and the verbal is designed to "hook" the reader and move him or her to the next level of the photo essay.

Once the reader activates the link and moves to the corresponding subsection, he or she finds a series of carefully selected and sequenced images that represent war photography from that time period. What is important about these subsections is that within them the photographs are the primary means of argumentation. Each subsection contains a single caption (see Figure 8.13) that remains constant for each subsequent image; the pictures change, but the print remains the same. In composing his photo essay, Ye Yuan carefully considered the ramifications of the relationship between words and images to a degree that influenced not only the design of the pages themselves but also the process by which the reader understood his central argument.

Following Ye, determine which medium best suits your needs, then you can experiment with different formats within that medium.

COLLABORATIVE CHALLENGE

Perform an Internet search on the term *photo essay*. In small groups, select one of the essays that results from the search and analyze the ways in which it creates an argument for its audience. What is the relationship between text and image? Which is given priority? What is the intended audience, and how does the design of the photo essay reflect attention to audience? How interactive is the experience; how much does the reader contribute to the construction of the text (i.e., does the photo essay follow a linear model or a networked hypertext model)? After assessing the properties of the photo essay as a group, together map out alternative strategies of arrangement—for either an electronic or paper photo essay—that this author might have followed. Present the original and your plan for an alternative version to the class, clarifying the rationale behind the changes you would make and suggesting which project—yours or the original—you feel is the most rhetorically effective photo essay and why.

Composing Websites as a Rhetorical Act

In creating your visual argument, you might decide to move your project online and produce a Website to reach a broader audience, one that addresses readers on a community, national, or even international level. Your readers will then encounter your argument as **hypertext,** or a series of interlinked Web pages. As a medium, Websites tend to be *open-ended*—that is, they focus more on opening up an argument rather than in resolving it through the linear process of moving from introduction, to evidence, to a definitive conclusion. Hypertext authors construct a framework for an argument through the **home page** (the site's introduction), the **navigation scheme** (the site's organizational structure), and the content of the individual pages, offering a proliferation of both internal and external links designed to guide the reader through the different levels of argument and evidence. In effect, a *hypertext argument* is produced by the collaboration between the author's direction and the reader's participation; in this way, the rhetorical situation of a Website as a visual argument becomes literally interactive, with the reader playing an active role in the construction of meaning.

Construct a Website as your visual argument if you are dealing with a complex, multilayered topic that may be either strongly argumentative or more interpretative in nature.

A term coined by T.H. Nelson in the 1960s . . . hypertext refers to the non-sequential arrangement of text-based information. Hypertexts are broken down into *nodes*, small units of text (screens of text, of text and graphics, or scrolling screens of text and graphics, for instance), which are *linked*, or connected to other nodes in *webs*, or connected sets of information.

—Richard Selfe

FIGURE 8.14. The Truth Crazyworld invites readers through a large arrow that they need to click to "enter" the Website.

We can see how this dynamic determines the reading experience for a site such as the Truth.com's Crazyworld home page, accessible through archives of past pages (see Figure 8.14). The site's target audience might be young people inclined towards smoking. By appearing on the Internet, the site conveys its argument to a wide ranging public, using the carnival motif to suggest what a "crazy world" we live in where tobacco companies continue to sell—and consumers continue to buy and smoke—cigarettes that contain chemicals like arsenic, benzene, and cyanide. The site's primary *level of decorum* is plain style; through simple language and engaging visuals, the Website seeks to instruct viewers in the dangers of tobacco usage to both smokers and nonsmokers. Although the Truth campaign is known for the in-your-face tone of its anti-tobacco campaign, little of that style or content appears in the primary site pages. The reader is drawn into the argument through the use of a moderate, inviting tone (indicative of Cicero's middle level of style), expressed through the carnival metaphor and engaging visuals; he or she only encounters the more explicitly argumentative indictments of Big Tobacco in the site's subsidiary content pages (that depend on the plain level of style) that focus on statistics, interviews, and indictments of cigarette companies.

Yet the power of this visual argument is in the flexibility of its format, which allows the reader to explore its many features. That is, while it resists relying on the sort of linear development typically found in paper texts, it still offers the reader a variety of structured and clearly delineated pathways into its central arguments against Big Tobacco.

On the surface, the site engages the reader through its striking graphics and visual **menu bar,** consisting of links to different aspects of the site. However, its primary **navigation toolbar,** the list of links that provide the reader most direct access to the interior of the Website, is actually hidden beneath the clown image. The toolbar only appears when the reader rolls the mouse over the word "Navigate," placed beneath the curved arrow that points at the clown. From the initial viewing of this Website, reading is a process of exploration; the reader has great responsibility for making logical sense of the text. In other words, there is no "right way" to enter or navigate this site.

AT A GLANCE

Principles for Web Analysis and Design

- *Audience Stance:* The ways in which the audience is invited to participate in online documents and the ways in which the author creates an *ethos* that requires, encourages, or even discourages different kinds of interactivity for that audience.

- *Transparency:* The ways in which online documents relate to established conventions like those of print, graphic design, film, and Web pages. The more the online document borrows from familiar conventions, the more transparent it is to the audience.

- *Hybridity:* The ways in which online documents combine and construct visual and verbal designs. Hybridity also encourages both authors and audiences to recognize and construct multifaceted identities as a kind of pleasure.

—Mary Hocks

Three Principles of Web Design

Websites as visual arguments profit from careful attention to audience, purpose, and form. Yet they also need to be constructed with particular attention to the properties of the medium. We might approach the principles of Web design through the terminology suggested by visual rhetoric scholar Mary Hocks; she frames the rhetorical properties of Websites in terms of *audience stance, transparency,* and *hybridity.*

If we were to assess the Truth site according to this rubric, we might arrive at the following conclusions:

- **Audience Stance:** The reader is invited in to be entertained as well as informed; the layout and text of the Truth site, through its Crazyworld motif, suggest a fun-house atmosphere that

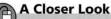

A Closer Look

For critiques of popular Websites, read Jakob Nielsen and Marie Tahir's *Home page Usability: 50 Web sites Deconstructed* (New Riders Publishing, 2002) or visit The Worst of the Web to see examples of poorly designed pages. www.ablongman.com/envision091

allows the reader freedom to browse the site's contents while underscoring the serious nature of the topic.

- **Transparency:** As a result of its reader-centered organization, this site offers multiple points of entry, taking full advantage of the flexibility of its medium. It therefore offers a less transparent structure than would a print ad or a conventional antismoking pamphlet.

- **Hybridity:** This site has a high level of hybridity of word and image, and in fact relies primarily on the visual for its persuasive force. Even many of the most prominent words on the site are rendered visually for effect: the retro neon sign, the old-fashioned roller-coaster ticket, the identifiable "truth" logo. In addition, the site offers the reader the possibility of experiencing its argument on many levels and in many formats by offering links to television ads, posters, and even a game site.

In this way, this site is well-tailored to appeal to its target audience of young people, whose experience with online formats would make them a ready audience for such multilayered and reader-directed arguments.

What makes the Truth Website so effective is not its flashy graphics or professional polish: it is the way in which the design reflects a careful consideration of the specific rhetorical situation. In creating your own Website, you can construct a similarly effective visual argument by considering your argument, purpose, audience, and context, and by implementing an appropriate style.

CREATIVE PRACTICE

Visit the most current Truth campaign and evaluate it according to the Principles for Web Analysis list in the At A Glance box. Assess whether or not the design is rhetorically effective for this site. Now, relying on the same content contained in the site, suggest a revision of the site that would alter how the reader experiences the site by changing at least two of the following properties: audience stance, transparency, or hybridity.

www.ablongman.com/envision092

Layout and Organization of Websites

When creating Websites, recognize that such texts cannot dictate how readers experience their arguments, nor can they control who enters the site or how they arrive at it. For this reason, although successful Websites, like all well-crafted rhetorical texts, are designed with attention to a specific target audience, they also tend to give some consideration through strategic use of **visual layout** to persuading the more unexpected readers that might come across their site. With Website layout, a crucial consideration of Web design is **usability**—namely how user-friendly it is and how accessible it is to users with disabilities. Even a site with professional design and state of the art graphic interface is ultimately ineffective if the audience cannot navigate it.

Perhaps even more important is the way the *level of decorum,* or *tone* of the piece, is managed to ease the audience into the site's argument.

Sometimes the visual layout or organization of a Website can hook viewers into becoming the audience for the argument. Figure 8.15, for instance, shows a Web page created during the U.S. war with Iraq that circulated widely over the Internet. Consider the following: How did the author rely upon the layout and organizational strategies of a well-known text—the error page—to engage readers? How does the layout and organization of the Website

> Consider users with disabilities when designing the layout of your Website.

 **A Closer Look**
To test a Website's usability, visit the Bobby Website for guidelines on improving Website accessibility for audiences with disabilities. www.ablongman.com/envision093

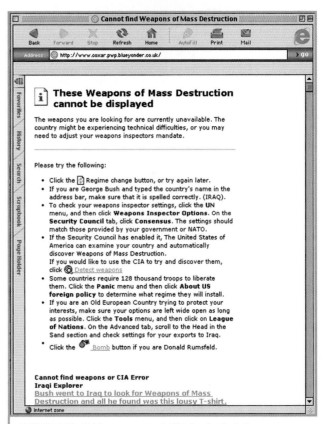

FIGURE 8.15. 404 Error page parody Website that fooled many.

mimic the well-known design of error pages and therefore suggest the larger "error" made, the author implies, by White House officials regarding the attacks on Iraq? How does the Website merge form and function to suggest the writer's point of view on international policy?

COLLABORATIVE CHALLENGE

Now go online and compare the 404 Error Page with either a White House parody site or the official White House Website. How does the parody site use visual layout, organization, and style or decorum to produce a certain rhetorical effect? Working collaboratively, draft a sample home page that makes the same argument as either the page in Figure 8.15 or one of the articles on the parody site. What rhetorical choices for layout, organization, and decorum did you make in constructing your page?

www.ablongman.com/envision094

After studying such examples, the process of authoring your own Web page or a complete Website may seem daunting at first. However, in many ways, drafting Web text resembles drafting the complex argument of a long research paper: in both cases, you need to follow a process of careful planning and organization. It makes sense, then, that many Web designers find storyboarding and brainstorming to be indispensable tools for constructing an effective Website. There are five main elements to consider when planning a Web text:

- Your target audience
- Your content and main argument
- Your purpose (to teach, persuade, or move to action)
- Your level of decorum, style, or tone
- Your site organization, navigation, and layout

This last item is of particular importance. Although the audience controls much of its reading experience, the site's navigation scheme needs to be clear and well designed so that you can guide the reader purposefully into your argument, rather than letting him or her wander aimlessly.

In storyboarding your Website, therefore, you need to account for three levels of information: a *home page* at the **primary level** (which will serve as the introduction to your site), a *series of topic pages* at the **secondary level** (which will contain both content and, sometimes, links to further, more specialized subtopic pages); and the *subtopic pages* at the **deep Web level** (which will contain content and perhaps even more links). Although most sites contain only one home page, some use a **splash page**—often featuring a single provocative quote, a flash animation, or gripping image—that functions as a hook or **gateway** to a more substantive introductory home page. There is no limit on the number of topic and content pages you can include; you should determine the scope of your project and pages based on your assessment of how to make your argument most effectively. The template in Figure 8.16 demonstrates one way in which a site can be organized.

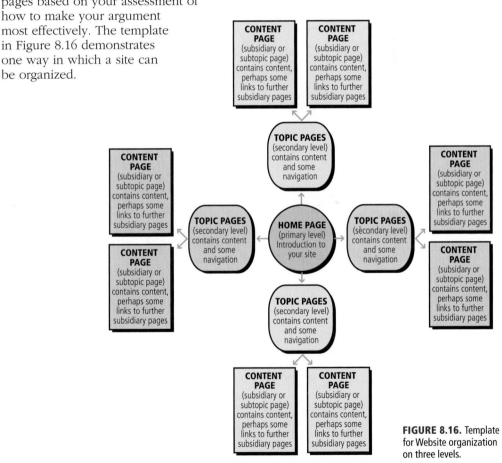

FIGURE 8.16. Template for Website organization on three levels.

Seeing Connections
For more details on
the techniques of
graphic brainstorm-
ing and storyboard-
ing, see Chapters 4
and 6.

In Figure 8.16, each topic branches into subtopics, so that the reader moves easily from general to specific. However, one of the unique properties of hypertext is its ability to move beyond such a linear construct. Figure 8.17 offers an example of a more complex model of organization, where secondary-level pages connect to multiple-content pages, and some of the subtopic pages point to external sources.

A structure like this one comes closer to maximizing the potentials of *electronic rhetoric*—what some call **e-rhetoric**—in that it allows

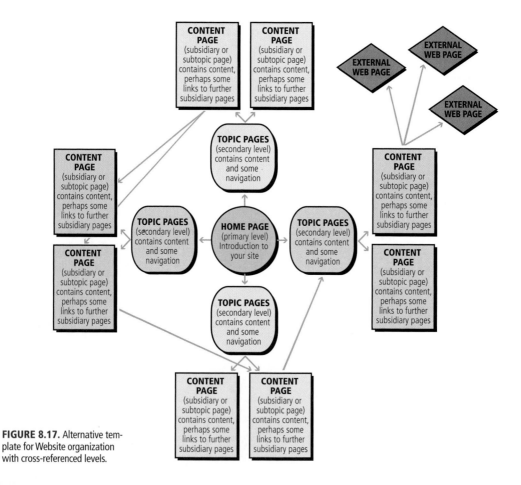

FIGURE 8.17. Alternative template for Website organization with cross-referenced levels.

> After you determine your content, you begin to plan how to divide and organize it. Information "chunking" involves breaking information into smaller units. A chunk usually consists of one topic, idea, or concept. By chunking information into small units, you make large topics more manageable. Furthermore, chunking makes information easier to revise and update. Readers can also decide which topics they need. Presenting small chunks of information that link to more detailed or complex information makes optimal use of hypertext.
>
> —Martha Sammons

the reader to move fluidly between different levels and categories of information, all related to the same topic.

From Figures 8.16 and 8.17, it should be clear that storyboarding a Website both resembles and differs from outlining a research paper. Yet there is one additional difference between organizing a print text and a hypertext, namely how you break down your information. When writing a formal paper, most writers outline their argument, dividing it into topics and subtopics that they later synthesize into long sections and paragraphs as part of the writing process. However, the writing process for a Website is different: as many researchers have noted, readers process information differently when they read it online. Accordingly, you'll need to consider ways to **chunk** your information—or divide it into manageable parts.

Effective Visual Choices

Once you have mapped out the organization of your larger site, it is time to turn to the finer elements of design and making effective visual choices for your Website. You may decide to design your site on tracing paper, in a spiral notebook, or using your favorite Web-authoring software; you may even create a Word document and then convert it to html code. The tools you use to design your Website are not as important as ensuring that the process is grounded in attention to the specific rhetorical demands of your project. We will focus on designing your home page simply because, just like the introduction to a paper, it is the place in which you initially begin your visual argument.

To a certain degree, some of the suggestions for "Writing for PowerPoint and Slide-Based Presentations" apply to Web pages as well: maintain a consistency of theme, font, and/or color throughout your site; avoid visual clutter and ineffectual use of images; think

Seeing Connections
To apply the specifics of PowerPoint to your Website design, see Chapter 7's guidelines on "Writing for PowerPoint."

> As with written compositions, Web pages must have an internal coherence; they must, in other words, be navigable. Unlike written compositions, the internal logic of a Web piece is likely to appear first in the visual construction of the page—not only in the images chosen but the colors, the placement of text or links, the font, the use of white space, and other elements linked more closely to the world of graphic design than to composition pedagogy.
>
> —Diana George

about the relationship between the word and image on the page. However, unlike a PowerPoint slide, which functions as a single unit in a timed presentation, a Web page must be designed for constant use and reuse. Therefore, in designing a home page that appeals to the reader in terms of both form and function, you might want to create a **template,** or visual precedent, for the rest of the site. Figures 8.18 and 8.19 offer two very simple strategies for designing a home page; although the format changes, you can see that the key elements remain constant.

In deciding on your layout, keep in mind that readers approach Web text differently than they do traditional print text. The design of the page, therefore, must do much more than look impressive. It needs to be founded on strong rhetorical principles so as to engage even the casual Web surfer immediately into argument of the site.

"Print readers start at the upper left; on Web pages, readers see the entire screen as a whole. Thus positioning of information is crucial."

—Martha Sammons

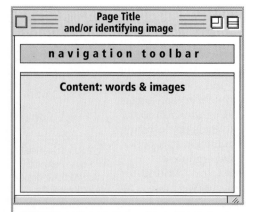

FIGURES 8.18–8.19. Two models for Web design showcasing visual choices.

COLLABORATIVE CHALLENGE

Visit Writing for the Web and read at least three of the articles listed there. Compose your top ten list of how to write for the Web. Now, as a group, evaluate your individual lists and collaborate on one main list that hits on the high points of effective rhetoric for Web-based visual arguments.

www.ablongman.com/envision095

Let's look at how two students merged a consideration of form and function in constructing research-based hypertexts. Sarah Douglas's project on Internet usage and isolation investigated several different topics: instant messaging, online dating, and **blogs** or **Weblogs,** a form of online journal published as a Web page. Her challenge was to encourage her reader to explore each form of electronic communication in depth without losing perspective on the overall argument. Her strategy was to use her design to structure her page effectively (see Figure 8.20). Notice the layers of navigation embedded at the top of her site: first, in black, the title bar that recurs from page to page; beneath that, a navigation bar, also constant throughout the site, that lists the major paths of her argument, color-coding each path with vivid, complementary colors. The third horizontal bar is the variable—it represents a secondary navigation bar for navigating within each node. Notice how the color reproduces that of the major path from which it is derived. Therefore, at a glance the reader knows exactly what path he or she is on. In addition, notice the use of the blue box to the right margin. In this box, Sarah embedded key quotes that commented on the issues contained in that particular page. By choosing a color not otherwise used by the site and also by setting the quotation box next to the main frame,

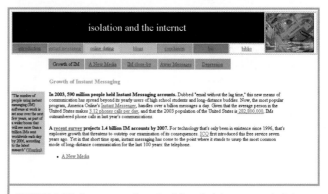

FIGURE 8.20. Content page from Sarah Douglas's hypertext on Isolation and the Internet featuring effective use of color for navigation.

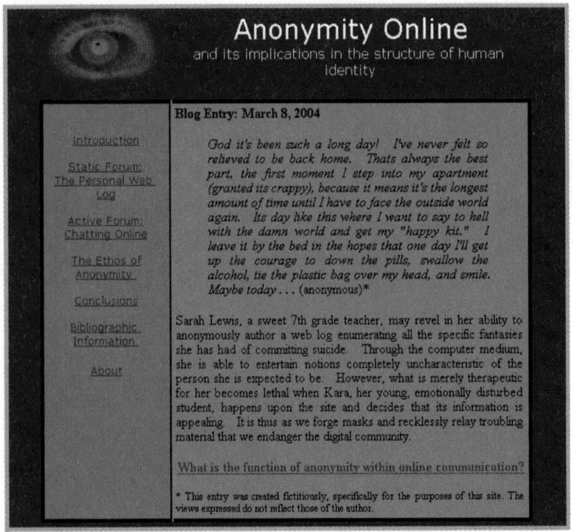

FIGURE 8.21. Home page for Monica Bhattacharya's research hypertext on anonymity and online identity, demonstrating a clean, user-friendly design.

Sarah creates a conversation with her sources and an argument that accurately represents the dialogic nature of her research project.

Monica Bhattacharya chose a different approach to maximizing the possibilities for effective e-rhetoric on her site (see Figure 8.21). Immediately striking is the use of complementary color to frame the central content, drawing the reader's attention inward to the fictional blog entry that serves as a hook into the hypertext's argument The color also corresponds to the iconic eye, positioned in the upper left corner. Notice how this image offers a powerful visual metaphor without overwhelming the page with graphics. Playing on the idea of the eye (or "I") as the window to

AT A GLANCE

Strategies for Designing a Website

• Design an identifiable header/title that may contain a signature image as well: consider how to create a sense of design consistency between your pages (use of color, same imagery, same header).

• Map a logical organization for your site to help readers find information easily and understand your site's purpose and argument.

• Include a navigation tool, usually either along the top right above or below the title, or along the left margin.

• Develop clear content, including images, words, or both.

• Consider the visual impact of your design: avoid jarring color combinations or visual clutter. Use purposeful and appropriate images, sized and formatted to be most effective on your page.

• Create a series of links, either to your own topic pages or to external sites.

• Provide a feedback link so users can email you comments, and consider including a "last updated" notation at the bottom of the page to give users date information about your site.

• Test your site for *usability*—both in terms of its general user-friendliness and its accessibility to users with disabilities.

identity and to the soul, Monica created a photonegative image of her roommate's eye and effectively led her viewers beneath the surface and into the heart of the anonymity. The rest of the Web design demonstrates a similar attention to detail; her rhetorically purposeful navigation bar to the left contains a clear hierarchical structure that gives the reader sense of a linear argument at the same time that it encourages him or her to browse; the central content culminates in her central research question—formatted both conceptually and electronically as a link into the body of her argument. This example illustrates excellent application of rhetorical principles in Website design. You might keep such models in mind as you begin to compose your own interactive Web text as a visual argument.

Student Writing
Follow links through the *Envision* Website to a variety of student-designed Web projects.
www.ablongman.com/envision096

Making Visual Collages, Montages, and Murals

In discussing op-ads, photo essays, and Websites, we have merely touched on the wide range of visual rhetoric texts you might compose for a class exhibit or as a multimedia version of your research argument. In this last section, we'll discuss a variety of additional visual projects—collages, murals, films, brochures, flyers, bound books, and more. In each case, the same rhetorical strategies that you've been experimenting with so far in this chapter can be used to devise effective visual arguments in these genres. The key lies in understanding not only your audience, argument, medium, and form, but also your goals for the project.

Depending on your underlying purpose, you may opt to produce your visual argument in the form of a **multimedia collage.** One student began his visual rhetoric project with the goal of creating a photo essay, but he soon found himself drawn to the graphic possibilities of a collage instead. Through juxtaposing and intertwining numerous images from 1960s China, Yang Shi created a powerful and complex argument about the causalities of Mao Zedung's Chinese Cultural Revolution (see Figure 8.22).

Yang recognized that in a collage, he could utilize not only the power of different images, but that he could crop and arrange the images for rhetorical purpose. Accordingly, he created an overtly chaotic layout, one that he felt reflected the lack of focus of the

FIGURE 8.22. Yang Shi's photomontage about Mao Zedong and the Chinese Cultural Revolution.

Chinese Cultural Revolution. Despite the initial impression of randomness, however, there is an underlying order to this collage: from the portrait of Mao heading the page, to the patriotic children surrounding him, to the paired statistics at the bottom, and finally the outline of China as a faint red background at the poster's center in front of the protestors, all the visual elements structure the text's visual argument. In one sense, China encompasses all these representations—struggles and tragedies, ideals and victories. Yet the collage's inclusion of Mao's choice of political imagery—the propaganda drawings of happy workers—suggests that he undermined his own anti-West stance by "marketing" himself along the same lines as traditional Western advertising. In this way,

Student Writing

Read Yang Shi's full reflection letter for further insight into his decisions in constructing this visual argument.

www.ablongman.com/envision097

Yang's strategic use of the collage form produces a powerful statement through a careful arrangement of images and color.

> The choice to avoid as much as possible the inclusion of my own text with the exception of the introduction and the list of credits at the end was a conscious one. My aim was to direct the thoughts of my viewers not necessarily to any given conclusion but to charge them emotionally in one way or another. I decided to do so with the exclusive use of photographs based on the idea that words would only detract from the vivid photography of others.
>
> —Derrick Jue, Stafford student
> reflection letter

Montages with Voice-Over or Music

For your visual rhetoric project, you might decide to construct a more dynamic text, using software applications to produce a moving montage, slide show, or animation. Each of these multimedia forms combines individual images to produce a powerful persuasive text. For example, in creating her visual argument on the enduring legacy of slavery on African-American women's self image, KiYonna Carr paired a dynamic **montage**—or sequence of still images—of historical and contemporary photographs with her own voice-over commentary.

Similarly, Derrick Jue chose a short-film format for his visual argument on war protests over the war against Iraq. In what might be described as a photo essay set to music, Derrick developed his montage by carefully selecting images from the news that depicted scenes from the war, from protest demonstrations, and from footage of politicians speaking about the war, and then arranging them into a slide show set to the song "Wake Me Up," by Evanescence. Everything in the piece, from the order of images to their relationship to the accompanying sounds, served a rhetorical purpose, working collaboratively to provide Derrick's argument on the American public's sometimes angry, sometimes ambivalent reaction to the 2003 war against Iraq. The persuasive appeal of Derrick's photo montage set to music was that it was designed specifically to rely on visual and aural elements; the rapid succession of images in the montage paired with stirring music intended to provoke an emotional reaction in its audience. The images and music carried the force of this powerful multimedia argument, without the need for written commentary.

To create a montage of moving images, use a software program such as Windows Movie Maker, i-Movie, or even PowerPoint.

Possibilities for Montages Set to Music

- Josh Schwarzapel created a montage of images exposing the strategies that alcohol advertisers use to target youth; he structured his images through three Beatles songs: "I'm Looking through You" (for his argument on their messages) "While My Guitar Gently Weeps" (for the effects of these lies—illness, sex, pregnancy, car accidents) "Yesterday" (for the concluding slide show of people who lost their lives because of alcohol).

- Monica Prieto displayed her argument about the conformity of women musicians on CD covers by juxtaposing images from their albums to a series of songs.

- Ashley Mullen's photomontage on the transformation of Aunt Jemima as a racial icon over the years displayed a series of images that merged into one another set to the music of "Thank You, Aunt Jemima," an old-time folk song that exposes the racism of the figure.

- Jake Cornelius created a powerful photomontage of newspaper images covering the aftermath of 9/11 set to "O Fortuna" from *Carmina Burana* by Carl Orff.

Murals and Tactile Visual Arguments

Seeing Connections
For more discussion on how the term *multimedia* refers quite literally to any media text, from illustrations on a chalkboard to the most advanced technological graphics or sound-enhanced documentary montage, see Chapter 7.

In addition to music montages, some of the most innovative visual arguments are not electronic but rather **tactile,** using touch or physical form, thereby suggesting ways that the medium itself can function as part of a text's argument. In other words, you should consider the word *multimedia* very literally, and don't rule out creating physical models, three-dimensional visual structures, and lifelike reproductions of your argument's focus.

Possibilities for Tactile Projects

- Jessica Vun produced a hand-sewn manners book to give readers the "feel" for gender roles in the 1800s, the subject of her visual rhetoric research paper.

- Albert Kueng pasted fake warning labels on lollipops to argue against genetically engineered high-fructose corn syrup and expose the dangers of modified foods.

- Allison Smith made drawings by hand and stained them with tea to suggest their age for a project on Margaret Sanger's political cartoons in her battle for legalized birth control.

Student Writing
See a selection of these projects through the *Envision* Website.
www.ablongman.com/envision098

- Dexian Cai, in a visual argument against the globalization of McDonald's into Asian markets, brought in traditional Chinese snacks as an alternative, food version of an op-ad.

In each of these cases, the student used the physical nature of the text itself (a model, a book, an eatable artifact, and a stained historical document) in a rhetorically purposeful manner.

Similarly, in a large-scale innovation, student Lauren Dunagan transformed her research argument about the visual rhetoric of graffiti into a mural (see Figures 8.23–8.24).

Her 14-foot-long hand-painted mural was indeed the most appropriate medium and format for exploring the issue of graffiti, social

FIGURE 8.23. Excerpt from the 14-foot mural on graffiti by Lauren Dunagan.

FIGURE 8.24. Close-up of the last panel of Lauren Dunagan's mural.

protest, and self-expression because it enabled her to merge form and content in a rhetorically effective way: she used graffiti itself to make an argument about the power of graffiti as a medium for social protest and self-expression. To paraphrase famous theorist Marshall McLuhan, in Lauren's project, the medium became the message.

While many community murals feature groups of symbolic images centered around a single theme—such as family, heritage, or social protest—Lauren Dunagan chose to use both symbolism and a chronological layout to produce what she calls a "graphic time line." She drew on her extensive research into public graffiti—from primitive drawings to Egyptian hieroglyphs, from Roman and Anglo-Saxon phrases to twenty-first-century war protest—in order to evoke the ongoing debate over the nature of unauthorized visual rhetoric in public places.

On her final panel (see Figure 8.24), she includes a single question, "Vandalism?" to focus viewers' reflections on these sequential images and ask the viewers to reassess their own assumptions about the social function of graffiti. This strikingly creative visual rhetoric project also allowed Lauren to inscribe her own persona into this discussion about self-expression; she incorporated a small phrase, "Lauren was here," at the end of the mural to indicate her own status as a social entity using graffiti as a way of presenting a public argument. Although the author's point of view invariably informs every rhetorical text, in this case, the medium itself offered Lauren a unique and powerful way to indicate her own purpose and stance in relation to the larger issue of her research project.

Student Writing

Read Lauren Dunagan's full reflection letter on her process of crafting this visual argument. www.ablongman.com/envision099

The chronology covered by Lauren Dunagan's project suggests the way in which writing has changed over time. As technology and media continue to evolve over time, so too will the possibilities for constructing innovative and effective visual arguments. From Weblogs to interactive multimedia exhibits and collaborative hypertext projects, the way we understand language, argument, and persuasion continues to change. With the changing face of modern media, you have an increasing number of choices for crafting an effective visual argument with purpose, power, and creativity.

A Closer Look

To explore a variety of tactile visual rhetoric projects, read Holly Harrison's *Altered Books, Collaborative Journals, and Other Adventures in Bookmaking* (Rockport Publishers, 2003).

Creating Your Visual Argument

In this chapter, you've learned how writing in a visual culture is an opportunity to experiment with producing your own innovative multimedia texts that exist as independent creations. You've worked through the key questions for determining your argument and your audience, then deciding upon your medium and your format, and having these choices support your purpose in constructing this visual argument. As we examined op-ads, photo essays, Websites, musical montages, and multimedia creations, you have seen that the rhetorical principles of audience, argument, form, and purpose carry across diverse media. It's time now for you to make your contribution. Write out your brainstorming ideas, and begin to shape your own visual argument.

PREWRITING CHECKLIST
Key Questions for Analyzing Visual Arguments

❏ **Argument:** What is the topic and the argument? What evidence is used to support the argument? What is the rhetorical stance and point of view on the topic? What role does the visual play in persuasion in this text? Are words and images complementary or does the argument work primarily through visual means?

❏ **Audience:** Whom is the argument intended to reach? What response seems to be anticipated from the audience? sympathetic? hostile? concerned?

❏ **Medium:** Is the medium used appropriate for the argument and its target audience? What type of interaction does the medium create with its audience? For instance, an advertisement suggests a hierarchical relationship, where the author presents the argument to the audience; a Web page, by contrast, engages the audience more interactively, allowing them a part in constructing the argument.

❏ **Form:** What are the specific characteristics of the medium? Consider layout, images, typography, style, captions. How are these elements organized?

❏ **Purpose:** What is the purpose in presenting the argument to the audience? To move them to action? inform or teach them? What type of decorum or style (grand, middle, or plain) is used to realize this purpose?

WRITING PROJECTS

Visit the *Envision* Website for expanded assignment guidelines and student projects.

1. Create a one-page op-ad featuring the argument from your research project. The op-ad should combine both pictorial and written elements to convey its point of view. As you devise your op-ad, keep in mind those elements important to successful advertising, including consideration of audience and purpose; use of space, color, and image; strategies of development; and an appropriate hook. Your goal is to produce an op-ad that both encapsulates your argument and moves your audience. Indicate in a written note the intended audience (who would read it) and context (what magazine or newspaper they would read it in) for your ad.

2. Create a photo essay based on the argument from your research paper or as part of an independent project. The images you use in your photo essay may be identical to the ones you use in your paper, a subset of the ones you use in your paper, or completely different from those that you use in your paper. Relatedly, your argument may mirror that in your research paper, or you may focus on a smaller portion of your overall argument. Your photo essay may be electronic or in paper form: but the style, arrangement, medium, and rhetorical strategies should be appropriate to your audience and your purpose. You may use written text in your photo essay, but remember that the images should be the primary mode of argumentation.

3. Create a Website about the topic you explored for your research paper or as part of an independent project. Be sure that rather than simply translating your argument to hypertext form, you consider the way in which you may need to reorganize it (rechunk it) to be appropriate for an Internet audience. Also consider the ways in which the visual design can be used to facilitate your argument.

FOR ADDED CHALLENGE

Visit the *Envision* Website for expanded assignment guidelines and student projects.

1. Create an op-ad as a visual rhetoric parody. Select an organization or product and review its advertising campaign and/or brand logo. Now create an op-ad that utilizes parody as its primary rhetorical strategy to argue against this company/product. Be sure to be clear in your purpose: Are you simply presenting information? Or is your op-ad a call to action? Once you have finished, write a one-page reflection on the strategies you used in your opinion advertisement.

2. Transform your photo essay into an electronic format that uses audio strategically as part of the text's persuasive power. You can match your images to a recorded argu-

ment. Alternatively, combine visual images with a sound track. Pick your music care-fully and time each image to match a particular mood or moment in the music or select music to match the sequence of your images. If you are transforming a paper photo essay into an electronic audio version, then feel free to modify your organiza-tion, arrangement, text selection, and even treatment of images to accommodate this shift in medium. Once you have finished, write a one-page reflection on how the shift in medium affected your argument.

3. Make a tactile argument by picking the best medium and format to display your argu-ment in physical form. This could include food, a three-dimensional model, a histori-cal replica of some sort, or even a box, such as the cigarette packs that Angel Cuevas handed out containing a warning to pick Mickey over Joe Camel as our cultural mas-cot, or the small mirror montages that Adel Jacobs created to argue for alternative responses to body image.

CHAPTER 8 ON THE WEB

Resources and Readings	Exercises and Assignments	Student Writing
• Closer Look links	• Visual argument possibilities worksheet	• Students' op-ads
• Links to sites on decorum, usability, and style	• Working with decorum	• Students-created paper and electronic photo essays
• Links to op-ad collections, photo essay archives, innov-ative Websites	• Experimenting with Web navigation	• Student-created Websites
• Guidelines for creating visual arguments	• Detailed guidelines for creat-ing visual arguments	• Collaborative Web texts and home pages
• Annotated readings	• Peer Review forms	• Collages, sound-enhanced montages, and tactile projects
	• Focus on diverse learners	• Self-reflection letters

www.ablongman.com/envision

CHAPTER 9

Writing for Public and Professional Communities

Pretend for a moment that you are walking through the scene depicted in Figure 9.1. Around you, amid the soft murmur of running water, people pace through the gently filtered sunlight, caught up in silent reflection. Removed from the academic setting and the loud crush of more media-saturated environments, you may feel quite distant from issues of writing and rhetoric; however, the setting itself exemplifies the powerful potential of visual rhetoric as a mode of community discourse. The drawing in Figure 9.1 represents a carefully designed tribute to the students murdered during the 1999 shooting at Columbine High School; behind this color rendition of a proposed memorial are embedded layers of sketches, written proposals, design sheets, three-dimensional models, blueprints, press releases, and many collaborative discussions. Figure 9.1 is, in fact, an act of writing realized on a very large scale, a public articulation in visual form of loss and healing.

In this final chapter, we'll look at how such innovative forms of writing—including monuments, design models, and multimedia community writing projects—are produced today for public audiences and in fulfillment of specific community needs. We'll examine a range of texts comprised of various media, from steel structures to electronic spaces, and explore how communities both shape and respond to the material possibilities in our world. Finally, we'll discuss ways in which you can produce texts that use your growing expertise in

FIGURE 9.1. The Design Board for the proposed Columbine Memorial conveys the power of visual rhetoric as a mode of community discourse.

visual rhetoric to contribute in meaningful ways to what we call the **public sphere,** a theoretical term for the process of debating ideas and opinions to produce consensus for the good of the community.

As we've seen in the numerous examples of political cartoons, advertisements, photojournalism, posters, and Websites that we've examined throughout this book, visual argumentation is hardly limited to the academic sphere. Often when we locate visual projects in a broader arena, outside a classroom or restricted academic audience, we call this work **public art** or **public discourse.** Material examples of public art or public discourse include monuments, memorials, community structures, and other public creations, both architectural and technological. Each consists of a multilayered process of development, design, creation, and exhibition. The end goal is *public communication;* each is designed for a particular community and hopes to move, persuade, or inform that specific public audience.

> Public art includes sculpture and other "visual art that uses both traditional and nontraditional media to communicate and interact with a broad and diversified audience about issues directly relevant in their lives."
>
> —Suzanne Lacy

Chapter Preview Questions

- What are discourse communities, and how do they determine writing acts?
- How can you use visual rhetoric as part of community writing projects?
- What are branches of oratory and how do they determine choice of media and form?
- How can you create multimedia structures for public viewing, from designs for monuments to proposals for complex Web texts?
- What is the future of writing in our multimodal society?

Anticipating Diverse Audiences

For you to begin to make such contributions, you'll need to anticipate the expectations you might encounter in different rhetorical situations and assess how diverse audiences overlap. The term **discourse community,** used by writers in various fields and professions to mean communicating to a specific audience, is useful here; it is a convenient term for referring to a given group of people who share goals, specific language or modes of communication, and knowledge. In other words, we say that a text belongs to a *discourse community* when it functions according to the conventions of that particular group. While we've stressed the importance of writing for a specific audience from the beginning of *Envision,* it's worth understanding the differences between groups, for as you head into more specific academic and professional contexts, you'll want to consider carefully how your writing across a range of media addresses the needs and expectations of the particular given community.

> Discourse communities, as a concept, links two useful notions—discourse and community. The concept of **discourse** relates to the influential role communicative practices play in constituting the social world. . . . Discourse interweaves language, action and identity in a way that engages and connects its participants, both immediately and over time and place, to give a sense of coherence and common purpose to a community. **Community,** as a concept, is often applied to describe social groups whose identity is supported by the affiliations people have to the ideas, beliefs and purpose that create a binding force for the group.
>
> —Alan Ovens

You probably participate in many diverse discourse communities, including your family, your neighborhood, your dorm, your classes, and your employment. Each of these spaces can be characterized as a group of people gathering together who share very specific **conventions** for communication (language preferences, jargon, terminology, gestures, reliance on charts, use of graphs, visual maps, or document styles). In many ways, the academic world is one large discourse community comprised of subsets organized by discipline, and we've covered many of the conventions of academic discourse throughout this book. Specifically, in academic circles, the standard mode of persuading an audience has been through the *analytical essay,* the *written argument,* the *research paper,* and the *presentation.*

"No writer can participate in a discourse community without adopting the genres of that community."

—Anne Beaufort

Yet the expectations of academic discourse communities—or groups that share language conventions as well as intellectual and cultural goals—are changing. More and more, we are seeing visual and multimedia texts, electronic presentations, and creative projects. In this way, the differences between academic and professional rhetorical situations are decreasing. As you look beyond your writing class to your professional future, you may wish to think about the ways in which your skills in visual rhetoric will help you navigate the demands and expectations of diverse discourse communities beyond college.

Using Visual Rhetoric in Community Writing

You might have already begun this process; the innovative visual arguments that you might produce within an academic setting, including op-ads, murals, photo essays, and even montages, also address real audiences in the public arena. Although we framed these projects as part of a final class assignment, you might be just as likely to produce such texts for a nonacademic discourse community, such as a nonprofit agency, your city council, or members of an outreach group. In fact, you might already be producing pieces of practical writing as part of your participation in a local organization or your volunteer work with a community group; perhaps you've authored a Website with narrative and images from a group trip, compiled a scrapbook of experiences from a religious retreat, or drafted a proposal for a new meeting place for an off-campus organization. Or maybe as part of your activism for a student group, you've created brochures, flyers or posters protesting injustice on campus.

While you might have created such texts as part of your own personal involvement with your community, it is also possible that you might find yourself learning to produce these texts as part of your academic course work. When such visual-verbal projects, aimed for the public good of a given community group or charity, are assigned within a classroom setting, we call it **community writing** or **service learning** because you combine learning (or writing) with service to the community. You'll find service-learning courses across various disciplines throughout the university. In such cases, you might compose documents for local community nonprofit agencies, often collaboratively. You might be asked to produce a grant letter, a newsletter article, a fact sheet, a brochure, or even a Web page. Such projects benefit both the nonprofit organization and the members it serves; in addition, it also provides invaluable preparation for producing the kinds of documents and projects that you'll often be asked to write throughout your professional career. In effect, community writing moves you beyond the academic environment. Your audience is part of the broader public community, and your writing assumes real-life, practical applications.

Seeing Connections
To review other possibilities for innovative visual arguments, look back at Chapter 8.

Service-learning and community writing projects often function as complements to your university course work and offer a unique dialogue between academic and public discourse communities.

"Community-based writing—whether it is practical or academic—is *writing for real.* It engages tangible issues, uniting thought and action, and it calls for new approaches to writing."

—Carolyn Ross and Ardel Thomas

Designing Projects for Service-Learning Courses

Some community writing projects are multilayered, just like many of the professional projects that you might encounter outside the university

A Closer Look

For more information on community writing projects and service learning, see Carolyn Ross and Ardel Thomas's book, *Writing for Real* (Longman, 2003).

setting. As part of your service-learning course, you might be asked to develop not *one* flyer, pamphlet, or poster, but rather a series of interconnected texts. For example, as part of their community writing project for the nonprofit organization, Alternative Spring Break (ASB)—a program that offers college students an opportunity to use spring break to help a specific community by working with the homeless, cleaning out land to grow plants, building affordable housing, etc.—students Gene Ma and Chris Couvelier created an interview questionnaire, a formatted feature article for online publication, and created a new "logo" as well as new design and content for the Alternative Spring Break (ASB) Website. The logo in Figure 9.2 features a sleek, minimalist approach to engage prospective students: the red and white letters replicate the university's colors (in place of the former blue and yellow); the faint image of students in San Francisco's Chinatown conveys the location of one of ASB's most successful community programs, focused on helping the Asian-American population.

FIGURE 9.2. Gene Ma's redesigned logo for the ASB Website.

The key to this project, as with many community writing tasks, was collaboration. Here's how it worked: Gene Ma and Chris Couvelier divided the tasks. Chris contacted past participants of ASB through a written survey and follow-up telephone calls and then created a newsletter suitable for publication on the Web page (see Figure 9.3). Then Gene analyzed the rhetoric of the ASB Website, and he found it dull and cluttered. He created a new logo, new content, different pictures, and 40 pages of updated materials to post on the Website (see Figure 9.4). Finally, he created a humorous PowerPoint presentation to convey to his colleagues in class the process of completing this community writing project. The multiple layers of this

FIGURE 9.3. Chris Couvelier's newsletter with visual layout.

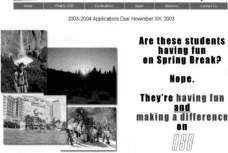
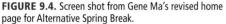

FIGURE 9.4. Screen shot from Gene Ma's revised home page for Alternative Spring Break.

service-learning project made it much more akin to the kind of work that both students might find in the workforce, whether they work for nonprofit or professional organizations. In each case, the total needs of a specific community dictated the various steps along the way to completion of the visual rhetoric project.

Student Writing
See the award-winning Website project for ASB.
www.ablongman.com/envision/100

Producing Work for Community Organizations

In another community writing project, students Daniel Balick and Mike Situ developed graphics for the advertising campaign of the university's public service organization, the Haas Center. As they explained, "our project was not a written one; instead it was a visual display consisting of a series of posters to promote community service through the Haas center." Their task was to design graphics that

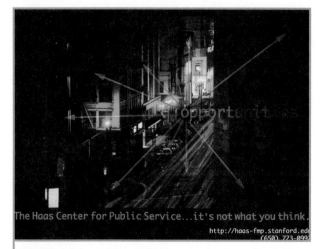

The Haas Center for Public Service...it's not what you think.

http://haas-fmp.stanford.ed(
(650) 723-099

FIGURE 9.5. Dan Balick and Mike Situ, new advertisement for the Haas Center for Public Service, created March 2003 with Photoshop.

 Student Writing

Explore the student-created Website, "Revolutionizing Healthcare," designed by Nicholas Giacomini, Monique King, Rebecca Pratt, and Radhika Zopey, a community-focused e-zine dedicated to promoting awareness about injustices in the U.S. healthcare system.

www.ablongman.com/envision101

would target male students in particular, and they created three different models using diverse strategies of visual rhetoric design. Figure 9.5 shows their preferred ad sample: a cool, clean modern image of a city street with lines directing the viewer towards sites of community service. By completing this project, Mike Situ and Dan Balick learned how to work effectively in a group at a professional level, and they produced quite innovative and different sample advertisements. As they reflected: "This project also taught us a lot of valuable information about advertising. We researched what interested our young male target group and we methodically designed our posters to appeal to the general interests of this group." The materials showcase how writing for the community in multimedia forms is a crucial skill and an important part of our changing curriculum as well as a bridge between academic and professional audiences.

COLLABORATIVE CHALLENGE

Contact the center for public service at your university and locate a community agency that might be interested in student writing projects—for instance, a battered women's shelter, a soup kitchen, or a low-cost after-school daycare program. Working with that organization, decide upon a visual-verbal text that could suit its needs. Be sure to consider the demands of your specific rhetorical situation in creating your text.

Attending to Time, Purpose, and Subject

It is helpful to turn to classical rhetoric for ways of understanding the needs of your specific writing situation as you begin to draft, design, and create a community writing project. Let's explore the way in which classical rhetoricians divided oratory into three branches based on time, purpose, and content, and apply these principles to visual and multimedia writing projects. According to Aristotle, each **branch of oratory** corresponds to a specific time, purpose, and topic of invention. Since these may not be familiar concepts, let's look at some contexts for these rhetorical branches that you might encounter in your writing:

- For **judicial** or **forensic discourse,** you might find yourself presenting a position on a past action in debate team, moot court, or law school, using verbal arguments as well as charts, graphs, photos, and other visual evidence arranged and designed in a way to persuade your audience.
- For **deliberative** or **legislative discourse,** you might exhort or dissuade an audience if you are trying to start your own business, develop new software or plan a cross-country trip; you would write a memo, a financial plan, and the specifications concerning the worthiness of the enterprise; you might also use PowerPoint "decks," charts, images, prototypes, models, and animation to persuade your audience visually.
- For **epideictic** or **ceremonial discourse,** you might engage in the rhetoric of display in a senior thesis, company report, advertising campaign, or political party statement, if you were to craft words and images that praise or blame your subject.

> ## AT A GLANCE
>
> ### The Branches of Oratory
>
> 1. *Judicial* or "forensic" discourse corresponds to the past and has to do with accusing or defending a subject; the content revolves around justice and injustice.
> 2. *Deliberative* or "legislative" discourse concerns the future and is used to exhort or dissuade subjects regarding good or unworthy subjects.
> 3. *Epideictic,* also called "ceremonial" or "demonstrative" discourse, deals with the present; it operates through praise or blame concerning virtue and vice.

Working with Branches of Oratory

As you can see, you'll work with these three rhetorical branches throughout your academic and professional career. Each of these branches of rhetoric governs the shape that words and images will take for writing in various discourse communities.

COLLABORATIVE CHALLENGE

Each class group should pick one of the following *branches of oratory* and create visual-verbal-multimedia texts for public viewing.

1. *The Judicial Group:* Set up a conference on campus to indict or defend a public figure's stance on a particular issue in social justice. You might, for instance, hold a conference about the charges made against elected or school officials concerning the treatment of janitorial workers on campus. For your writing project: create flyers, reserve a hall, make a documentary film, compile an audio montage, and design a Website to collect student responses.

2. *The Deliberative Group:* Set up a forum for public discussion about a pressing social issue, such as the need to build more homeless shelters or a new student union on campus, or the drafting of a new state policy granting education to migrant workers. For your writing project: create a newsletter presenting various views that exhort or dissuade voters on the issue, that showcase photos and testimonials, that offer sound clips, data, and blueprints of the proposed buildings.

3. *The Epideictic Group:* Establish space to assess the merits of a current situation, such as alcohol use on campus or the value of a program such as Alternative Spring Break, or to negotiate the decision to give an honorary degree to a present school official or public service leader. For your writing project: survey students and community members, create a report with images and narratives, design a proposal and include visual rhetoric to convince your audience.

Seeing Connections
To practice your presentation skills and make your oral rhetoric as strong as your multimedia project, see Chapter 7.

As each of the options for the Collaborative Challenge reveals, writing for community audiences entails a high degree of innovation on your part. Use in combination all the tools you've learned throughout this book, but pay careful attention to the mode of rhetoric that you are using to complete your project.

The branches of oratory show how rhetoric, which by now we know includes more than speech but also written, visual, and hybrid texts, is fundamentally a *purposeful* and *public act*. The importance of rhetorical texts (as opposed to aesthetic texts) is that they serve very concrete goals and meet the needs of a particular community.

We find this to be true from your class community, to your professional work community, to the "public at large."

Public Discourses and Changes in "Writing"

The three branches of oratory provide us with a helpful framework for assessing and producing a range of persuasive texts, both academic and public in nature. They suggest, moreover, the way in which in our increasingly visual, multimodal world, the most powerful pieces of modern rhetoric come in a variety of forms—visual, tangible, aural, electronic, or material. Today, many innovative forms of multimedia texts act as public statements for people to use in communicating across nations and cultures. A rapidly growing number of multimedia "monuments" and public structures are being produced not only in print form but also on the Web, on the streets of our cities, and in our town halls and schools. People are turning to this type of hybrid, visual rhetoric to reflect on world events—to respond to issues by writing about them through visual and multimedia projects that challenge us to think in new ways about what writing means today. "Writing" has expanded across the possibilities of multiple media. The rhetorical strategies apparent in such texts suggest ways that you can harness the tools of persuasion for powerful, public writing of your own.

Today, writing is becoming increasingly visual and multimedia in form.

Some of the most famous forms of public writing appear in the shape of **monuments.** Consider representational structures of statues or memorials that use the human form to commemorate events or moments of history. From the Lincoln, Jefferson, or FDR memorials in Washington DC, to war memorials such as the Iwo Jima Memorial monument in Connecticut, to the Crazyhorse monument in South Dakota, the representation of the human body in

A Closer Look
Look through the *Envision* Website at the descriptions of two recently established memorials: The Irish Hunger Memorial in New York City's Battery Park and the World War II Memorial in Washington, DC.
www.ablongman.com/envision102

action provides a memorable message about the event through the form of visual rhetoric. Abstract structures carry similar potency. The Vietnam War Memorial, for instance, transforms a polished and expansive black granite slab into a medium of remembrance and reflection. The human form appears as a reflection of the viewer echoed in the black mirror of the monument wall, at once both a witness to and an eerie participant in the loss of life commemorated by the monument. More recently,

electronic memorials provide new possibilities for public writing about events of national and international significance; consider Websites designed to commemorate the victims of the Oklahoma City bombing, the death of Princess Diana of Wales, or the legacy of Kurt Cobain. But once you begin to look, you find memorials in visual form everywhere—from online tributes to lost loved ones to more **tactile manifestations of writing** such as handmade crosses left at the sides of the road, plaques attached to trees, and benches with dedications on the sides of school yards or parks. Public memorials today use visual rhetoric to reach a broad audience, commemorate those now lost, and shape a community's sense of itself.

CREATIVE PRACTICE

Compare three different types of online memorials through the *Envision* Website:

- The Vietnam Veterans Memorials Around the World
- The Vietnam Veterans' Memorial Wall Page
- Virtual Memorials

Analyze the rhetorical functions of each; assess both representational and abstract monuments, compare war-based to community-based memorials; consider the difference between these and more personal forms of public writing. What branch of oratory is operational in each case? How can people respond to similar events or convey similar emotions using different media and different forms?

 www.ablongman.com/envision103

A Closer Look

See "Advocates Debate the First Amendment, Ten Commandments," the debate over the monument that made a religious argument and challenged notions of church and state.

www.ablongman.com/envision104

Monuments and Community Conflicts

Working through the Creative Practice, you may have begun to realize that sometimes individual and community memorials overlap or can even be in conflict with one another. We may find instances of such contradictory public discourse in war demonstrations, where families of killed soldiers march for peace. Similarly, a battle over the visual rhetoric of a given location can happen with the display of flags in churches, crosses in schools, or, more specifically, in the 2003 debate over the placement of a monument to the Ten Commandments in the lobby of the rotunda at the State Judicial Building in Montgomery, Alabama. In this conflict between a religious community and a community of elected government officials, both sides viewed the 3500-ton visual structure as *an argumentative text.* As the photos in Figures 9.6 and 9.7 suggest, the center of the firestorm was a piece of visual rhetoric and two different community interpretations about the nature of public space. Here again we see that the *kairos* of the rhetorical situation—a government building at a time of ongoing debate over the separation of church

FIGURE 9.6. Moving the Ten Commandments Monument off government property.

and state—made creating and installing the Ten Commandments in that building a form of "writing," a deliberate visual argument about the relationship between the government and the place of Judeo-Christian beliefs in public locations.

The outpouring of public response shown in Figure 9.7 to the removal of the monument (in Figure 9.6) suggests that public visual rhetoric takes the form not only of the structure itself—the slab of marble shaped into two tablets—but also the form of *embodied rhetoric,* here expressed through the bodies on the floor. More importantly, perhaps, the debate over the monument shows us that memorials are always much more than the personal expression of religious values or individual loss. They serve an argumentative function; they convey a shared ideology or collective belief. For this reason, the design, construction, and response to memorials are often hotly debated. These structures *shape* a community's sense of itself even as they *emerge*

FIGURE 9.7. Dozens of people outside the Alabama Judicial Building hold a vigil and lament the removal of the monument.

Seeing Connections
For an extended discussion of embodied rhetoric, refer to Chapter 7.

out of that community's needs and stated objectives.

Multimedia Expression of National Mourning

Perhaps one of the most memorable instances of public and purposeful writing happened on a national scale and occurred with the visual, verbal, and multimedia texts produced in response to the September 11, 2001 attacks on the United States. These diverse forms of visual writing, significantly, served in turn to create a community among the mourners and survivors. In the wake of the attacks, the world witnessed the creation of Websites, murals, music tributes, physical monuments and even interactive flash-based graphic applications that show us how writing itself is changing, bridging media and audiences, and spanning international communities and diverse political purposes. Consider the way in which each textual creation also operates as public discourse. Sometimes it is a mural, such as that featured Figure 9.8, which evokes Picasso's famous painting *Guernica* in terms of the abstracted figures suffering under an attack from another country. Other times, it can take the form of a less tangible medium: a song, such as Bruce Springsteen's "The Rising," or an architectural design such as the "Tribute of Light," which we will look at in Figure 9.11. It might be a Website: an electronic exhibit like the New York Historical Society's "WTC: Monument" or an online memorial quilt to the victims and heroes of 9/11, composed of 20,000 individual pages.

The text might even combine several different media; the Patriot's

FIGURE 9.8. The Academy of Mt. St. Ursula Art Club created a mural as a collaborative project in response to 9/11.

Day Anthem in Figure 9.9, for instance, represents a union of sound and image, audio and Internet links. The Anthem itself is a version of "The Star Spangled Banner" with its lyrics updated to reflect the events of 9/11. In addition to being available on CD, the song has its own Website, one that visually demonstrates the song's rhetorical purpose through pairing the lyrics with a modified image of the World Trade towers. The site links to a recording of the Anthem, sung by a female voice and accompanied by a dynamic scrolling text. Looking

FIGURE 9.9. Patriot's Day Anthem Web collage of visual, verbal, audio, and flash-graphic materials.

at the image in Figure 9.9, we can see how the text addresses a public audience on the Web, shows membership in an American discourse community through the selection of images and words, and reveals a deliberate rhetorical purpose—to commemorate and honor—in its combination of words and graphics. At the same time, the visual text fosters a community by suggesting that its viewers are bound together by shared ideals and values.

It is important to recognize these many examples, not only for their formal diversity, but also for their commonality as purposeful instances of public rhetoric. In each case, the author or collaborative team uses writing and visual rhetoric in an innovative way to communicate, inform, and persuade. Each text emerges out of a particular context, addresses a specific rhetorical situation, communicates with a very specific audience, and conveys a very focused argument. In this way, we can consider each text a form of "writing" for our increasingly visual, multimedia world. In fact, many people call such innovative writing **multimodal** specifically because of the way that these texts utilize many different media or modes of communication in producing forceful arguments.

A Closer Look

Take time and browse through the September 11 Digital Archive, an expansive collection of online materials generated in response to the 9/11 tragedy.

www.ablongman.com/envision105

CREATIVE PRACTICE

Explore online for public visual rhetoric and writing produced in response to the 9/11 attacks, such as that found through the September 11 Digital Archive. Using the left navigation bar, click first on Still Images to look at the user-contributed drawings and paintings, then return to the home page and follow the Guide to Websites link and examine these multimedia responses. Write up a brief analysis of the many forms of "writing" you have seen and the argument made by each one. Then, use the rhetorical elements of design and composition that you find most powerful, and sketch your ideas for your own possible multimedia response to this event.

www.ablongman.com/envision106

As you noticed in the Creative Practice, the aftermath of 9/11 produced powerful forms of public, multimedia writing that appeared across the Web, in city billboards, on T-shirts, even as patriotic tattoos. These kinds of public discourses mark a historical shift enabled by new technologies and the increasing sense of our world as what Marshall McLuhan called "a global village." It seems that such texts are one sure sign that our very understanding of what it means to communicate in the public sphere, or to "write," is indeed changing.

Design as a Collaborative Process

In order to understand more fully how "writing" is transforming, as well as how visual texts work *as writing,* let's analyze more closely the public reaction to 9/11 and examine New York City's installation of a deliberate visual response to the collapse of the buildings and the consequent gaping absence, a public visual rhetoric text called "Tribute of Light." As Figures 9.10 and 9.11 show, the new memorial was created to provide a deliberate visual echo or "ghosting" of the fallen towers. In this way, the image of the burning buildings conveyed by Figure 9.10 would be replaced with the beautiful light of the memorial.

We may not think of a light installation as a form of "writing," but in fact the steps that contributed to the final installation had *everything* to do with the tools of analysis, argument, research, collaboration, presentation, and visual design that we've discussed in this book.

Understanding the memorial structure as a powerful rhetorical statement helps us begin to appreciate the many writing components that contributed to its creation. For beneath the finished product lies the entire process of developing, designing, and implementing the idea. As architect Gustavo Bonevardi explained in a *New Yorker* interview with Calvin Tomkins, the project was collaborative from the beginning: "There was even a sense of inevitability about collaborating—the way the firefighters and the police and the whole city have done in the rescue effort." It started with emails sent by Bonevardi and his colleague John Bennett to friends in New York and concluded with a team effort to produce "a virtual re-creation, in projected light, of the World Trade Center towers, silhouetted against the nighttime skyline."

In addition to being collaborative at every stage of the multimedia project—from written emails to drafts of visual plans to the physical securing of space and equipment—the point of this public multimedia project was to send a persuasive message: "And it's key that this is not a memorial. A memorial needs to be done, but that's not what this is. This is a statement to the rest of the world and to ourselves," Bonevardi told Tomkins. Most of all, the community that the team hoped to address was a very broad one, and the construction of a physical structure—visible to

FIGURE 9.10. World Trade Center towers burning.

FIGURE 9.11. "Tribute in Light," World Trade Center memorial project.

A Closer Look
Read Gustavo Bonevardi's own words, describing the process of designing the Tribute of Light.
www.ablongman.com/envision107

a global audience—therefore needed to convey a powerful rhetorical point. "The international aspect was key: It was the *World* Trade Center, after all, and people of many nationalities had perished there. We even proposed that, in solidarity, similar light towers be erected in cities around the world: London, Paris, Buenos Aires. The original towers were destroyed. Now virtual ones would sprout up all over the world." Virtual towers function, then, as a form of public discourse, writing a new script for the meaning of the architecture and the city of New York. In other words, the monument serves as a public act of writing in three-dimensional space. It uses visual rhetoric to communicate with a specific community.

> We set out to "repair" and "rebuild" the skyline—but not in a way that would attempt to undo or disguise the damage. Those buildings are gone now, and they will never be rebuilt. Instead we would create a link between ourselves and what was lost. In so doing, we believed, we could also repair, in part, our city's identity and ourselves.
>
> —Gustavo Bonevardi

Producing Public Visual Rhetoric as a Team

"The aesthetics were secondary to the statement."

—Gustavo Bonevardi

In a research project on the design of the new, permanent public structures to memorialize the World Trade Center, student Michael Rothenberg argued that "the public became an active and inseparable part of this design process to make certain that the new World Trade Center plans would visually and symbolically reinforce American values and appropriately memorialize the victims" (2–3). Michael's point that architecture is transforming and becoming a more community-driven act of creation is worth noting. It means that all of us participate in the shaping of our public discourses as visual structures.

Consider, for instance, Figure 9.12, one of hundreds of submissions people drafted and submitted as designs for a new memorial. These writers were responding to a specific rhetorical situation (the needs of New Yorkers) and producing visual texts as part of an ongoing dialogue about national values and human community. The image in Figure 9.12, posted on CNN.com as part of a showcase of online proposals for the new World Trade Center, reveals that each writer relied on visual rhetoric to make an argument about the memorial's significance to the local and global community; each, however, approached the task in different ways. While other designs proposed six buildings in a circular embrace arranged around a memorial pillar, or two impressive globe-topped monuments showing international solidarity, the strong fortification of Sieb's united pillars in Figure 9.12 suggests his emphasis on national strength and resistance. We learn from such models that designers use public visual discourse to assert different interpretations of what it means to memorialize the fallen World Trade Center towers and to produce powerful, permanent monuments for the public.

FIGURE 9.12. The proposed World Trade Center Memorial by Eric Sieb shows his attention to the needs of New Yorkers.

CREATIVE PRACTICE

Read Michael J. Lewis's essay, "How to Avoid a 9/11 Memorial Disaster," from *The Wall Street Journal,* August 12, 2003, in which he outlines the difficulties of constructing a successful memorial to the 9/11 disaster. Having read his article, compare his argument to that made by student Michael Rothenberg, available through the *Envision* Website, entitled "Rising from Rubble: New York Citizens Engineer the Symbolic Rhetoric of the New World Trade Center," a research paper focused on the way in which the new structural memorial designed by Daniel Libeskind, "eventually won the Ground Zero commission due to its meaningful symbolism and careful study of public opinion" (3). Finally, assess the memorials yourself by exploring the Websites for the design of the new WTC and the Webcast of public hearings. What is your opinion of the rhetorical situation facing the designers? of the final choice of Libeskind's memorial? of the way in which the memorial both reflects and creates a public community?

www.ablongman.com/envision108

As you can tell from your work in the Creative Practice, the search for an appropriate design showcases the power of effective visual rhetoric as a form of public discourse and writing in the twenty-first century. Today, public participation in the production of the memorials such as the one for the World Trade Center reveals in a dramatic way the fact that acts of writing, drawing, producing, and viewing in society are increasingly collaborative and complex.

Visual Rhetoric for Local Communities

The community of Columbine, in suburban Colorado, has struggled with similar complex questions about audience, purpose, visual form, collaboration, and message in its efforts to construct a memorial to the students who died in the 1999 Columbine High School shooting. The Design Board shown in Figure 9.13 represents only one small piece of this effort. In order to commemorate those lost in the tragedy, the Columbine Memorial Committee designed a permanent community structure to be built in a park adjacent to the high school. From its earliest stages, the project was a collaborative one. The design team invited members of the community to participate in the process. First they spoke with families of those killed and next those injured in the shootings. Then the team held design workshops and collected surveys, and finally they held an open house with the community at large. Intended both to memorialize the victims of the tragedy and to facilitate the healing for family and friends, the plan from its inception involved, we learn from the Columbine Memorial Website, the goal to "create a memorial with content and purpose 100% derived from members of the Columbine community." The design boards themselves reflect this collaborative focus (see Figure 9.13): the visual argument intersperses a summary of the project's purpose and design with brief quotes from survivors, longer reflections on the lost students, an aerial sketch of the memorial itself, and a striking photograph showing how a stone monument can both inscribe memory and touch the lives of its visitors.

A Closer Look

Read about the planning process, goals, and the award-winning design of the Columbine Memorial through the link available on the *Envision* Website

www.ablongman.com/envision109

The visual rhetoric of the design boards reproduce in miniature the way that the larger structure of the monument will embody a public reflection

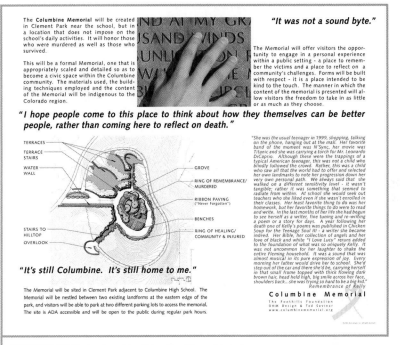

The **Columbine Memorial** will be created in Clement Park near the school, but in a location that does not impose on the school's daily activities. It will honor those who were murdered as well as those who survived.

This will be a formal Memorial, one that is appropriately scaled and detailed so as to become a civic space within the Columbine community. The materials used, the building techniques employed and the content of the Memorial will be indigenous to the Colorado region.

"It was not a sound byte."

The Memorial will offer visitors the opportunity to engage in a personal experience within a public setting - a place to remember the victims and a place to reflect on a community's challenges. Forms will be built with respect - it is a place intended to be kind to the touch. The manner in which the content of the memorial is presented will allow visitors the freedom to take in as little or as much as they choose.

"I hope people come to this place to think about how they themselves can be better people, rather than coming here to reflect on death."

TERRACES
TERRACE STAIRS
WATER WALL
STAIRS TO HILLTOP
OVERLOOK

GROVE
RING OF REMEMBRANCE/ MURDERED
RIBBON PAVING ("Never Forgotten")
BENCHES
RING OF HEALING/ COMMUNITY & INJURED

"She was the usual teenager in 1999, shopping, talking on the phone, hanging out at the mall. Her favorite band of the moment was N'Sync, her movie was Titanic and she was carrying a torch for Mr. Leonardo DiCaprio. Although these were the trappings of a typical American teenager, this was not a child who blindly followed the crowd. Rather, this was a child who saw all that the world had to offer and selected her own landmarks to note her progression down her very own personal path. We always said that she walked on a different sensitivity level - it wasn't tangible; rather it was something that seemed to radiate from within. At school she would seek out teachers who she liked even if she wasn't enrolled in their classes. Her least favorite thing to do was her homework, but her favorite things to do were to read to see herself as a writer, fine tuning and re-writing a poem or a story for days. A year following her death one of Kelly's poems was published in Chicken Soup for the Teenage Soul III - a writer she became indeed. Her Bible, her collection of angels and her love of black and white "I Love Lucy" reruns added to the foundation of what was so uniquely Kelly. It was not uncommon for her laughter to shake the entire Fleming household. Every morning her father would drive her to school. She'd step out of the car and there she'd be, carrying herself in that small frame topped with thick flowing dark brown hair, head held high, big smile across her face, shoulders back...she was trying so hard to be a big kid."
Remembrance of Kelly

"It's still Columbine. It's still home to me."

The Memorial will be sited in Clement Park adjacent to Columbine High School. The Memorial will be nestled between two existing landforms at the eastern edge of the park, and visitors will be able to park at two different parking lots to access the memorial. The site is ADA accessible and will be open to the public during regular park hours.

C o l u m b i n e   M e m o r i a l
The Foothills Foundation
OHM Design & Ted Savinar
www.columbinememorial.org

FIGURE 9.13. Design board for Columbine Memorial.

on the tragedy. As designed, the memorial's primary structures will consist of two stone walls: an Inner Ring of Remembrance and an Outer Ring of Healing. The walls themselves literally incorporate the community perspective: the Inner Ring will be inscribed with narratives about the victims, excerpted from interviews with their families and friends; the Outer Ring will record first-person testaments to healing, change, and renewed faith in the face of tragedy. The memorial will function as a carefully planned piece of public discourse, a structured rhetorical experience designed to move the visitor through the community's own experience—from the remembrance of the victims, to reflections on healing, and, finally, up a staircase to a scenic overlook, where the panoramic views of the majestic Rocky Mountains are intended to leave the visitor with a sense of faith and connection to a larger community.

COLLABORATIVE CHALLENGE

Explore monuments and memorials on your campus and in your town. Take photos, create a design board or post the photos on the Web, and write up text addressing the following questions: How do the monuments or memorials address a particular community? What is the persuasive message and how does it in turn foster community through conveying shared values? Now, as a team, research the steps of planning, production, and implementation for the structure. Set up interviews with architects, art historians, or campus administrators. You might also want to interview students on campus or people in town to get a sense of audience responses to such structures. How are these monuments or memorials a form of public writing in three-dimensional space?

Visual Rhetoric for the Professional Sphere

As you can tell from the work that you've done in this chapter so far, the skills you develop as a rhetorician will make you an effective contributor to your own community through the analysis, research, and production of compelling visual-verbal texts. As you look beyond your writing classroom and campus community to your professional career and your broader participation in the public sphere, you will find yourself asked to produce effectively persuasive texts that rely on the visual and verbal as modes of argumentation for both business and nonprofit purposes. From writing business proposals and grant applications, to designing Websites and company newsletters or drafting blueprints and three-dimensional architectural models, you can create an effective piece of "writing" relevant to time, purpose, and subject.

The architectural firms led by Gustavo Bonevardi or Daniel Libeskind are only two examples of locations in the professional sphere that call for expertise in visual rhetoric. From nonprofit organizations aimed at improving living conditions in a given community to consulting companies engaged in business mergers and the sale of IPOs such as Google.com, professional working environments

Student Writing

See examples of student projects, produced collaboratively for public audiences, on the *Envision* Website. These include

- A multimedia magazine about global news for local campus audiences
- An ezine on healthcare issues
- Proposal "pitches" for various social entrepreneurship projects
- Community outreach projects

www.ablongman.com/envision110

today are more and more reliant on **hybrid discourses**—creative combinations of word, image, and sound—to conduct transactions and communicate between diverse audiences. As you look ahead to work in these spheres, the principles of visual rhetoric will guide you in using these discourses effectively and purposefully. Consider how you might use these skills to begin to make your contribution to the larger world in innovative ways. Forms of writing for professional situations might include:

Seeing Connections
For detailed guide-
lines on creating
Websites and other
multimedia texts, see
Chapter 8.

- Formal business proposals that include graphic mock-ups and models
- Grant applications with careful arrangement of sections and materials
- Website demonstrations of prospective business ventures
- Design memos with physical samples, architects' blueprints and models
- 3D samples for new buildings (from hotels to amusement parks)
- Multimedia memos to politicians on behalf of a lobbying group

Nonprofits and companies are in essence specific discourse communities, and you can apply the skills you have learned in this chapter for your work in this professional sphere. Explore your possibilities through the Creative Practice.

CREATIVE PRACTICE

Select from the list above the form of professional visual rhetoric that interests you most and search online, in the bookstore, on your campus, or in the community at large for relevant models related to a project or topic that interests you. You might consult the Amnesty International Website, examine brochures from the Peace Corps, or recruitment newsletters by Doctors Without Borders; alternatively, if you are interested in Social Entrepreneurship or business, explore the Business library, browse design competitions in the Engineering School, and look at multimedia exhibitions at your school. For each case, assess the model by asking the following questions:

- Who is the author (or collaborative author) and intended audience?
- What are the elements of design, layout, visuals, links, navigation, and other formal properties?
- What is the text's public service or purpose?

COLLABORATIVE CHALLENGE

Building on your analysis of an intriguing model text in the Creative Practice, create a piece of professional writing to launch your own venture, whether it be for nonprofit purposes (to begin a "Designated Drivers Network" in your community, for example) or for business purposes (to sell singing telegrams to support your school drama production). What elements would you include? How would you "brand" your business through a particular design, format, font, language, and choice of graphics? Who is your intended audience? How could you collaborate with others to create a design memo, distribute the tasks, speak to members of the community, create advertising, and oversee the time line to completion?

As you examined nonprofit or professional writing models and then composed your own visual-verbal professional project, you probably noticed that each professional text has its own particular language, look, and design motif. These verbal and visual elements all respond to the conventions of that discourse community and shape the way it is received by a given audience. From businesses creating new technologies to improve global communications, to scientific labs discovering cures for disease, to urban shelters advertising their open-door policies to community members in need, we find visual rhetoric performing important, practical work in the public and professional sphere.

Consider, for instance, a collaborative student project such as the multimedia magazine, Angles, featured in Figure 9.14. To begin their project, the authors developed a business plan to raise awareness about important community issues. Implementing this plan involved presenting a multimedia collaborative proposal pitch, designing a mock table of contents using both visual and verbal rhetoric (see Figure 9.14), creating a sequence of four radio advertisements, interviewing faculty and conducting research, drafting articles with appropriate visuals, making op-ads, and formatting their work into the prototype of a viable magazine. For their magazine's first issue, they composed hybrid articles concerning community activism, children and homelessness, and environmentalism. They used all the strategies you have learned in this book in order to fully realize the potential of visual rhetoric to make powerful contemporary arguments for a practical purpose. Their writing project was truly a dynamic, multimedia contribution to the public sphere.

FIGURE 9.14. The initial table of contents for *Angles* magazine shows careful
attention to the power of visual rhetoric in professional writing.

Writing into the Future

As we progress further into the twenty-first century, "writing" will
continue to evolve, to include texts in various media, to bridge communities by various modes of communication, and to explore means
of expressing, informing, and persuading diverse audiences. New

innovations like i-pod audio books are making print a more dynamic medium; instant messaging is transforming the look and rhythms of the English language; highly interactive computer interfaces continue to redefine what it means to "read" a text; recently developed picture-phones—cell phones equipped with digital cameras—now allow the instant transmission of photographs and visual-verbal voice messaging; live streaming video and audio wraps around our buildings, keeping us informed of the most current world events; Web-broadcasting opens up a new forum for public and private discourse; and, increasingly sophisticated gaming and graphics software brings us one step closer to the virtual realities of science fiction. With advances in technology and what we call "new media" pushing hybrid discourses into uncharted terrain, we are on the threshold of a new age of innovation and public expression. And yet, despite the evolution in the *forms* of writing, the principles of argumentation and rhetoric remained unchanged. For this reason, your understanding of and ability to work with visual rhetoric will become increasingly important. For no matter what forms writing may take in the future, your skills as a *rhetorician*—using verbal, visual, and oral means to craft effective arguments—will serve you well.

As we've seen, classical rhetoric provides us with a solid foundation that informs the way that we engage in private and public discourse, from *invention* to *publication*. The skills you've accumulated through your work in *Envision* have prepared you for such work; your understanding of the dynamics of the rhetorical triangle, of *kairos*, persona and stance, of research and organization methodologies, of the canons of rhetoric, of the levels of decorum, and of the branches of oratory will help you choose the best means of persuasion in any given situation. Through an understanding of the principles behind purposeful visual rhetoric, you can meet the challenges that lie ahead by writing and working with visual and multimedia texts.

Forging Your Own Public Writing

This chapter's specific focus on public writing has covered the importance of writing for diverse communities, including nonprofit organizations that serve the public, and it has considered the way in which rhetoric functions as a *practical art* for *public good*. You've learned how to produce visual rhetoric texts such as a project that requires multiple components of writing such as a service-learning project that benefits the community and requires multiple components of writing, including grant proposal, formal newsletter, brochure, or even a Web page. You've also explored the process of constructing memorial projects for public viewing. These collaborative ventures entail working with design boards, constructing models, revising blueprints, and balancing visual and verbal texts in a three dimensional space. This work has in turn prepared you for the kind of professional writing projects that you may face in your future such as in nonprofit or business environments in which you may be asked to produce diverse forms of public writing through collaborative work.

In effect, this chapter has taken us beyond the realm of your writing classroom by looking at the power and potential of visual rhetoric in various public and professional environments. Through acquiring the skills you need to meet the demands of different nonacademic rhetorical situations, you can now begin to produce complex and compelling texts that contribute in important ways to our ever-changing society.

PREWRITING CHECKLIST
Analyzing Monuments and Memorials

❑ Who designed the monument? Was it collaborative or a single person's vision? Who constructed it? Was it made by individual members of a community or by a professional company? How does the form or function of the monument reflect these aspects of its design and creation?

❑ What motivated the creation of the monument? Was it a personal incident or a public event? Does the monument itself reflect the personal or public nature of the event? What is the purpose of the structure: to memorialize a person or event? to inspire its audience? to suggest a model for change? What is its argument or message?

❑ Was there any debate over the creation or installation of the monument? What were the contested areas—aspects of the design, the act of memorializing that particular event, the placement of the monument itself?

❑ Where is the monument located? What is the significance of the location? Does the physical context of the monument affect how an audience reacts to it? How does the physical context influence the monument's central argument or message? Was the monument designed with that location in mind? If not, how was the design modified to accommodate that location?

(continued)

❑ Is the monument abstract (like the Vietnam War Memorial) or representational (like the Lincoln Memorial)? What is the rhetorical effect of this choice?

❑ Is the monument obviously symbolic (such as the Statue of Liberty) or does it seem realistic? Does it contain any deeper levels of symbolism (for instance, a monument that includes figures of people from different ethnic groups to signify a multicultural society)?

❑ From what materials is the monument made? What symbolism do the materials themselves lend to the structure (for instance, use of marble might signify endurance, while use of water might suggest the alteration or passage of time)? Does it use mixed media or one type of material? If the monument uses mixed media, how do the different media (for instance, water and rock) work together to produce a unified statement?

❑ What are the tactile properties of the monument? Is it rough and coarse? Smooth and glossy? What colors are used the monument? What rhetorical effect does the feel and look of the monument produce?

❑ What is the size of the monument? What impact does the scale and proportion of the monument have on its viewer?

❑ Does the monument include any print text? Is it an integrated part of the structure or is it an afterthought, such as a plaque? What makes the main argument of the monument: the visual elements or a combination of visual and verbal?

❑ Is the monument a static or dynamic object? For instance, does the monument include moving parts, or does its appearance change at different times of the day? How does motion (or immobility) operate as a rhetorical strategy?

❑ What is the audience's relationship with the monument? Does the viewer look at it from a distance, or has it been designed to bring the viewer into the monument itself? Can the viewer change the monument (sign a section of the monument, rearrange pieces, add a note to a wall, or contribute a panel to a quilt)?

❑ Do visitors to the monument or memorial engage with it as the creators intended? For instance, a series of sculptures of human figures may be intended to be looked at, but in practice, viewers might wander among them, hold their hand, sit on their laps, decorate them with flowers or signs. How does this type of encounter change the meaning of the monument? What is the new argument that the memorial makes?

WRITING PROJECTS

 Visit the *Envision* Website for expanded assignment guidelines and student projects.

1. Produce a Community Writing Project with several colleagues from class. After you have established a contact with your university's center for public service and decided to help a particular community agency via a writing project, brainstorm with your agency mentor the way that your skills in visual rhetoric, research, and argumentative writing can benefit them the most. For instance, you might translate a brochure into Spanish, update a Website, write articles for a newsletter, or compose a quarterly report. Work in teams on this project, keeping your communication channels open between team members and the agency. Write up a reflection of your project as the student examples did in this chapter.

2. Design a community memorial or monument. First, choose your topic; check out local events in your hometown. Then, decide on the audience, argument, medium, and format your memorial will take. Draft a plan, include a list of materials, a rationale, a sketch of the memorial, physical samples of the materials to be used, a time line, and a budget. Finally, design your memorial. Realize that it might take many forms: you can produce a documentary film, compile an audio montage, and design a Website, or create a showcase of photos and testimonials using sound clips, data, and historical documents. You will probably find this project perfect for collaborative work, as you can benefit from the ideas and unique skills of different members in your group to produce one final, compelling public visual rhetoric text.

3. Create a multimedia writing project for a specific discourse community. After consulting several models of effective professional or community writing endeavors, determine a social or business need, develop a concept, and begin to write up the elements to fulfill your project. These might include a formal business proposal, a visual model, a grant application with supporting visual evidence, interviews with photographs, 3-D samples, or online components such as an interactive Website. Divide up the tasks, set yourself a timeline, and this project to develop your practical skills in writing to meet real world needs.

FOR ADDED CHALLENGE

 Visit the *Envision* Website for expanded assignment guidelines and student projects.

1. Compose a multimedia memo to a politician or related official about a key public issue. First, decide on your topic. It can be something to do with the environment, social issues, racial discrimination, homelessness, living wage disputes, or gun laws. Then, working collaboratively or by yourself, create a memo or report that includes

photos, charts, recorded testimony from interviews you conduct, blueprints or drawings for proposed new buildings, and a written cover letter to frame your multimedia
memo. Annotate each of your visual arguments with a supplementary verbal rationale. Use the branches of oratory to persuade your audience.

2. Propose a public service or commercial Website. After you know what you wish to
pursue in this entrepreneurial project, establish a Website to present your ideas in
nonlinear dimensions. You might include survey results with photos, computer animation of your product, flash graphics of your potential customers, potential "press
releases" about your company, and a compelling, easy to follow script for each page
of your dynamic, multimedia creation. Realize that your audience will be not only
your potential customers, but also the public at large. Save your Website on a CD and
create an index.htm page as the proposal cover page, offering links to each of the
pages and dynamic cross references that take the viewer deeper into your model.

CHAPTER 9 ON THE WEB

Resources and Readings	Exercises and Assignments	Student Writing
• Closer Look links	• Rhetoric progress worksheet	• Service learning posters, newsletter, Websites
• Links to sites on the branches of oratory	• Brainstorming for multime-dia project	• Collaborative radio and video spots
• Links to community writing and service learning resources	• Detailed guidelines for col-laborative ad campaigns	• Business plans and group proposals
• Guidelines for new media writing	• Group proposal pitch assignment	• Multimedia magazines
• Professional writing resources	• Community writing or pro-fessional writing project directions	• Community-focused e-zines
• Memorial and monument Websites	• Focus on diverse learners	• Research projects on monuments
• Annotated readings		• Self-reflection letters

 www.ablongman.com/envision

Works Cited

Chapter 1

Aristotle. "Rhetoric." The History and Theory of Rhetoric. By James A. Herrick. Boston: Allyn & Bacon, 1998.

Blakesley, David, and Collin Brooke. "Introduction: Notes on Visual Rhetoric." Enculturation 3.2 (2001): Node 4. <http://enculturation.gmu.edu/3_2/introduction.html>.

Diamond, Matthew. "No Laughing Matter: Post-September 11 Political Cartoons in Arab/Muslim Newspapers." Political Communication 19 (2002): 251-72.

Gellis, Mark. "Six Ways of Thinking about Rhetoric." The Rhetoric Page at Kettering University. Par. 1 <http://www.gmi.edu/~mgellis/HANDT001.HTM>.

Horn, Robert. Visual Language: Global Communication for the 21st Century. MacRovu Inc., 1999.

Lehrer, Jim. "Illustrated Men." Online Focus. Transcript. 31 Oct. 1996. <http://www.pbs.org/newshour/bb/election/october96/cartoonists_10-31.html>.

Moore, Art. "'What would Muhammad drive?': Pulitzer-winner's cartoon terrorist spurs death threats from Muslims." WorldNetDaily.com. 28 Dec. 2002. 18 Mar. 2003 <http://www.worldnetdaily.com/news/article.asp?ARTICLE_ID=30197>.

McCloud, Scott. Understanding Comics. New York: HarperPerennial, 1993.

Melandri, Lisa. "Drawing the Line." Philadelphia, PA. 18 Mar. 2003. <http://thegalleriesatmoore.org/publications/cartoons/politicalcartoons.shtml>.

Mitchell, J. T. "The Pictorial Turn." Picture Theory. Chicago: U of Chicago P, 1994.

Plato. Gorgias. Trans. Robin Waterfield. New York: Oxford UP, 1994. 21.

Villanueva, Victor Jr. Bootstraps: From an American Academic of Color. Urbana: National Council of Teachers of English, 1993.

Watterson, Bill. Calvin and Hobbes Sunday Pages 1985-1995. Kansas City: Andrews McMeel Publishing, 2001.

Chapter 2

Burgin, Victor. "Art, Common Sense, and Photography." Visual Culture: The Reader. Eds. Jessica Evans and Stuart Hall. London: Sage Publications, 1999. 41–50.

Caputi, Jane. "Seeing Elephants: The Myths of Phallotechnology." Feminist Studies. 1988.

Hacker, Andrea. New York Times 14 June 1984.

Kinneavy, James. "Kairos in Classical and Modern Rhetorical Theory." Rhetoric and Kairos: Essays in History, Theory and Praxis. Eds. Phillip Sipiora, James Baumlin, and Carolyn Miller. Albany: State U of New York P, 2002. 58–76.

"Merchants of Cool." Frontline. PBS. 27 Feb. 2001. Dir. Barak Goodman. <http://www.pbs.org/wgbh/pages/frontline/shows/cool/>.

Messaris, Paul. Visual Persuasion: The Role of Images in Advertising. Thousand Oaks, CA: Sage Publications, 1997.

Twitchell, James B. Adcult USA. New York: Columbia UP, 1996.

---. "Listerine: Gerard Lambert and Selling the Need." Twenty Ads That Shook the World. New York: Three Rivers Press, 2000. 60-69.

Williams, Roy H. "The Wizard of Advertising." Secret Formulas of the Wizard of Ads. Bard Press, 1999.

Chapter 3

Boese, Alex. <u>Museum of Hoaxes</u>. <http://museumofhoaxes.com>.
Harris, Christopher, and Paul Martin Lester. <u>Visual Journalism</u>. Boston: Allyn & Bacon, 2002.
Smith, Anna Deavere. "Twilight: Los Angeles." <u>Stage on Screen</u>. PBS Home Video. 2001. <http://www.pbs.org/wnet/stageonscreen/twilight/twilight.html>.
Sontag, Susan. "Looking at War: Photography's View of Devastation and Death." <u>New Yorker</u> 9 Dec. 2002: 82-98.

Chapter 4

Bizzell, Patricia and Bruce Herzberg. "Research as a Social Act." <u>Background Readings for Instructors Using The Bedford Handbook</u>. Ed. Glenn Blalock. 6th ed. Boston: Bedford/St. Martin's, 2002. 321-26.
Booth, Wayne. <u>Craft of Research</u>. Chicago: U of Chicago P, 1995.
Drew, Elizabeth. <u>Poetry: A Modern Guide</u>. New York: Dell Publishing, 1959.
Gorgias. "Encomium of Helen." <u>The Older Sophists: A Complete Translation by Several Hands of the Fragments</u>. Ed. Rosamond Kent Sprague. Columbia: U of South Carolina P, 1972. 50-54. Online. 7 Apr. 2003. <http://www.phil.vt.edu/mgifford/phil2115/Helen.htm>.
Hunt, Douglas. <u>The Riverside Guide to Writing</u>. Boston: Houghton Mifflin, 1991.

Chapter 5

Ballenger, Bruce. <u>The Curious Researcher</u>. 4th ed. NewYork: Longman, 2004.
Bowen, Catherine Drinker. <u>Adventures of a Biographer</u>. Boston: Little, Brown, 1959.
"Bush vs. Bush." <u>The Daily Show with Jon Stewart</u>. <http://www.comedycentral.com/tv_shows/ds/videos_corr.jhtml?startIndex=13&p=stewart>.
Clark, Jocalyn. "Babes and Boob? Analysis of JAMA Cover Art." <u>British Medical Journal</u> (18 Dec. 1999): 1603.
Gonser, Sarah. "Revising the Cover Story." <u>Folio: The Magazine for Magazine Management</u> 1 Mar. 2003.
Huff, Darrell. <u>How to Lie with Statistics</u>. New York: Norton, 1993.
Rea, Alan, and Doug White. "The Changing Nature of Writing: Prose or Code in the Classroom." <u>Background Readings for Instructors Using The Bedford Handbook Sixth Edition</u>. Ed. Glan Blalock. Boston: Bedford/St. Martin's, 2002. 217-30.
"Statistical Significance." Creative Research Systems, 2000. <http://www.surveysystem.com/signif.htm>.
"Stem Cells, Regenerative Medicine and Cancer." The Beckman Symposium. 14-15 Apr. 2003. <http://beckman.stanford.edu/events/symp_videos.html>.
Zimbardo, Philip G., Ann L. Weber, and Robert. L. Johnson. <u>Psychology: Core Concepts</u>. 4th ed. Boston: Allyn & Bacon, 2003.

Chapter 6

Adamson, Eric. "Malleability, Misrepresentation, Manipulation: The Rhetoric of Images in Economic Forecasting." Boothe Prize Essay, Winter 2003. Program in Writing and Rhetoric, Stanford University. <http://pwr.stanford.edu/publications/>.
Antohin, Anatoly. "Storyboard." <http://afronord.tripod.com/film/storyboard.html>.

Burke, Kenneth. "Rhetoric—Old and New." New Rhetorics. Ed. Martin Steinmann. New York: Scribner, 1967. 59-76.

Collier, John, Greg Daniels, and Paul Lieberstein. "Homer, Hank & the American Dream: Social & Political Satire on American Television." The Program in American Studies. Stanford University, California. 7 Nov. 2003.

Gibaldi, Joseph. MLA Handbook for the Writers of Research Papers. 6th ed. New York: Modern Language Association, 2003.

Goodwin, Doris Kearns. "How I Caused That Story." 27 Jan. 2002. <http://www.time.com/time/nation/article/0,8599,197614,00.html>.

Hilligoss, Susan. Visual Communication. 2nd ed. New York: Longman, 2002.

Kaplan, Deborah. "Mass Marketing Jane Austen: Men, Women and Courtship in Two Film Adaptations." Jane Austen in Hollywood. Eds. Linda Troost and Sayre Greenfield: U of Kentucky P, 1998. 177-87.

Lamott, Anne. Bird by Bird: Some Instructions on Writing and Life. New York: Anchor, 1995.

"Merchants of Cool." Frontline. PBS. 27 Feb. 2001. Dir. Barak Goodman. <http://www.pbs.org/wgbh/pages/frontline/shows/cool/>.

Morgan, Peter W., and Glenn H. Reynolds. "A Plague of Originality." The Idler. <http://www.the-idler.com/IDLER-02/1-23.html>.

Phillips, William H. Film: An Introduction. 2nd ed. Boston: Bedford/St. Martins, 2002.

Paton, Alan. National Observer 8 Nov. 1965.

Chapter 7

Burton, Gideon. Silva Rhetoricae The Forest of Rhetoric. <http://humanities.byu.edu/rhetoric/silva.htm>.

Byrne, David. "Learning to Love PowerPoint." Wired Magazine Sept. 2003. <http://www.wired.com/wired/archive/11.09/ppt1.html>.

Hocks, Mary. "Understanding Visual Rhetoric in Digital Writing Environments." CCC 54.4 (June 2003): 629-56.

Ingleman, Kelly. "Delivery." Rhetoric Resources at Tech. Georgia Institute of Technology. <http://www.lcc.gatech.edu/gallery/rhetoric/terms/delivery.html>.

Jean Kilbourne. Slim Hopes: Advertising and the Obsession with Thinness. Dir. Sut Jhally. Northampton, MA: Media Education Foundation, 1995.

Parker, Ian. "Absolute PowerPoint." The New Yorker 28 May 2001: 76-87.

Shugart, Stephen. "Beyond PowerPoint." Educator's Voice 15 Aug. 2001. <http://www.title3.net/TechTips/misusingpp.html>.

Tufte, Edward. "PowerPoint Is Evil: Power Corrupts. PowerPoint Corrupts Absolutely." Wired Magazine Sept. 2003. <http://www.wired.com/wired/archive/11.09/ppt2.html>.

Chapter 8

Adbusters: Culturejammers. <http://www.adbusters.org>.

Agee, James. Foreword. Let Us Now Praise Famous Men. Boston: Houghton Mifflin, 1969.

Burton, Gideon. Silva Rhetoricae The Forest of Rhetoric. <http://humanities.byu.edu/rhetoric/silva.htm>.

Cody, Anthony. "Teaching Practices: Digital Photoessays." Apple Learning Exchange. <http://ali.apple.com/ali_sites/ali/neccexhibits/1000308/The_Lesson.html>.

Crowley, Sharon, and Debra Hawhee, <u>Ancient Rhetorics for Contemporary Students</u>. New York: Longman, 1999.

George, Diana. "From Analysis to Design: Visual Communication in the Teaching of Writing." <u>CCC</u> 54.1 (2002): 11-39.

Mitchell, W. J. T. "The Photographic Essay: Four Case Studies." <u>Picture Theory: Essays on Verbal and Visual Representation</u>. Chicago: U of Chicago P, 1994.

Lanham, Richard. <u>The Electronic Word: Democracy, Technology, and the Arts</u>. Chicago: U of Chicago P, 1993.

Landow, George. <u>Hypertext</u>. Baltimore: Johns Hopkins UP, 1992.

Nielsen, Jakob, and Marie Tahir. <u>Homepage Usability: 50 Websites Deconstructed</u>. Indianapolis: New Riders Publishing, 2002.

Sammons, Martha. <u>The Internet Writer's Handbook</u>. New York: Longman, 2004.

Stephenson, Sam, ed. <u>Dream Street: W. Eugene Smith's Pittsburgh Project</u>. New York: Norton, 2001.

Chapter 9

"Advocates Debate the First Amendment, Ten Commandments." CNN.com. 21Aug. 2003. <http://www.cnn.com/2003/LAW/08/21/cnna.commandments.debate/index.html>

Beaufort, Anne. <u>Writing the Organization's Way: The Life of Writers in the Workplace</u>. Diss. Stanford University, 1995.

Bonevardi, Gustavo. "'Tribute in Light' Explained." <u>Slate</u> 11 Mar. 2002 <http://slate.msn.com/id/2063051/>.

<u>Columbine Memorial Website</u> <http://www.columbinememorial.org/default.htm>.

<u>Irish Hunger Memorial: A Reminder to Millions</u> <http://www.batteryparkcity.org/ihm.htm>.

Lacy, Suzanne, ed. <u>Mapping the Terrain: New Genre Public Art</u>. Seattle: Bay Press, 1995.

Lewis, Michael J. "In the Fray: How to Avoid a 9/11 Memorial Disaster." <u>The Wall Street Journal</u> 12 Aug. 2003: 8.

Ovens, Alan. "Discourse communities and the social construction of reflection in teacher education." 8 July 2002. HERDSA Conference. Australia. <http://www.ecu.edu.au/conferences/herdsa/main/papers/ref/pdf/Ovens.pdf>.

Rothenberg, Michael. "Rising from Rubble: New York Citizens Engineer the Symbolic Rhetoric of the New World Trade Center." Program in Writing and Rhetoric. Stanford University, June 2003.

Ross, Carolyn, and Ardel Thomas. <u>Writing for Real</u>. New York: Longman, 2003.

Tomkins, Calvin. "Towers of Light." <u>The New Yorker</u> 1 Oct. 2001. <http://www.newyorker.com/talk/content/?011001ta_talk_horizon_dept>.

Credits

Page x, Figure 1: The Board of Trinity College Dublin

Figure 1.1 and Contents: Mike Thompson, Detroit Free Press

Figure 1.3: Courtesy of Scott McCloud

Figure 1.8: Courtesy of Doug Marlette

Figure 1.11: Daryl Cagle, Cagle Cartoons, Inc.

Figure 1.12: Gary Markstein and Copley News Service

Figure 2.1 and Contents: Linda A. Cicero/Stanford News Service

Figure 2.2: Courtesy of Clairol nice 'n easy

Figure 2.4: © The Procter & Gamble Company. Used by permission.

Figure 2.5: Courtesy of Escort

Figure 2.6: Courtesy of AT&T Wireless

Figures 2.7-2.8: © The American Legacy Foundation

Figure 2.9: The Advertising Archive Ltd.

Figure 2.11: © The American Legacy Foundation

Figure 2.12: The Advertising Archive Ltd.

Figure 3.1 and Contents: © Telegraph Group Limited 2003

Figure 3.2: Library of Congress

Figure 3.3: Library of Congress

Figure 3.4: Library of Congress

Figure 3.5: Cordell Hauglie

Figure 3.6: Library of Congress

Figure 3.7: William Gladstone

Page 71: Suddam Hussein. AP/Wide World Photos

Figures 3.8–3.10: Photography by Ken Friedman, Photo courtesy of Berkeley Repertory Theatre

Figure 3.11 and pages 2–3: Abed Omar Qusini/Reuters

Page 79: "The Boston Photographs." Reprinted by permission of International Creative Management, Inc. Copyright © 1978 by Nora Ephron.

Figure 3.13: Courtesy of the *Boston Herald*

Figure 4.1 and Contents: Patrick Broderick/ModernHumorist.com

Figure 4.2: Hoover Institution Archives Poster Collection

Figure 4.4: Library of Congress

Figure 4.5: The Art Archive/Musée des 2 Guerres Mondiales Paris/Dagli Orti

Figure 4.6: Library of Congress

Figure 4.7: The Advertising Archive Ltd.

Figure 4.8: Courtesy National Archives, 513533

Figure 4.9: Courtesy National Archives, 516102

Figure 4.10: Courtesy National Archives, 514597

Figure 4.14: Hoover Institution Archives Poster Collection

Figure 4.15: Poster designed by Stevan Dohanos. Minneapolis Public Library, Special Collections

Page 118, Figure 1: Courtesy National Archives, 513533

Figure 5.1 and Contents: Time Life Pictures/Getty Images

Figure 5.2: Reprinted cover logo and text only with permission from *Science* (vol. 290, no. 5500 22 December 2000). Copyright 2000 AAAS. Illustration reprinted with the permission of Peter Steiner.

Figure 5.3: Steve Bronstein/The Image Bank/Getty Images: Creative Collection

Figure 5.5: Courtesy CNN. "Usage of this CNN material does not constitute an implied or expressed endorsement by CNN."

Figure 5.6: Image appears courtesy of the Stem Cell Research Foundation.

Figure 5.7: Reprinted with permission of The Coalition of Americans for Resarch Ethics.

Figure 5.9: *Rocket Blitz from the Moon* by Chelsey Bonestell. Bonestell Space Art.

Figure 5.10: Time Life Pictures/Getty Images

Figure 5.11: Time Life Pictures/Getty Images

Figure 5.12: Time Life Pictures/Getty Images

Figure 5.13: *Global Environment Politics* cover, Volume 3: Number 1 (February 2003) © the Massachusetts Institute of Technology.

Figure 5.14: Courtesy of www.alternativesjournal.ca

Figure 5.16: *Song of Unity* mural, a three-dimensional mural depicting the unity of the people of the Americas in a common cultural bond against oppression. Mural painted by Anna de Leon, Osha Neumann, Ray Patlán, and O'Brien Thiele. Courtesy of La Pena Cultural Center, photography by Karen Kerschen.

Figure 6.1 and Contents: Reprinted by permission of HarperCollins Publishers Ltd. © Estelle Daniel 2000.

Figure 6.5: Photofest

Figure 6.6: Courtesy Everett Collection

Figure 6.7 and pages 92–93: *Bowling for Columbine* © 2002 Iconolatry Productions Inc. All Rights Reserved. Courtesy of MGM CLIP + STILL

Figure 6.8: Polygram/Spelling/The Kobal Collection

Figure 6.9: Courtesy Everett Collection

Figure 6.10: Danjaq/Eon/UA/ The Kobal Collection/Keith

Index